Wartime Origins and United Nations

CW01083248

The creation of the UN system during World War II is a largely unknown or forgotten story among contemporary decision makers, international relations specialists, and policy analysts.

This book aims to recover the wartime history of the United Nations and explore how the forgotten past can shed light on a possible and more desirable future. To achieve this, each chapter takes three snapshots:

- "Then," the imaginative and transnational thinking about solutions to postwar problems demonstrated a realization that victory in World War II required an intergovernmental "system" with enough power and competence to work—that is, the UN was not established as a liberal plaything and public relations ploy but rather as a vital necessity for postwar order and prosperity.
- "Now," which often seems a pale imitation of wartime thinking that nonetheless reflects a growing and widespread recognition of the fundamental disconnect between the nature of transboundary problems and current solutions seen as feasible by 193 UN member states.
- "Next steps," or the collective wisdom about the range of new thinking and new institutions that, in fact, may well have antecedents in wartime thinking and experimentation and could be labeled blueprints for a "third generation" of intergovernmental organizations.

This work will be essential reading for all students and scholars of the United Nations, International Organizations, and Global Governance.

Dan Plesch is Director of the Centre for International Studies and Diplomacy at SOAS, University of London.

Thomas G. Weiss is Presidential Professor of Political Science and Director Emeritus of the Ralph Bunche Institute for International Studies at The City University of New York's Graduate Center.

Routledge Global Institutions Series

Edited by Thomas G. Weiss
The CUNY Graduate Center, New York, USA
and Rorden Wilkinson
University of Sussex, Brighton, UK

About the series

The "Global Institutions Series" provides cutting-edge books about many aspects of what we know as "global governance." It emerges from our shared frustrations with the state of available knowledge—electronic and print-wise, for research and teaching—in the area. The series is designed as a resource for those interested in exploring issues of international organization and global governance. Since the first volumes appeared in 2005, we have taken significant strides toward filling conceptual gaps.

The series consists of three related "streams" distinguished by their blue, red, and green covers. The blue volumes, comprising the majority of the books in the series, provide user-friendly and short (usually no more than 50,000 words) but authoritative guides to major global and regional organizations, as well as key issues in the global governance of security, the environment, human rights, poverty, and humanitarian action among others. The books with red covers are designed to present original research and serve as extended and more specialized treatments of issues pertinent for advancing understanding about global governance. The volumes with green covers—the most recent departure in the series—are comprehensive and accessible accounts of the major theoretical approaches to global governance and international organization.

The books in each of the streams are written by experts in the field, ranging from the most senior and respected authors to first-rate scholars at the beginning of their careers. In combination, the three components of the series—blue, red, and green—serve as key resources for faculty, students, and practitioners alike. The works in the blue and green streams have value as core and complementary readings in courses on, among other things, international organization, global governance, international law, international relations, and international political economy; the red volumes allow further reflection and investigation in these and related areas.

The books in the series also provide a segue to the foundation volume that offers the most comprehensive textbook treatment available dealing with all the major issues, approaches, institutions, and actors in contemporary global governance—our edited work *International Organization and Global Governance* (2014)—a volume to which many of the authors in the series have contributed essays.

Understanding global governance—past, present, and future—is far from a finished journey. The books in this series nonetheless represent significant steps toward a better way of conceiving contemporary problems and issues as well as, we hope, doing something to improve world order. We value the feedback from our readers and their role in helping shape the ongoing development of the series.

A complete list of titles appears at the end of this book. The most recent titles in the series are:

International Judicial Institutions (2nd edition, 2015)
by Richard J. Goldstone and Adam M. Smith

The NGO Challenge for International Relations Theory (2014)
edited by William E. DeMars and Dennis Dijkzeul

21st Century Democracy Promotion in the Americas (2014)
by Jorge Heine and Brigitte Weiffen

BRICS and Coexistence (2014)
edited by Cedric de Coning, Thomas Mandrup and Liselotte Odgaard

IBSA (2014)
by Oliver Stuenkel

Making Global Institutions Work (2014)
edited by Kate Brennan

Post-2015 UN Development (2014)
edited by Stephen Browne and Thomas G. Weiss

Wartime Origins and the Future United Nations

Edited by
Dan Plesch and Thomas G. Weiss

Routledge
Taylor & Francis Group

LONDON AND NEW YORK

First published 2015
by Routledge
2 Park Square, Milton Park, Abingdon, Oxon OX14 4RN

and by Routledge
711 Third Avenue, New York, NY 10017

Routledge is an imprint of the Taylor & Francis Group, an informa business

British Library Cataloguing in Publication Data
A catalogue record for this book is available from the British Library

Library of Congress Cataloging in Publication Data
A catalog record for this book has been requested

ISBN: 978-0-415-71265-1 (hbk)
ISBN: 978-0-415-71267-5 (pbk)
ISBN: 978-1-315-88380-9 (ebk)

Typeset in Times New Roman
by Taylor & Francis Books

MIX
Paper from
responsible sources
FSC   **FSC® C013604**
www.fsc.org

Printed and bound by CPI Group (UK) Ltd,
Croydon, CR0 4YY

Contents

viii *Contents*

List of contributors

Manu Bhagavan is Professor of History at Hunter College and The Graduate Center, The City University of New York. The author or (co-)editor of five books, most recently of *The Peacemakers: India and the Quest for One World* (2012), he also serves as Chair of the Human Rights Program at the Roosevelt House Public Policy Institute at Hunter College. He has been a fellow of the American Council of Learned Societies and President of the Society for Advancing the History of South Asia.

Stephen Browne is Co-Director of the Future UN Development System Project and Senior Fellow at the Ralph Bunche Institute for International Studies at The CUNY Graduate Center. He worked for more than 30 years in different organizations of the UN development system, sharing his time almost equally between agency headquarters and country assignments. He has written books and articles on aid and development throughout his career, his most recent being *The UN Development Programme and System* (2011), *The International Trade Centre* (2011), and *The United Nations Industrial Development Organization* (2012).

John Burley read History and Economics at the University of Cambridge. He worked for four years as an economist for the newly independent government of Uganda before joining the United Nations in 1972. He worked for UNDP in New York, for the Office of the United Nations Director-General for Development and International Economic Cooperation, and for UNCTAD in Geneva. He has authored numerous reports on the UN's support for development. He is now the International Development Law Organization Chargé d'affaires to the United Nations in Geneva and Conseiller Municipal in Divonne-les-Bains, France.

Miriam Intrator is Special Collections Librarian at Ohio University. She received her PhD in Modern European and Jewish History in 2013 from the Graduate Center of the City University of New York. A 2011 recipient of a Social Science Research Council International Dissertation Research Fellowship, her dissertation investigated the role of UNESCO in post-World War II library reconstruction and rehabilitation. Her research interests include the prewar forced selling of library collections and the postwar fate of looted and displaced library materials, including current developments in provenance research for still unaccounted-for materials.

Ruth Jachertz is a PhD candidate in History at Humboldt University Berlin. Her dissertation, which is part of the Volkswagen-sponsored research group on the role of food in globalization, examines the emergence of an international food aid regime between the 1940s and 1970s. She holds an MA in American Studies, History and Political Science from the University of Bonn and was a DAAD student at the University of Austin. Before returning to university for her PhD, she worked for several years as a managing director for an association that empowers young people to become active in politics.

Eli Karetny is a PhD candidate in Political Science at the CUNY Graduate Center. He teaches International Relations, Political Theory and American Politics at Baruch College and is writing a dissertation on the counterrevolutionary conception of freedom in the work of Leo Strauss, whose critique of global institutions and universal values has influenced conservative thinking about the United Nations. He has a JD/MBA from Temple University, served in Ukraine as a Peace Corps volunteer, and has done research in Israel on the Middle East peace process.

Dan Plesch is Director of the Centre for International Studies and Diplomacy at the School of Oriental and African Studies (SOAS), University of London. His most recent book is *America, Hitler and the UN* (2011). His follow-on research includes articles on the UNWCC. He previously worked for the BBC and CNN, the Royal United Services Institute, and was the founding director of the British American Security Information Council (1986–2000). His other publications include *The Beauty Queen's Guide to World Peace, A Case to Answer* (2004) and *Preparing for the First Use of Nuclear Weapons* (1987). He is co-director of the Wartime Origins and the Future United Nations Project.

J. Simon Rofe is Senior Lecturer in Diplomatic and International Studies in the Centre for International Studies and Diplomacy at SOAS,

University of London. His research interests lie in the field of US diplomacy and foreign relations in the twentieth century, with a focus on the era of Franklin D. Roosevelt, and more specifically on international organization and postwar planning. His books include *International History and International Relations* (with Andrew Williams and Amelia Hadfield, 2012), and *Franklin Roosevelt's Foreign Policy and the Welles Mission* (2007).

Pallavi Roy is a lecturer in International Economics at the Centre for International Studies and Diplomacy at SOAS, University of London. Her research focuses on the political economy of growth and liberalization in developing countries, especially Southasia, Institutional Economics, financing and capability development, corruption, mining and metallic commodities markets. She has previously had ten years of experience as a journalist with *Businessworld* magazine in India, covering mining and commodities policy, steel and heavy industries as well as some of the recent landmark political movements against land acquisition for mining and industry in Eastern India.

Giles Scott-Smith is senior researcher with the Roosevelt Study Center and holds the Ernst van der Beugel Chair in the Diplomatic History of Transatlantic Relations since World War II, at the University of Leiden. His research interests cover the development of transatlantic relations through the twentieth century, with a focus on the role of nongovernmental organizations and public diplomacy. His books include *Western Anti-Communism and the Interdoc Network: Cold War Internationale* (2012), and *Networks of Empire: The US State Department's Foreign Leader Program in the Netherlands, France and Britain 1950–1970* (2008).

Thomas G. Weiss is Presidential Professor of Political Science and Director Emeritus of the Ralph Bunche Institute for International Studies at The City University of New York's Graduate Center. Past President of the International Studies Association (2009–10), his most recent single-authored books include *Governing the World? Addressing "Problems without Passports"* (2014), *Global Governance: Why? What? Whither?* (2013), *Humanitarian Business* (2013), *What's Wrong with the United Nations and How to Fix It* (2012), and *Humanitarian Intervention: Ideas in Action* (2012). He is co-editor of the Routledge "Global Institutions Series" and co-director of two research projects: Wartime Origins and the Future United Nations, and of the Future UN Development System.

Foreword

This book throws refreshing new light on aspects of the United Nations hitherto little explored. It traces the discussions that took place, both during World War II and its aftermath, which laid the foundations of the much more complicated organizational structures that we know today. The various chapters examine the origins of a wide range of organizations—the UN War Crimes Commission, the UN Relief and Rehabilitation Administration (UNRRA), the financial and development institutions, and those dealing with trade, food and agriculture, and education. I started working for the United Nations soon after its creation so that much of the history encapsulated here is well known to me, but there are also fresh insights. In their Introduction and Conclusion, the editors, Dan Plesch and Thomas G. Weiss, use the wonderfully apt phrase "past as prelude." The essays in this book constitute a treasure trove not only for those engaged in research about the world organization but also for more general readers.

It is astounding that so much thought and time were dedicated to the planning of a new and better world even in the darker days of a vast and unpredictable war, when the outcome was far from certain and the specter of defeat often loomed. After 1942, when eventual victory at last seemed possible, these activities intensified. There was a general realization that peace could only be sustained through multilateral cooperation between countries. Similar visions had informed thinking after World War I, albeit in a more embryonic reform, and had led to the creation of the ill-fated League of Nations. Analysis not only of the causes of the League's failure, but also of some of its successful initiatives, constituted an important part of the planning, as many chapters point out.

Inevitably, the United States and the United Kingdom took the lead, particularly the former. In those days there were fewer countries interested in creating the United Nations, since a large part of the world was still under colonial rule. The United States was the superpower with the massive resources needed to make the dream become reality. Yet it is interesting that smaller countries, as well as China, were not without voice or influence. This reality was particularly evident in the case of the UN War Crimes Commission: rather than a purely Western creation, it owed much to initiatives by China and other victim states that persuaded London and Washington to support this forerunner of today's International Criminal Court.

One of the most interesting revelations of all the chapters is the extent to which the discussions of that time, both within and between the various countries involved, were riven by the same disagreements and tensions as those that bedevil proposals for the reform of the United Nations today. They still remain unresolved and the experiences of seven decades ago have important lessons for current thinking.

Then the need for multinational cooperation as the key to sustainable peace was the main guiding theme for those intent on setting up the new international system, but it was not universally accepted. There were divided opinions within the Roosevelt administration between the realists, who favored a postwar liberal order that the United States would naturally dominate, and the idealists, who envisaged a new order of international cooperation dawning. The fundamental difference was between the multilateral ideal and national self-interest. The former could not be successfully pursued without US support, while the latter forced President Franklin D. Roosevelt to accept compromises in order to ensure Congressional support. Thus, the United States played, at one and the same time, the contradictory roles of indispensable backer and occasional "spoiler." With the advent of the Cold War, the emphasis on putting national interests first inevitably became more powerful and political considerations exercised a greater role.

One of the great bones of contention concerned the manner and extent of coordination needed to harmonize the activities of the growing number of new organizations, some already in existence before the war, others being created for the first time. Here the argument was between a decentralized system and a central coordinating organization. It became particularly acute in the area of development cooperation, which came into being as an "add-on" to the other functions of the various institutions being set up. The idea of an International Development Authority was mooted, but by then it was too late to interpose a central institution to control this area of work that developed rapidly, and soon extended throughout all the entities of the system. Instead, a loose framework was instituted, operating by consensus. From the start it was doomed to be only partially effective, and it proved incapable of avoiding duplication or ensuring the optimum use of resources. The legacy of that compromise is still with us today. Every one of the frequent proposals for UN reform in the intervening years has identified coordination as a central problem; they have all recommended remedial measures, but the centrifugal forces, by now deeply entrenched in the system, have prevented their implementation.

One of the many virtues of the book is to remind us of some of the forgotten stars of that enormously creative time. Roosevelt and Winston Churchill were at the helm, but there were many brilliant movers and shakers, not only civil servants within national administrations but also intellectual leaders in the vanguard of political and economic thought. To single out a few of that stellar cast, there was John Maynard Keynes and Harry Dexter White, clashing in the negotiations to establish the World Bank and the International Monetary Fund; Gunnar Myrdal, the Swedish economist and Nobel laureate; David Owen, who established the UN Development Programme (UNDP) field network; Raúl Prebisch of Argentina, for long head of the Economic Commission for Latin America and subsequently the creator and first head of the UN Conference on Trade and Development; Sir John Boyd Orr, the brilliant nutritionist and early head of the Food and Agriculture Organization; Sir Robert Jackson, a logistical genius who led UNRRA, the postwar relief organization, and still the largest UN operation of this kind, who combined a flair for strategic thinking with effective leadership and outstanding operational skill. I had the privilege of working closely with Prebisch and Jackson, and can testify to their outstanding leadership and creative thinking.

Sadly, as the book also points out, few such giants were appointed to top positions at the headquarters in New York when the first Secretariat members were recruited because already the preference was given instead to bureaucratic and political choices. This key factor explains, then and now, the increasing gap between ideas and operations. In the 1940s and early 1950s, the United Nations was a pioneering center of creative thinking about development but, over time, with the explosion of bilateral assistance programs and of development research in academic institutions, this primacy declined. The fragmentation of the multiple organizations of the so-called UN system, the increase in their operational functions to the detriment of their original role as centers of excellence and storehouses of knowledge, their quasi-autonomous status and the lack of any effective coordinating mechanism all contributed to this process. The recognition of each new global challenge has led to the creation of new organizations to deal with them and thereby exacerbated problems of coordination, duplication, and less than optimum use of resources. It is easier to introduce new organizations than to dissolve or merge bodies that are not working well or even are no longer relevant.

It is sobering to observe that the problems that confound would-be reformers today have their roots in decisions taken seven decades ago but now are immensely more daunting. Why is this so? There are many reasons. However, to my mind the main obstacle is the continuing dominance of national interests over international cooperation likely to benefit the world as a whole, when that involves some concessions. The paradox of our age is the strength of national sovereignty although the very concept is undermined by increasing globalization. No government can stand alone or single-handedly manage its economy in today's world of split-second communications that do not observe frontiers and the multitude of what are now accurately described as "problems without passports."

Everything points to a crying need for robust multilateral cooperation, even greater than that envisaged at the end of World War II. How can this be brought about? One chapter ends, to strengthen the multinational system, "Must we wait for another San Francisco moment?" Others echo the same dismal message. Heaven forbid if that means another war must come first. The only way—and it is a dauntingly rocky path—is for government attitudes to undergo a sea change. They must be made to recognize that international development and cooperation are in every country's interest, as well as that of the international community of states and of ordinary people all over the world.

Needless to say, such a sea change will not happen without massive public pressure on governments everywhere. Given the troubled state of the world today, it is high time to make a reality of the clarion call at the beginning of the UN Charter: "We the peoples of the United Nations ... " The essays collected in this volume are essential reading for understanding that most vital of public policy challenges today: how to move from narrow national interests to broader collective ones as the basis for better global governance. I trust that the publication of this well-documented history on the eve of the 70th anniversary of the San Francisco conference will inspire readers to comprehend the gravity of our current situation. We should all urge our governments to learn the lessons of the past and take action to strengthen the United Nations, our best hope for the future peace and security of humanity.

Margaret Joan Anstee
Former UN under secretary-general
September 2014

Acknowledgments

This book grows from our own analytical experiences with the United Nations—past and present—and a commitment to building a world organization that is fit for purpose. It is part of preparations for the 70th anniversary of the United Nations Conference on International Organization, the April 1945 gathering in San Francisco where delegates forged the Charter for the UN Organization. Building on the wartime experience of the successful experiment in multilateral cooperation to defeat fascism, we were convinced about the relevance of those years for the transnational problems that plague the planet. Hence, the decision by the Centre for International Studies and Diplomacy at SOAS, University of London, and the Ralph Bunche Institute for International Studies at The City University of New York's Graduate Center to collaborate on this book.

Fortunately, the Carnegie Corporation of New York understood the logic of probing history to help improve contemporary and future international society. We are grateful to Vartan Gregorian and Steve del Rosso for their encouragement and support, and to Brian Urquhart for having helped to make the case for this research endeavor.

As in many such undertakings, the list of persons to whom the editors owe an intellectual debt is lengthy. More people than we can possibly mention here contributed to this timely conversation. We cannot mention all the generous colleagues who attended seminars, conferences, and other gatherings during the two-year duration of this project; it will have to suffice to name those to whom we owe the most.

At the Centre for International Studies and Diplomacy, Rohit Gupta provided thoughtful administrative support for the October 2013 workshop and the gathering of authors in May 2014. At the Ralph Bunche Institute for International Studies, Eli Karetny helped administer the grant and co-authored a chapter, and Danielle A. Zach patiently helped to edit and shape the chapters.

This support and background was especially in evidence during the authors' workshop to solicit comments from knowledgeable experts on the wartime period, on the United Nations, and on historiography. The input from discussants at those sessions was especially important, and so we and the authors would like to thank: Margaret Joan Anstee, Leon Gordenker, Laura Hammond, Andrew Johnstone, Richard Jolly, Mushtaq Khan, Angus Lockyer, Rahul Rao, Jessica Reinisch, Katharina Rietzler, and Thomas Zeiler.

We express our appreciation to our contributors not only for their insights and evident commitment but also for the collective journey of learning through their respective disciplines and life experiences. Despite geographic, disciplinary, and personal diversities and logistical challenges, the project was a pleasurable team effort.

Finally, we are indebted to our friend and colleague Margaret Joan Anstee for gracing these pages with a substantive foreword that reflects her experience, knowledge, and insights from many years as a pioneer and practitioner working in the vineyards of UN development. Her integrity is a source of inspiration along with her willingness to call into question organizational shibboleths.

Dan Plesch and Thomas G. Weiss
London and New York
October 2014

Abbreviations

ACPFR	Advisory Committee on Problems in Foreign Relations
ARA	American Relief Administration
BBC	British Broadcasting Corporation
BoP	balance of payments
BWS	Bretton Woods System
BW2	Bretton Woods 2
CAME	Conference of Allied Ministers of Education
CROWCASS	Central Register of War Criminals and Security Suspects
DPI	Department of Public Information
ECE	Economic Commission for Europe
ECLA	Economic Commission for Latin America
ECOSOC	Economic and Social Council
EFO	economic and financial organization
EIS	Economic Intelligence Service
EPTA	Expanded Programme of Technical Assistance
ERO	European Regional Office
EU	European Union
FAO	Food and Agriculture Organization
FDI	foreign direct investment
G20	Group of 20
GATT	General Agreement on Tariffs and Trade
GDP	gross domestic product
IABC	Inter-Allied Book Centre
IAIC	Inter-Allied Information Committee and Center
IBRD	International Bank for Reconstruction and Development
ICA	international commodity agreement
ICC	International Criminal Court
ICCH	International Commodity Clearing House

ICHP	International Clearing House for Publications
ICRC	International Committee of the Red Cross
ICTY	International Criminal Tribunal for the former Yugoslavia
ICU	International Clearing Union
IDA	International Development Association
IEFC	International Emergency Food Council
IFAD	International Fund for Agricultural Development
IFI	international financial institution
IGO	intergovernmental organization
IIIC	International Institute for Intellectual Cooperation
ILO	International Labour Organization
IMF	International Monetary Fund
IMS	international monetary system
IMT	International Military Tribunal
IRO	International Refugee Organization
ITC	International Trade Centre
ITO	International Trade Organization
MDGs	Millennium Development Goals
MESC	Middle East Supply Centre
NAACP	National Association for the Advancement of Colored People
NGO	nongovernmental organization
NIEO	New International Economic Order
NWICO	New World Information and Communication Order
OECD	Organisation for Economic Co-operation and Development
OEEC	Organisation for European Economic Co-operation
OWI	Office of War Information
SBAA	standard basic assistance agreement
SDGs	Sustainable Development Goals
SGBV	sexual and gender-based violence
SUNFED	Special UN Fund for Economic Development
TAA	Technical Assistance Administration
TAB	Technical Assistance Board
TAC	Technical Assistance Committee
TNC	transnational corporation
UNCTAD	United Nations Conference on Trade and Development
UNDP	United Nations Development Programme
UNEP	United Nations Environment Programme
UNESCO	United Nations Educational, Scientific and Cultural Organization

UNFPA	United Nations Fund for Population Activities (later UN Population Fund)
UNICEF	UN Children Fund
UNIDO	United Nations Industrial Development Organization
UNIO	United Nations Information Organization
UNO	United Nation Organization
UNRRA	United Nations Relief and Rehabilitation Administration
UNWCC	United Nations War Crimes Commission
USSR	Union of Soviet Socialist Republics
WFB	World Food Board
WFP	World Food Programme
WHO	World Health Organization
WTO	World Trade Organization

Introduction

Past as prelude, multilateralism as a tactic and strategy

Dan Plesch and Thomas G. Weiss

"We mean business in this war in a political and humanitarian sense just as surely as we mean business in a military sense. This is one more strong link joining the United Nations."[1] Such was US president Franklin D. Roosevelt's clear message in November 1943, a few weeks before his first meeting with Soviet premier Joseph Stalin in Tehran, and almost two years before the United Nations Charter entered into force in October 1945.

Roosevelt was referring to the political-military alliance that began with the 1 January 1942 signing by 26 states of the "Declaration by United Nations"; he was speaking at a White House conference that created the UN Relief and Rehabilitation Administration (UNRRA). Between 1943 and 1947, the governments of 51 states participated in this first operational UN organization—in fact, it remains the world's largest integrated, post-conflict aid and reconstruction body. It dispensed 1 percent of member states' gross domestic products in the years immediately following the war to support activities from China to Belarus that were as diverse as self-managed refugee camps to the replacement of industrial machinery. The initial purpose of these efforts was to strengthen the political will of Allied populations and the diplomatic bonds between their leaders by demonstrating that the rhetoric of war aims in the Atlantic Charter were manifest even at the height of the fighting. UNRRA pursued its quintessentially liberal work out of Realist necessity rather than as an optional accessory. Nonetheless, its pioneering multilateral efforts are all but invisible in contemporary scholarship,[2] largely eclipsed by a focus on the bilateral Marshall Plan. Moreover, UNRRA was just one of the economic, political, and humanitarian challenges successfully addressed by the United Nations during World War II, most of which are largely overlooked today.[3]

Others include issues ranging from education to agriculture, from trade and finance to criminal justice; these are discussed in this volume in order to explore the pertinence of the UN's wartime origins for insights about improving its future. One of the supposedly distinguishing characteristics of humanity is its ability to adapt to change and to anticipate it. Indeed, even deoxyribonucleic acid (better known by the acronym "DNA") was originally thought to be set in stone but is now found to be adaptable within a living creature. If even DNA is not immutable, we should not allow ourselves to think that our own international political order is fixed permanently. The examples and lost prototypes of the 1940s should give us the courage to have comparably ambitious visions about improving future world orders.

Today, a key question that ought to be in bold-faced type on the agenda of global governance is: "Do we need another cataclysm to re-kindle the imagination and energy and cooperation that was in the air in the 1940s, or are we smart enough to adapt in anticipation?" International order has been built and rebuilt on numerous occasions, and yesterday's institutions often are ill-equipped to tackle today's problems. The question is whether a new generation of multilateral organizations will arise quickly and as a result of unnecessary and unspeakable tragedies—as such crisis innovations as the League of Nations or the United Nations arose phoenix-like from the ashes of the twentieth century's world wars and the Congress of Vienna from the Napoleonic wars—or more deliberately on the basis of more modest functional bases.

The editors are betting on the human capacity for learning and adapting to prevent suffering on a scale that could well dwarf the twentieth century's wars. Why? "Whether our accumulated connectivity and experience has created fresh perspectives on global governance and an ability to transcend national orders," Ian Goldin answers, "remains the most critical question of our time."[4]

Both the practical vision of the 1940s and the general ignorance of its value should shock us from the twin complacencies that we are doing the best that we can and that our best today is better than yesterday—an assumption of steady progress epitomized in George Trevelyan's history of England.[5] It would be a tragedy that the Ancient Greeks would appreciate if we allow ourselves to drift into catastrophe in the twenty-first century having discarded or forgotten lessons learned at such cost in the last.

Peering through the lenses of global governance offers a way to identify substantial, albeit inadequate, past efforts to fill major gaps in governing the globe: in knowledge, norms, policies, institutions, and compliance.[6] Too often ahistorical examinations of global problems might well depress Voltaire's Dr. Pangloss. We clearly are not living in what that unwarranted optimist viewed as the best of all possible worlds. At the same time, we are not starting at square one, and things could be far worse; past efforts, successful or less so, provide important stepping stones toward a better future.[7] The wartime experience is essential in this regard. We need to understand the intricacies of structures and interactions by numerous agents in order to learn lessons from the past and apply them to improve future global governance.

This volume moves beyond the substantial investigations of World War II that have stressed almost exclusively the military efforts by the "greatest generation" while largely ignoring the "softer" side of the wartime efforts by the United Nations. Liberal, even socialist, ideas and programs played a critical role in Allied cohesion and prompt war termination.

Liberal international institutions were designed to create a peaceful and prosperous world. According to Craig Murphy, John Maynard Keynes and others "convinced the victors in the Second World War, the original 'United Nations,' to retain and expand the League's economic and social activities in their postwar 'United Nations Organization'."[8] Both Michael Howard and Edward Mortimer agree that this perspective makes an important reassessment of both the conduct of the war and the origins of the Cold War, thereby challenging assumptions that underpin military-centric policymaking to this day.[9]

US Lend-Lease military supplies to its allies began in March 1941 and were critical to a prompt victory, but they were under attack from Congressional Republicans throughout the war, on grounds ranging from unalloyed isolationism, reluctance to support a Communist army against the Nazis, and objections to bolstering British and other imperialism. One should recall the formal title of the legislation, "An Act to Further Promote the Defense of the United States." Roosevelt gave the same name, "United Nations," to war making and peace making, which helped to mobilize Congressional support for Lend-Lease at home and on the back of Lend-Lease to build political alliances abroad. One could summarize: no United Nations, no Lend-Lease; and no Lend-Lease, no victory in the war within four years of the attack on Pearl Harbor in December 1941.

Rapid reference is often made to the collapse of the idealism prevalent at the end of the war in the face of the double shock of Hiroshima and of the growing confrontation between the West and the Soviet Union. Little if any attention is given to that idealism, apparently irrelevant in Washington today, for instance, where the echo resounds, "We don't do social work." However, it was an essential US contribution in World War II, and it worked at home and abroad.

This volume discusses international crimes, postwar reconstruction, international development, regulated world economic and agricultural policy, education, and public diplomacy. They were strategies for the prevention of yet another world "war to end all wars"—the some-what premature billing for World War I—and viewed as foundations for postwar stability and prosperity that also helped sustain the wartime effort. In the twenty-first century, if these policy areas are considered part of security, it is often through the analytical frameworks of human security, securitization, or soft power.[10] In the common and perhaps debased usage, soft power connotes a weakness that is ultimately secondary to hard power. Yet *this* United Nations had not only defeated fascism but laid the foundations for the emergence of multilateral civilian organizations since 1942. As such, international cooperation for economic and social policies was at the core of Allied national security strategy for the postwar world, and not on the periphery where "human security" or "human development" are currently located.

Our review of wartime thinking and work peers through the other end of the telescope. The processes were, to create a word as ugly as "securitization," the "civilianization" of security as a means of war prevention. Part I of the book concerns "Planning and propaganda." In Chapter 1, "Prewar and wartime postwar planning: antecedents to the UN moment in San Francisco, 1945," J. Simon Rofe explores the strategic approach of US officials to a postwar world even before the United States was at war. No one sought a return to the chaotic pre-1914 order among the powerful despite the failure of the first generation of universal-membership international organizations—the League of Nations. Unilateral military might was not regarded as a viable option. Whatever the mindset, the Roosevelt administration adhered to the precept: if at first you don't succeed, try, try again. It battled isolationists and "America-firsters" to that end, just as it fought Congressional Republicans to increase military spending.

The second generation of intergovernmental organizations, the UN system, was not peripheral but rather absolutely essential in the minds of policy and decision makers alike—not least as a means of reducing direct requirements on Washington. At a moment when one might have expected the disaster of the failed Kantian experiment of the League to have produced a Hobbesian reaction on steroids, those at the helm were resolute in their conviction that multilateralism and the rule of law, not the law of the jungle, were essential for future world order. The contrast was Hitler, who epitomized the right of might.

A vital part of building multilateralism abroad included strengthening it at home. In the United States, this meant constructing Roosevelt's 1941 messages of the Four Freedoms and developing a system to transmit internationalist messages to the wider public, as Giles Scott-Smith explores in Chapter 2, "The UN and public diplomacy: communicating the post-national message." The idea that governments might fund a multilateral body tasked with transmitting the ideas of other governments into their own media in wartime runs counter to the usual assumption that public diplomacy by a state concerns projecting its interests abroad and that of international bodies is to promote themselves. Scott-Smith concludes by wondering whether the United Nations could attempt a similar propaganda exercise with the post-2015 development agenda, the "sustainable development goals" that will have universal dimensions and aspirations.

Yet that counterintuitive role was the task of the UN Information Offices in the United States, the United Kingdom, and elsewhere during World War II. The key aim was to share and project government views among the states of the UN coalition, numbering more than 40 by the end of 1944. US radio and newsreels featured concerts of music from the United Nations, and newspapers received briefing notes on key issues of concern to member states. Today, virtually none of the myriad satellite channels available worldwide in 193 member states includes the productions of the UN Department of Public Information. There is no UN channel among the hundreds available in Brasilia or Boston or Brighton. In 1943 movie newsreels featured in upper New York State for hosting not just a UN Day but a UN week, with visits from troops of the Allies to the lakeside community of Oswego.

UN Days from 1942 onward were state occasions around the world. Today, UN Day is celebrated on 24 October but is left to nongovernmental organizations (NGOs) to organize; it is not an event celebrated by the whole of society as during the war. True there are now also numerous "days" and "years" for many special topics in the UN system, but none of them comes near to the impact of those that took place from 1942 to 1945. In 2010, Britain's Queen Elizabeth II chose to address the UN General Assembly, a priority some commentators found puzzling, but during the war she had taken part in a vast global celebration of the wartime alliance, as her office explained: "The Queen's attendance in June 1942 at the United Nations Day Parade at Buckingham Palace … illustrates the very long connection which the Queen has with the movement and later the institution of the United Nations."[11]

The point of departure for the final chapter in Part I is education rather than economics as the priority for building a culture of peace. The national representatives at wartime educational conferences saw war as starting in the minds of men and women and regarded exaggerated nationalism as a key contributor to war and violence. Consequently, the founders of what became the United Nations Educational, Scientific and Cultural Organization (UNESCO) pursued war prevention through internationalist education. Thus, we might usefully view the development of what became UNESCO's strategy of "civilianization" of security, thereby building a culture of peace as a foundation of what today we call conflict prevention. Such a strategy could well be seen as the antithesis of today's justifications that might entail increasing education against extremism, reporting extremist students to the authorities, and increased support for nationalism and the armed forces.

In Chapter 3, "Educators across borders: the Conference of Allied Ministers of Education, 1942–45" (CAME), Miriam Intrator explores how participants in that gathering of Allied ministers, meeting in London beginning in October 1942, sought to identify the means and to lay the groundwork that they imagined would be necessary to reconstructing their countries' educational systems. Their aim was not simply to recreate what had existed prior to the outbreak of war but also to generate new pathways that would contribute to building a more tolerant and peaceful future. Their concerns ranged from ensuring that students would have access to accurate and authoritative textbooks, to building cooperative networks of transnational communication, sharing, and exchange. As the war progressed, the notion to broaden CAME into a cultural branch of the United Nations gained traction and culminated in the November 1945 establishment of UNESCO.

The focus of Part II of this volume is "Human security." Dan Plesch's Chapter 4 focuses on international criminal justice, and more specifically on the United Nations War Crimes Commission (UNWCC) of 1943–48, which comprised 17 countries. The UNWCC considered some 30,000 cases of "minor" war criminals. According to the former chief prosecutor of the International Criminal Tribunal for the former Yugoslavia (ICTY), Richard Goldstone,[12] the ICTY and other tribunals that have pursued key issues, including sexual violence, would have approached collective-joint criminal responsibility more resolutely had recent archival research into the UNWCC been available at the beginning of the 1990s.[13]

It was common throughout the UNWCC, for instance, to prosecute ordinary soldiers for torture in national tribunals. Attempts to prosecute rank-and-file perpetrators of atrocities constituted a practical recognition that such efforts could have a deterrent effect and provide a glimmer of hope to those suffering. Today, there often is not even that—prosecutions follow the Nuremberg model of pursuing the top leadership with no prosecution of the foot soldiers who commit mass atrocity crimes. At the level of leadership, states have even excluded the crime of aggression from the remit of the International Criminal Court until 2017—two decades after the court's establishment—to maintain their freedom to consider all military options.

In Chapter 5, "UNRRA's operational genius and institutional design," Eli Karetny and Thomas G. Weiss's discussion indicates why this experiment is an apt illustration of how lessons can be gleaned from revisiting wartime achievements. Among other things, this research could help shed light on the fraught contemporary notions of "One UN" and "Delivering as One," from the central oversight of UNRRA, which aimed to create self-managed and democratically run refugee camps, set up divisions for industrial and agricultural reconstruction, and provide emergency relief in the areas of food, welfare, and health. With today's booming "humanitarian business" and veritable industry of post-conflict peace-building challenges,[14] the current UN system could and should learn much from UNRRA's policies and practices. They provide potent lessons for the contemporary global governance of humanitarian action and post-conflict peace building.

In addition, the disappearance of a temporary agency—UNRRA terminated its operations in 1947 while the other "temporary" inter-governmental and nongovernmental organizations continued—may hold lessons for thinking about possible sunset clauses for other inter-governmental bodies. The 2010 creation of UN Women from four smaller UN bodies was an almost unprecedented event in UN history, shuttering existing institutions.

In light of its preponderant economic and military power, the United States is prevalent in these pages as in all books about World War II. Nonetheless, this reality does not mean that we view the multilateral framework created in the 1940s as either an affirmation only of American exceptionalism or as a hegemonic imposition of Western ideas and power.[15] Quite the contrary, which is why Manu Bhagavan's Chapter 6 explores "Toward universal relief and rehabilitation: India, UNRRA, and the new internationalism." Building on the preceding chapter's analysis of that immense UN operational experiment, he spells out how a pre-independent India made its voice heard and exercised a surprising degree of agency in deliberations about UNRRA's financing and operations. Although circumscribed by colonial status, Indian delegates worked in tandem with allies, a reality that has been given scant attention in the criticisms of international organization and the United Nations, in particular, as Western driven or even imposed. In examining and understanding decolonization in India and elsewhere in wartime, there is less of a tendency to see the UN as an imperial exercise, a claim that taints the world organization to this day.[16]

Bhagavan analyses the effort to establish offices in India, one that he judges to be in good faith, by the United States as a way to send signals to London; he also sees that Washington was essentially blind to the most pernicious aspects of the imperial stranglehold. Moreover, he examines the decision to contribute to UNRRA in the midst of a famine in Bengal, as a precursor of Jawaharlal Nehru's idealistic—although he judged realistic—stance towards international society, "One World."[17]

At US insistence, India—albeit Imperial India—participated as a full member of the wartime UN organization on war crimes and post-war relief, at Bretton Woods and San Francisco. In addition, the United States and China encouraged Indian independence as a post-war if not intra-war expectation. It was the resilience of the Chinese people in resisting the Japanese that convinced Washington at a time of institutionalized racism in America that this Asian state should occupy one of the five permanent seats at the Security Council's high table in the postwar organization.

Our consideration of the specific economic and social projects of the wartime United Nations leads to the conclusion that what is now called "human security" was for policymakers and public conceptions of the fundamentals of national and international security rather than as a fringe concern of the major powers. The concept grew from a post-Cold War, multifaceted understanding of security that merged a number of disciplinary and research efforts, including development studies, international relations, strategic studies, and human rights.[18] The United Nations Development Programme's (UNDP) *Human Development Report 1994* is considered a milestone publication in the field of human security, harking back to Roosevelt's 1941 State of the Union Address[19] with its argument that ensuring "freedom from want" and "freedom from fear" for all persons is the best path to tackle the problem of global insecurity: "The concept of security has for too long been interpreted narrowly ... It has been related more to nation-states than to people."[20] Roosevelt's rhetorical flourishes are almost three-quarters of a century old, but there is little sense today that his catch-phrases launched a contemporary global strategy. However, then secretary-general Kofi Annan's document for the 2005 UN World Summit gave at least a more conscious nod to World War II history in the key background document on the occasion of the world organization's 60th anniversary.[21]

Part III of the book continues with other elements of people's security under the heading of "Economic development." It begins with Chapter 7, "The United Nations and development: from the origins to current challenges," by John Burley and Stephen Browne. Our affection for the achievements of wartime internationalism should not blind us to the structural flaws in the design of what would become the postwar system of universal but atomized intergovernmental organizations. As

Robert Jackson wrote in the first few pages of his 1969 overview of the UN development system, "the machine as a whole has become unmanageable in the strictest sense of the word. As a result, it is becoming slower and more unwieldy like some prehistoric monster."[22] That lumbering dinosaur is now almost a half-century older and no better adapted to the climate of the twenty-first century.

What we now call "international development" did not exist in its modern form when states gathered in San Francisco for the UN Conference on International Organization—indeed, the first edition of Paul Samuelson's classic textbook *Economics* in 1948 devoted only three sentences to the topic.[23] Adamant US anticolonialism died with Roosevelt, and paternalism within the context of trusteeship sought, unsuccessfully, to put the lid back on the cauldron of national liberation struggles in Africa, Asia, and the Middle East. There was a desire to keep and build on the best of the League of Nations, but fundamentally the attention was on the Security Council and its relationship with the General Assembly. Quite deliberately, the system was allowed to be decentralized and to overlap from the start.

The US State Department's wartime UN planners drew on the experiences of the New Deal and the League of Nations as well as "functionalism" to propose what became the Charter provisions for the promotion of economic and social cooperation. However, the subject of "development of less-developed areas" barely registered. Browne and Burley revisit the reasons for both the expansion and the fragmentation of UN activities for development, which quickly became the main UN activity once the Cold War virtually paralyzed the Security Council, and the influx of newly independent countries emphasized development as essential in and of itself and not merely as a foundation for peace.

It has become an ineffective cliché to contrast ever-growing military spending in the trillions with development aid stagnating in the billions. On this, as on many issues, arguments for progressive reform today can more effectively engage adherents of hard security realism by drawing on the policies of the leading states during the archetypal Realist struggle of World War II. The contrasts between then and now become still starker when considering the global economic and financial system. When financial crises reach the point of panic, as in the 2008 global meltdown or the earlier 1997–98 one in Asia, the cry is likely to be, "We need a new Bretton Woods!"

It is thus fitting that Chapter 8 is Pallavi Roy's "Financing gaps, competitiveness, and capabilities: why Bretton Woods needs a radical rethink." Today, powerful states meet as the G7 (formerly G8 until

Russia's suspension in 2014 over Crimea), or as the G20.[24] The once-critical voice of the UN Conference on Trade and Development is largely silent. At the UN Monetary and Financial Conference, the proper name for the 1944 gathering in Bretton Woods, the powerful thought it was important to include a seat at the financial high table for Liberia and Panama. Roy explores in particular the contributions by and limits placed on Imperial India. These and other seemingly insignificant states made their contributions to the new global economic efforts. She explores the pertinence of the Keynesian consensus among the "G44" (the number of states present) for today's ongoing financial and monetary crises with the G20's efforts to reform international financial institutions. Among other things, she challenges us to explore such questions as: Is it useful to re-introduce the securitization of global monetary, financial, and trade policy? What is the role of state oversight of an autonomous international monetary system?

However, rarely are the concrete ideas of that time given a full and fair airing. They are worth in-depth examination, however, whether to ensure economic stability narrowly defined, to reinforce a more equitable society as a moral good, or to act as a source of deep-rooted human security for war prevention. In 1944 high employment and social development were set as economic priorities to ensure international peace and security. International security concerns drove economic policy rather than security policy being devoted to the spread of the market. To meet security concerns, overall well-being rather than wealth creation was the priority.

Indeed, it is important to remind ourselves of the extent to which current expectations for intergovernmental organizations are remarkably feeble in comparison with previous proposals from highly respected commentators. At Bretton Woods in 1944, for instance, John Maynard Keynes and the British delegation proposed a monetary fund equal to half of annual world imports while Harry Dexter White and the American side proposed a smaller fund of *only* one-sixth. One of the first economists recruited by the United Nations, Hans Singer, sardonically noted two decades ago: "Today's [International Monetary] Fund is only 2 per cent of annual world imports. Perhaps the difference between Keynes's originally proposed 50 percent and the actual 2 percent is a measure of the degree to which our vision of international economic management has shrunk."[25]

The G20 decision in 2009 to alter International Monetary Fund (IMF) voting rules was a step toward "regime change" in that institution although the agreed changes to representation remain tied up in the US Congress. Nonetheless, even after the 2009 infusion of close to

1 trillion during the financial meltdown, the IMF still had one-twenty-fifth of the capital considered sensible by arguably the twentieth century's most able economist. Furthermore, foes and some friends of the IMF regularly lambaste its excessive leverage resulting from the conditionality tied to loans. If so, what adjectives should we apply to capture the discrepancy between demonstrated and supposedly agreed needs and the actual wherewithal of such institutions as the Office of the High Commissioner for Human Rights and UN Environment Programme? If we had Keynes's or even White's expectations, how cavernous would the institutional gaps be for human rights and the environment?

Among the conferences that laid the foundations for the postwar order was the very first in Hot Springs, Virginia, the 1943 United Nations Conference on Food and Agriculture. Ironically, it also may be among the least known, as Ruth Jachertz points out in Chapter 9, "Stable agricultural markets and world order: FAO and ITO, 1943–49." For contemporaries of that event, though, a re-ordering of agricultural markets and an increase in agricultural production worldwide were pre-requisites for lasting international peace; for the Roosevelt administration, it was a way to demonstrate the concrete benefits that effective multilateral cooperation could bring all countries, including the United States and its producers and consumers. Few at the center of power see this as a top concern nowadays, and yet hunger was one of the drivers of the so-called Arab Spring beginning in 2010–11.

The ideas debated at Hot Springs and later refined in the UN Food and Agriculture Organization (FAO), which was founded as a direct result of the conference, also deeply influenced the commodity policy envisioned in the Charter of the still-born International Trade Organization (ITO). Jachertz discusses the worldwide solutions to problems of food distribution and commodity trading suggested by FAO and the ITO. Solutions suggested today from the margins of policy for making agricultural markets more conducive to growth in developing countries such as commodity agreements, reserves, food aid, and protective tariffs had already been thoroughly discussed during World War II, and it is high time to ponder the alternative vision these plans entailed.

The final chapter consists of our "Past as prelude, whither the United Nations?" As the companion bookend of this Introduction, we attempt to draw together the wealth of lessons from these intriguing examinations of the UN's wartime origins and their implications for the future of the world organization.

We end this Introduction with the implications of this collection of essays for studying and teaching international relations. They are published for the 70th anniversary of the conference convened in San

Francisco in April 1945 which agreed the UN Charter whose Preamble's opening lines spells out the purpose: "to save succeeding generations from the scourge of war, which twice in our lifetime has brought untold sorrow." Our investigation into material about which we were unaware through much of our working lives leads us to reconsider how our academic disciplines do business, and how we teach. We are persuaded that a more thorough consideration of wartime history could help inform the study and practice of the future United Nations and of international relations more generally.

Andrew Hurrell usefully reminds us about the "relentless present-ism" that afflicts political science and international relations.[26] It has become a sort of inverse Alzheimer's disease. Short-term memory is retained while the contexts that crafted these memories have slipped away. So, in the spirit (but hopefully not the jargon) of postmodernism, we seek value in pertinent experiences of earlier times. A possible source of optimism is that we are not, in fact, starting from scratch. In some ways many current global problems ironically reflect past successes with interna-tional cooperation—for instance, more states as a result of decoloniza-tion, more globalization as a result of trade liberalization, more institutions as a result of the processes of collaboration and specialization, and more environmental degradation as a result of growth.[27]

As scholars and educators, in short, there are numerous lessons about how we as a profession go about our trade.[28] The overarching ones are that present policy needs to be better informed by history, and that history should not be shy of policy. The Cold War eclipsed the brief and brilliant wartime internationalism to an extent barely realized by many analysts today. Three authors of an international relations text-book, one of whom contributes to this volume, scold us appropriately: "One of the often-perceived problems of the social sciences is their lack of historical depth."[29]

There is enough in these chapters already to suggest that we review some cherished notions prevalent in our theorizing and policy analyses of world politics. Not least is the stark reality that evidence from the wartime origins of the United Nations indicates that in the heat of war states were wise enough to adopt multilateral liberal institutionalism to help ensure the classic Realist objectives of state survival.

Notes

1 Franklin D. Roosevelt, "The Nations Have Common Objectives," 9 November 1943, available at www.ibiblio.org/pha/policy/1943/1943-11-09c. html.

2 An exception is Jessica Reinisch, "'We Shall Rebuild a Powerful Nation': UNRRA, Internationalism and National Reconstruction in Poland," *Journal of Contemporary History* 43, no. 3 (2008): 371–404; "Internationalism in Relief: The Birth (and Death) of UNRRA," *Past and Present*, supplement 6 (2013): 258–89; and "'Auntie UNRRA' at the Crossroads," *Past and Present*, supplement 8 (2013): 70–97. For contemporary lessons, see Thomas G. Weiss, "Renewing Washington's Multilateral Leadership," *Global Governance* 18, no. 3 (2012): 253–66.

3 Dan Plesch, *America, Hitler and the UN* (London: Tauris, 2011).

4 Ian Goldin, *Divided Nations: Why Global Governance is Failing and What We Can Do about It* (Oxford: Oxford University Press, 2013), 166–67.

5 George Macaulay Trevelyan, *English Social History: A Survey of Six Centuries: Chaucer to Queen Victoria* (London: Pelican Books, 1968).

6 Thomas G. Weiss and Ramesh Thakur, *Global Governance and the UN: An Unfinished Journey* (Bloomington: Indiana University Press, 2010).

7 Thomas G. Weiss, *Governing the World? Addressing "Problems without Passports"* (Denver, Colo.: Paradigm Publishers, 2014).

8 Craig N. Murphy, *International Organization and Industrial Change: Global Governance since 1850* (Cambridge: Polity Press, 1994), 17.

9 Plesch, *America, Hitler and the UN*, i–ii.

10 Joseph S. Nye, Jr, *Soft Power: The Means to Success in World Politics* (New York: Public Affairs, 2004).

11 Letter from Buckingham Palace addressed to Dan Plesch, 22 October 2010.

12 Richard Goldstone, "Foreword: The United Nations War Crimes Commission Symposium," in *The United Nations War Crimes Commission: The Origins of International Criminal Justice*, ed. William Schabas, Carsten Stahn, Dan Plesch, Shanti Sattler, and Joseph Powderly, special double issue of *Criminal Law Forum* 25, nos. 1 & 2 (2014): 9–15.

13 Dan Plesch and Shanti Sattler, "Changing the Paradigm of International Criminal Law: Considering the Work of the United Nations War Crimes Commission of 1943–48," *International Community Law Review* 15, no. 2 (2013): 203–23.

14 Thomas G. Weiss, *Humanitarian Business* (Cambridge: Polity Press, 2013).

15 See, for instance, Edward C. Luck, *Mixed Messages: American Politics and International Organization 1919–1999* (Washington, DC: Brookings, 1999); and G. John Ikenberry, *Liberal Leviathan: The Origins, Crisis, and Transformation of the American System* (Princeton, N.J.: Princeton University Press, 2011).

16 Mark Mazower, *No Enchanted Palace: The End of Empire and the Ideological Origins of the United Nations* (Princeton, N.J.: Princeton University Press, 2009).

17 Manu Bhagavan, *India and the Quest for One World: The Peacemakers* (New York: Palgrave Macmillan, 2013).

18 S. Neil MacFarlane and Yuen Foong Khong, *Human Security and the UN: A Critical History* (Bloomington: Indiana University Press, 2006).

19 Franklin D. Roosevelt, "The State of the Union Address," 6 January 1941, available at voicesofdemocracy.umd.edu/fdr-the-four-freedoms-speech-text/.

20 UNDP, *Human Development Report 1994: New Dimensions of Human Security* (New York: Oxford University Press, 1994), 22–24.

21 Kofi A. Annan, *In Larger Freedom: Towards Security, Development, and Human Rights for All* (New York: UN, 2005).

14   *Dan Plesch and Thomas G. Weiss*

22 United Nations, *A Capacity Study of the United Nations Development System* (Geneva: UN, 1969), volume I, document DP/5, iii.
23 Louis Emmerij, Richard Jolly, and Thomas G. Weiss, *Ahead of the Curve? UN Ideas and Global Challenges* (Bloomington: Indiana University Press, 2001), 27; see also Richard Jolly, Louis Emmerij, and Thomas G. Weiss, *UN Ideas that Changed the World* (Bloomington: Indiana University Press, 2009).
24 Andrew F. Cooper and Ramesh Thakur, *The Group of 20 (G20)* (London: Routledge, 2012).
25 Hans Singer, "An Historical Perspective," in *The UN and the Bretton Woods Institutions: New Challenges for the Twenty-First Century*, ed. Mahbub ul Haq, Richard Jolly, Paul Streeten, and Khadija Haq (London: Macmillan, 1995), 19.
26 Andrew Hurrell, "Foreword to the Third Edition" of Hedley Bull, *The Anarchical Society* (New York: Columbia University Press, 2002), xiii.
27 Thomas Hale, David Held, and Kevin Young, *Gridlock: Why Global Cooperation is Failing When We Need it Most* (Cambridge: Polity Press, 2013).
28 See Thomas G. Weiss and Rorden Wilkinson, "Rethinking Global Governance: Complexity, Authority, Power, Change," *International Studies Quarterly* 58, no. 2 (2014): 207–15; and "Global Governance to the Rescue: Saving International Relations?" *Global Governance* 20, no. 1 (2014): 19–36.
29 Andrew J. Williams, Amelia Hadfield, and J. Simon Rofe, *International History and International Relations* (London: Routledge, 2012), 3. See also Barry Buzan and George Lawson, "The Global Transformation: The Nineteenth Century and the Making of Modern International Relations," *International Studies Quarterly* 57, no. 3 (2013): 620–34.

I
Planning and propaganda

1 Prewar and wartime postwar planning

Antecedents to the UN moment in San Francisco, 1945

J. Simon Rofe[1]

- **The antecedents of international organization**
- **An embryonic association, 1937–43**
- **Conclusion: looking back to look forward**

"Fortunately, there is always liberty to dream, even if the result is nothing but dreams."[2] Then US assistant secretary of state Adolf Berle uttered these words in the spring of 1940 when contemplating the future of an "international organization." The international organization about which Berle spoke with his colleagues in President Franklin D. Roosevelt's State Department would become the United Nations Organization (UNO) at the San Francisco conference of April 1945, although it was by no means pre-ordained during the course of World War II. Berle's remarks were part of a broad-ranging, complex, and often heated discourse surrounding the shape of the postwar world and the place of an international organization within it.

Importantly, these discussions were not isolated to the chief executives of the United Nations' main protagonists—the likes of Franklin D. Roosevelt, Joseph Stalin, and Winston Churchill at their wartime summits. Instead, as indicated in the opening words of this chapter, it was at the operational level—what Erik Goldstein has called the "marzipan" level—that the full breadth of the discourse about a future international organization becomes evident. The most complete records are to be found in the US and UK archives, particularly the former, as seen in the conceptual discussions of the US State Department in the late 1930s and early 1940s.[3] Of course, discussions of the postwar world were not limited to the State Department; the huge expansion of the federal government during World War II meant that other facets of Washington's bureaucracy, such as the War and Treasury departments, were intimately involved in planning for the postwar world.

Furthermore, opinion from nongovernmental organizations such as the Council on Foreign Relations, and other governments, particularly those with experience in the League of Nations, were considered. Their views are also included in this historical examination of the UNO's emergence.

The chapter explores the discussions on international organization that preceded the world organization's creation, not only at San Francisco in April 1945, but also before the 1 January 1942 Declaration by United Nations. It begins by looking at the genealogy of international organization through the Progressive era and World War I, and into the interwar period, providing a critical reading of the interwar legacy of the League of Nations to the United Nations itself. Central is the influence of the Woodrow Wilson administration, the Versailles conference, and the birth of the League of Nations. Particularly, they shaped the educational and professional experiences of a generation of diplomats who would find themselves deliberating about a postwar world by 1939.

Then this chapter looks at the period between 1937 and 1943 as the world accelerated into global war. This period was critical in illustrating the importance of preparing for the postwar world in political and economic dimensions while the war was being fought by an increasing number of protagonists. The failings of the League to prevent conflict were laid bare, before the Declaration by United Nations would emphasize the Alliance's dual war aims. Before then, the challenge was how to reconcile the future parameters of an international organization against immediate security threats: a dilemma that has confronted the call for reform at the United Nations ever since.

The chapter concludes that the legacy bequeathed to the United Nations by statesmen and diplomats before Pearl Harbor has been overlooked and requires repositioning in our understanding of the UNO that resulted from San Francisco. Only by understanding the breadth and depth of the debate of this previous era can the eventual shape of the United Nations as it unfolded be fully understood, and hence its position in the twenty-first century. A parallel story can be told of the creation of the Allied Supreme War Council in the closing stages of the Great War on the Allied military interest in formalized cooperation after 1939. The debates about an international organization during the latter part of World War II are well documented, but to understand the link between them and the implications for the immediate postwar world and beyond, it is salient to consider the words of one of the League's architects, Robert Cecil, at that institution's final meeting in 1946: "The League is dead. Long live the United Nations."[4]

The antecedents of international organization

The planned international organization that emerged from the Dumbarton Oaks conversations in late summer 1944, and which would go on to become the United Nations Organization the following year, had long-term antecedents. Predating the nation-state's recognized birth date in 1648 in the Treaty of Westphalia, bodies such as the Roman Catholic Church through the Holy Roman Empire operated in a fashion that we now recognize as being analogous to an international organization. The mid-nineteenth century saw the founding in 1865 of the International Committee of the Red Cross (ICRC), which sought to establish universal standards of medical care for wounded combatants. The ICRC, along with the Universal Postal Union founded in 1874, brought international levels of cooperation in an alternative realm to the Concert of Europe, which itself was important in "innovating international affairs." Mark Mazower continues that influenced by the likes of German philosopher Immanuel Kant, who held "that humanity not only possessed reason but would ultimately be guided by it," the Progressive movement of the end of the nineteenth century believed in the human race's capacity to organize itself to trade peacefully and to arbitrate conflicts.[5] These ideas, the latter discussed at the Hague Conferences in 1899 and 1907, were widespread in the Anglosphere and in the empires they governed around the world.[6] Although contested by disaffected groups within Western society, the inevitable "triumph" of progress would be challenged by the catastrophe of the Great War that blighted these same societies. Remarkable in many ways, the pervasiveness of the concept of an organized international framework transcended the carnage of World War I and endured.

The clearest evidence of the concept of an international organization becoming manifest was seen in US president Woodrow Wilson's January 1918 address to a joint session of the US Congress. Coming as the final point of his "14 points," Wilson called for "A general association of nations" to be formed "under specific covenants for the purpose of affording mutual guarantees of political independence and territorial integrity to great and small states alike."[7] His address drew upon the endeavors of the "Inquiry" that his proto-national security adviser, Colonel Edward House, had initiated in the autumn of 1917. House called upon a then 28-year-old Walter Lippmann to coordinate leading scholars in an effort to provide guidance to the pressing dilemmas of international affairs. Within the inquiry's discussions, the prospect of an international organization was prominent, and although debate exists as to how far Wilson listened, there is a self-evident link to the "general association of nations" that the president espoused in 1918. The inquiry was the foundation for the Council on Foreign Relations, which came into existence in July 1921—a link between the interwar period, the deliberations that ended with the United Nations, and postwar international affairs.[8]

With the end of the Great War in November 1918, the 14 Points were the Allies' only publicly stated war aims. When the peace conference began in Paris in 1919, many, including the defeated Germans, expected them to form the basis of the peace agreement. The tale of Wilson's feted arrival in Europe and the "old" diplomacy of Versailles have been told elsewhere. Suffice to say that it was no little achievement for the American president to secure the agreement of the European, née global, powers to the establishment of a League of Nations by the Treaty of Versailles.

The League, which met for the first time in November 1920 in Geneva, with 54 members signing its Covenant, began its work with a near universal sense of hope and good will. That its hopes would not be fulfilled is a story that need not be retold. What is significant here is the legacy that those debating a future international organization drew from their experience of the League of Nations.

The genealogy of the United Nations can be identified in at least two key areas. First, the League bequeathed to World War II policymakers a blueprint for issues that would face a future international organization in the postwar world. There is a remarkable similarity to the issues that the League actually addressed in the 1920s and 1930s—for example, repatriation of refugees, freedom of trade, regional security, minority rights, and disarmament—to be tackled on the basis of collective security.[9] Inis L. Claude's seminal text points to the link between international organization and the concept of collective security: "If the movement for international organization in the twentieth century can be said to have a preoccupation, a dominant purpose, a supreme ideal, it is clear that the achievement of collective security answers that description."[10] The League and the United Nations grappled with this concept, and the continuities did not end there. Striking similarities can be found in the solutions being proffered in engaging with these issues in the interwar years and by the planners of the post-1945 international order, to the extent that Mark Mazower argues that "the truth is that the UN was in many ways a continuation of the earlier body."[11]

The League itself provided a platform for its own evolution better to meet the requirements of managing international affairs. These suggested "reforms"—a term without its late twentieth-century baggage—were based on the reflective qualities to the League's Geneva-based secretariat. Patricia Clavin's *Securing the World Economy* reveals how the League was able to exert a new and material influence in economic and financial affairs in the interwar years providing substance for her subtitle, *The Reinvention of the League of Nations 1920–1946*. Furthermore, the League provided a stage for debate about the shape of an international organization in international affairs—a "multiverse," as she describes it. The League of Nations, she writes, "became a site where a plurality of views about global and regional coordination and cooperation were generated, and where they could be compared and could compete."[12]

At the time Joseph Avenol became the League's second secretary-general in the summer of 1934, and in the face of the failures of the World Disarmament Conference, the London Economic Conference, and the challenges arising from totalitarian regimes, a series of discussions on the League's structure and performance were formalized in an eponymous report. The essential tenor of Avenol's recommendations was to separate the "technical" and "humanitarian" issues from those of a "security" and "political" variety. Avenol did not make this distinction dogmatically by ignoring the implications of one upon the other—he had previously been deputy secretary-general from 1923 to 1933—but did so in order to advance the League's efforts to alleviate the plight of humanity by addressing "social and economic" issues. An experiential reading of the League in the mid-1930s could point to a notable body of work across a "myriad of programs concerned with relief and resettlement of refugees, commerce, health, transit and communications, finance, the Opium trade, prostitution, child welfare, and intellectual cooperation."[13] As Roosevelt himself said in the 1920s, the League had become "the principal agency for the settlement of international controversy, for the constructive administration of many duties which are primarily international in scope, and for the correction of abuses that have been all too common in our civilization."[14]

The second legacy of the League and the interwar period bequeathed to the United Nations was the involvement of the United States with the cause of a postwar international organization: the vision of the postwar world was quintessentially American, according to Michael Howard.[15] Here, this author disagrees with Mazower's suggestion that US centrality to the founding of the United Nations is an "optical illusion."[16] Famously absent from the official membership of the League of Nations, the United States became increasingly involved in the workings of the League in Geneva during the interwar period. As a small example, by 1938, New Deal veteran and future US ambassador to the United Kingdom John G. Winant would be elected head of the International

Labour Organization (itself unique within the UN system as a direct carry-over from the League era).[17] Before practical and institutional links were manifest, the idea of an international organization, and the US relationship with it, were intertwined at the culmination of the Great War in the shape of Wilson.

From the outset of that conflict "America's mission centered on neutrality and mediation, not preparation for war," Justus Doenecke writes, with the president desiring to "serve as the world's peace-maker."[18] Upon returning from Paris in the summer of 1919, Wilson's adherence to the League of Nations—which ultimately drove him to tour the United States pleading its case and the subsequent breakdown of his health—blended the cause of an international organization with US domestic politics. This would have repercussions for the fate of the League in 1919 and 1920 as the Senate rejected US membership and then the Democratic ticket lost the 1920 election; however, they also form a backdrop 20 years later for those debating the merits of US involvement in international affairs.

It is difficult to overstate the impact of World War I on the American body politic. While sheltered from the war's immediate ravages, the collective narrative of "returning home" built in an added poignancy as tales were retold, and memories waned. For the American people, as Michael Carew states, "The First World War was their most immediate reference point in relation to American foreign and defense policy."[19] Importantly, and underpinning the overly simplified debates about isolationism and internationalism, the war and the international organization that followed provided first-hand experience for those Americans who came together to deliberate the shape of what became the United Nations.[20] Clavin's account of the League's wartime home in Princeton from 1940 points to the number of Americans with League experience in the halls of officialdom. Alongside the number of veterans who had served in the conflict itself, both the League and the war were not easily overlooked by the 1940s.[21]

The significance of the earlier period on the future shape of the United Nations alliance and the subsequent organization on one protagonist in particular is noteworthy. Long before Roosevelt led the United States as a wartime leader, he stated "I have seen war" and "I hate war."[22] His experience of the Great War as assistant secretary of the navy, on visiting Europe, and being present at Versailles, and in the vehemence of the debates about the League as part of the 1920 election, would be formative in Roosevelt's understanding of affairs beyond US borders. Arthur Schlesinger, Jr., attributes a great deal of the global perspective that Roosevelt exhibited during World War II to his tenure as assistant secretary of the navy, during which he "learned the strategic necessities of international relations. He learned how to distinguish between vital and peripheral interests."[23]

As Roosevelt contemplated re-entering public life after his health travails of the early 1920s, his appreciation of the "global" was evident in a 1928 article in *Foreign Affairs*. Outlining the Democratic Party's position, he argued that the United States "should cooperate with the League as the first great agency for the maintenance of peace and for the solution of common problems ever known to civilization, and, without entering into European politics, we should take an active, hearty and official part in all those proceedings which bear on the general good of mankind."[24] This passage provides insight into Roosevelt's attitude toward a multifaceted international organization, mindful of domestic political pressures that would also come to bear during his presidency. Importantly, for its later implications on debates surrounding the United Nations and spheres of influence, was the article's approach toward the Western hemisphere. Roosevelt stated that US policy toward Latin America should be "aimed not only at self-protection but, in a larger sense, at continental peace." Such sentiment carries the hallmarks of what became Roosevelt's Good Neighbor policy and would be exhibited in the agreement on Principles of Inter-American Solidarity and Cooperation, at Buenos Aires in December 1936. The passage on Latin America was drafted by Franklin's close confidant Sumner Welles, an expert in Latin American affairs who would go on to become under secretary of state in 1937 and a key foreign postwar planner after that.[25] By the time that the Roosevelt administration was contemplating the United Nations Organization after Pearl Harbor, the Good Neighbor precedent of the United States as a strong international citizen working in conjunction with a concert of other countries was important in discussions of a postwar world in relation to the idea of "sphere of influence," given the term's "strong pejorative connotation." As Susan Hast notes, although "as a foreign policy tool [sphere of influence became] morally unacceptable, representing injustice,"[26] it was a referent term in burgeoning discussions about a postwar order in the 1930s and would shape the United Nations itself. This was not least because Roosevelt was mindful of how appealing it was to Joseph Stalin as postwar planning became part of their discussions in 1944 and his later promotion of the approach of "Three Policemen" (the United States, United Kingdom, and Soviet Union) as an alternative to a universal international organization (the Three became "Four" with the inclusion of China).[27]

There were not only differences in opinion between Washington, London, and Moscow on regional approaches to the postwar world as harbinger of the Cold War, but also cleavages in Anglo-American understanding too. Commenting on an aide-memoire from British foreign secretary Anthony Eden, State Department officials were categorical in a memorandum to the president: "the basis of international organization should be world-wide rather than regionaly [sic]; that there are grave dangers involved in having the world organization rest upon the foundation of previously created, full-fledged regional organizations; and that while there may be advantages to setting up regional arrangements for some purposes, such arrangements should be subsidiary to the world organization and should flow from it."[28] The preeminence of a universal international organization to the postwar thinking by 1943 is addressed in the next section.

The UN's genealogy from the League's interwar experiences and the consideration of an international organization in US political thinking is born out in a swath of recent literature. The likes of Patricia Clavin, Mark Mazower, Katharina Rietzler, Zara Steiner, Daniel Gorman, Justin Hart, and Barbara Keys constitute a reappraisal of the interwar period with the League playing a facilitating part in creating a level of international society that allowed for an exchange of ideas.[29] An important feature of these exchanges was the emergence and consolidation of foreign policy "think tanks" with their foundation funding. The Round Table, the Royal Institute of International Affairs—better known as Chatham House, in the United Kingdom—and the Council on Foreign Relations in the United States all readily discussed the League and the concepts underpinning an international organization.[30] The latter would go on to have a significant influence on US postwar planning efforts by preparing a series of papers for the State Department during the war. One such paper in 1941 called for a future organization to be coherent and have strong powers of review over its constituent bodies because "problems are so interrelated that they cannot be compartmentalized."[31] The author's reading of the League experience was that "separation and dispersal" in line with individual national interests had constrained its effectiveness. The League's role beyond its failure to inhibit totalitarian regimes, and a sophisticated understanding of US international involvement beyond isolationism, allow for consideration of previously dismissed continuities about international society of the era. Whether consciously or not, these historians are contributing to the "new" diplomatic history by alerting readers to the multiplicity of actors and processes beyond formal government-to-government channels, comprising what Claude identified as the "Second UN" and what Thomas G. Weiss, Tatiana Carayannis, and Richard Jolly have more recently expanded beyond international secretariats to the "Third UN."[32]

An embryonic association, 1937–43

This chapter now looks at the period from 1937 to 1943 preceding the Declaration by United Nations as regional conflicts expanded to engulf the globe, and the focus on what would constitute the postwar world was sharpened. The period outlines the difficulties of considering the postwar order while hostilities were ongoing. Remarkably, as the League of Nations operations in Geneva became more moribund, the issues for which it provided a stage could be found in the deliberations of officials and experts addressing the matter both within and without national governments.

The continuity of thinking from the interwar to the wartime period was remarkable. As examples, this section focuses on two instances of the relevance of the economic dimension of thinking to postwar developments. They can be found in the Bruce report of August 1939 on the League's ability to act as host for economic development and forebear to the UN's Economic and Social Committee, and separately in US State Department deliberations on international organization, including the Special Subcommittee on International Organization (July 1942–June 1943), which formed part of the Advisory Committee on Postwar Foreign Policy. For the United States, the period prior to Pearl Harbor was further complicated by the ongoing concern in the Roosevelt administration that the United States appear aloof from the trials of the Old World's conflicts. The American people were grappling with the extent of an internationalist future, at the same time as officials and experts had scope to "think the unthinkable" in terms of what the postwar world could look like. So while the higher echelons of the Roosevelt administration "foresaw the need for long-term American involvement in shaping international politics and economics when the war ended," according to Leon Gordenker, they worked "silently in a political atmosphere that remained coloured by isolationist reaction to Wilson's programme."[33]

The Bruce Committee and its report—*The Development of International Co-operation in Economic and Social Affairs: Report of the Special Committee*—known eponymously after the former Australian prime minister and then high commissioner in London, was published less than two weeks before Adolf Hitler's invasion of Poland.[34] A result of Avenol's sporadic desire to reform the League, with Bruce's own ambition, the report "reflected a growing global interdependence which had transformed the League into a center for the study of great national socio-economic concerns." It also advocated for closer involvement with non-members of the League—i.e., the United States.[35] According to David Lee, the committee's work laid "the foundations of the economic and social work of the United Nations today."[36] Bruce himself was a League enthusiast from the outset: "If the League of Nations goes, the hope of mankind goes also." However, he was not blindly evangelical about it during his time as Australia's representative 1932–39.[37] "The League counted less to Bruce than the contacts he established there," and it is his appreciation of this point that facilitated the cross-pollination of thinking—particularly at the "marzipan level"—on the shape of the postwar world that would see the ideas for economic and social cooperation be incorporated into the Economic and Social Council (ECOSOC, envisaged as a stronger UN body before Cold War politics saw the Soviet Union scale back its scope).

Despite the League's failings by the end of 1939, Bruce persevered in discussing the economic dimension to a future settlement. In March 1940, he told US under secretary of state Sumner Welles in London: "we should be prepared immediately to discuss both our political and economic objectives when the war was over."[38] In a memorandum composed at the time that the heritage of the Bruce report was clear, and alongside his concern for the end of the war, he wrote:

> If the legitimate desires of the people are to be met, it is necessary to secure international agreements, covering both the political and economic planes. This will involve the elaboration of new methods of international co-operation and new conceptions of the limitations of national sovereignty. The opportunity will arise at the conclusion of the war but unless immediate steps are taken to examine the problems and to propose a solution, it is more than probable that the opportunity will be missed.[39]

Bruce therefore welcomed burgeoning US efforts to consider the postwar world. "He said that of all the nations," State Department officer Jay Pierrepont Moffat records, "the United States alone was doing some thinking on what was to become of the world after the war. The Allies were so busy winning the war that they were not even risking possible divergence of view between themselves over peace terms."[40] Such a concern was a masterstroke in unifying those fighting the Axis into the United Nations in the 1 January 1942 Declaration. Bruce continued to correspond with US officials—including Leo Pasvolsky as the special assistant to the secretary of state and from 1942 the chair of the State Department's Committee on Post-War Planning—on the "problems of post-war reconstruction." With his particular interests, Bruce was invited to inaugurate and then chair the World Food

Council of the Food and Agriculture Organization of the United Nations, 1946–51.[41]

The significance of Bruce and his report is that the United States shared the concerns raised about economic diplomacy at the end of the world conflict. Those in the State Department saw in Bruce's report an opportunity to gather "all relevant LON [League of Nations] committees under a new Central Committee for Economic and Social Questions ... thus avoiding the 'debate on foreign politics'."[42] "The central objective of the settlement should be to lay the foundation for an expansion of economic activity," Pasvolsky wrote, "especially in the field of international trade, as a means of relieving the existing tension making for possible military conflict and of providing a basis for orderly and constructive development within individual nations."[43] This assessment of how security could be achieved came not on the eve of war but at the outset of 1937. It could equally have been written at any point from then until World War II ended, and would have chimed with Bruce. For those in Washington, as in Geneva, the importance of economic diplomacy to deliberations on the postwar world is clear.

The State Department's concerns in identifying an economic dimension to the postwar discussion can be seen in the work of the Advisory Committee on Problems in Foreign Relations (ACPFR).[44] Convened at the end of 1939, it was the US forebear to the more celebrated Advisory Committee on Postwar Foreign Policy.[45] The ACPFR itself was structured so that economic matters were discussed under a subcommittee, chaired by Pasvolsky, due to the influence of American public opinion at the beginning of an election year. Welles and his colleagues rationalized in the same way as many in Geneva thought, that Americans "would go further in support of United States participation in international economic cooperation than in international political arrangements."[46] The committee's concluding proposals were far-reaching and included a European "Regional Political, Economic and Security Organization," a "Permanent Court of Justice," and more speculatively, even an "International Air Force."[47] In each case the antecedents to provisions of the postwar environment are evident (and the latter came under Article 45 of the UN Charter, the moribund Military Staff Committee). Equally, there was scope for the evolution of State Department thinking in Pasvolsky's committee after it came into existence in February 1942 just weeks after Pearl Harbor and then the Declaration by United Nations.

One area that did exhibit the evolution of State Department thinking toward the United Nations was the Special Subcommittee on International Organization in the Subcommittee on Political Problems, both chaired by Welles.[48] Not originally planned, its institution itself showed the need for the process to be adaptable. It assumed "a position of major importance and status," according to Harley Notter's official history of US postwar planning, in providing the parent subcommittee with "something tangible before it."[49] The work involved considering all and any alternatives for an international organization and the breadth of alternatives considered is remarkable, making it worthy of Notter's remarks. The lengthy agenda from August 1942 gives an indication of the breadth of the material discussed by the seven-man committee in their weekly meetings: "General Smuts Memorandum of 16 December 1918; the Kellogg-Briand Pact; the Geneva Protocol of October 1924; the General Act for the Pacific Settlement of International Disputes of 1928; the latest edition (1939) of *Essential Facts About the League of Nations*; League Reform by S. Engel (Geneva Research Centre); the Open Door; and the Mandate System by B. Gerig of the Staff of SR [Division of Special Research] (for possible interest in Woodrow Wilson's views pages 101–3)."[50]

In October 1942, the special subcommittee offered its parent body a "Provisional Outline of International Organization" as a "basis for discussion," with the aim of constructing "a stronger, not a weaker, organization than is the League of Nations." This was immediately followed by the acknowledgment: "The necessity for this is admitted by all thoughtful observers."[51] By November 1942, the subcommittee was in a position to fulfill a founding requirement of all committees and complete a wiring diagram outlining the form of a new international organization.[52] With organs to address security, economics, social welfare, trusteeship, culture, and with an "Executive Council" and "Staff," it does not require a huge leap to identify today's UN system, even with its twenty-first-century trappings.

Those ignoring the League's legacy in the planning for the United Nations overlook the readiness of the United States to acknowledge, albeit within their postwar planning process, the heritage that Washington took from the League. In August 1942, with the League reduced to its Princeton presence, and the war that many people attributed to the League's failings still delicately poised, there was still "considerable discussion of the advantages and disadvantages of reviving the League" in the State Department. That the League warranted "considerable discussion" is notable. Indeed, subcommittee members each appraised "article by article" the League's Covenant in terms of "its strength or weakness in international action."[53] In reading the extensive files that comprise the US postwar planning effort, there is a clear appreciation of the League's work across a range of issues. Among the strengths that were readily identifiable to those in Washington was the League's work in the realm of health and social welfare: "It would be a calamity if the fine work which has been carried on in these fields under the auspices of the League of Nations should not be maintained and developed."[54] This work would be "maintained and developed," alongside many of the other attributes of the interwar period, through the course of 1944 and the gatherings at Bretton Woods and Dumbarton Oaks, and into 1945.

Conclusion: looking back to look forward

A 1942 draft of the Preamble to the Charter for a postwar international organization asserted:

> Having defended by force of arms the principle of peaceful relations between states, and
>> Having subscribed to a common program of human rights,
>> Undertake to establish the instrumentalities by which peace and human rights man be secured.

It also came with the following clarification: "The Preamble has been drafted to cover both the immediate and the ultimate war aims of the United Nations and has been limited to these two statements in order to secure united support for what follows."[55] That the clarification was warranted provides ample support to Dan Plesch's assessment of the United Nations Organization's emergence in San Francisco in the early summer of 1945 as "realist necessity, not liberal accessory." Realism, particularly in the post-Morgenthau understanding of the term, has not normally been associated with the United Nations at any stage of its history, or pre-history. Nonetheless, as Mazower reminds us, "[w]hat emerged in 1945 at San Francisco was the League reborn, only now modified and adjusted—thanks to the Big Three conversations at Dumbarton Oaks—to the frank realities of a new configuration of great power politics."[56] What is also clear from the antecedents to San Francisco is the pragmatism that the postwar planners had deployed in drafting what became the UN Charter. It was married to their repeated application and resourcefulness to adapt and learn from their immediate past. It is these latter two qualities that have been such a challenge to identify in the membership of the United Nations in more recent times and have plagued its twenty-first-century endeavors.

At the outset of a book that seeks to reprise the thoughtful analysis that saw many historians play a role in contributing to policy in the postwar planning process in the United States and elsewhere, this chapter has highlighted continuities not only with the interwar period but also the nineteenth century and even before. The chapter ceases before the "Advanced Preparation" stage in US postwar planning begins in late 1943, as that is a familiar tale in the run up to the conferences at Bretton Woods and Dumbarton Oaks because by then it was agreed that an international security organization would be the "basic instrumentality to keep the peace."[57] Given an E.H. Carr-inspired reading of the League's interwar performance and with World War II still unfolding, the United Nations' faith that the answer in the postwar world was a reinforced international organization is remarkable.

"Like the League, the United Nations was much more than a mere alliance, an international organization with global aspirations," Mazower remarks; "like the League, it spoke for humanity but acted through national governments. Like the League it talked about international law but deliberately avoided turning rhetoric into substance. But this time round, both the commitment to national self-determination and the turn away from law were more extensive. Tension and ambiguity were hardwired into the UN from the start."[58] It is perhaps the notion of inbuilt tension and happy ambiguity that is required to counter those seeking clear-cut answers to the intractable issues only the UN has to face. This would seem to be the case for those working at the United Nations today. As Lourdes Arizpe, a former assistant director-general for culture at UNESCO, has pointed out, "Certainly you have to be a dreamer to work in the United Nations with conviction. It is only if you have this sense of mission that you can withstand the constant battering by governments who are afraid that the United Nations will become a world government." Indeed, for Arizpe, "someone who works in the United Nations has to be a magician of ideas."[59]

Notes

1 The author would like to thank Thomas G. Weiss and Dan Plesch for the opportunity to contribute to the project and to the helpful comments from John Burley, Andrew Johnstone, Leon Gordenker, Katharina Rietzler, and Tom Zeiler.

2 Memorandum by Adolf Berle, 19 April 1940, box 211 Adolf Berle Papers, Franklin D. Roosevelt Library, Hyde Park, New York.

3 In a 1943 confidential report, John Foster Dulles noted of the British attitude toward postwar planning: "There is less interest in this than in the United States. This is explicable by the greater proximity to the area of hostilities and a greater sense of the precariousness of the outcome." John Foster Dulles, Confidential Report to the Commission to Study the Bases of a Just and Durable Peace, 30 July 1943, box 190, Postwar Foreign Policy

Files, 1940–43, Sumner Welles Papers, Franklin D. Roosevelt Library, Hyde Park, New York.

4 Quoted by M. Patrick Cottrell, "Lost in Transition, the League of Nations and the United Nations," in *Charter of the United Nations: Together with Scholarly Commentaries and Essential Historical Documents*, ed. Ian Shapiro and Joseph Lampert (New Haven, Conn.: Yale University Press, 2014), 91.

5 Mark Mazower, *Governing the World: The History of an Idea* (New York: Penguin Press, 2012), 4, 18.

6 David Armstrong, Lorna Lloyd, and John Redmond, *International Organisation in World Politics* (Basingstoke: Palgrave Macmillan, 2004), 5.

7 Woodrow Wilson, 8 January 1918, Library of Congress, Washington, DC.

8 For an account of the Council on Foreign Relations, see Inderjeet Parmar, *Think Tanks and Power in Foreign Policy: A Comparative Study of the Role and Influence of the Council on Foreign Relations and the Royal Institute of International Affairs, 1939–1945* (Basingstoke: Palgrave Macmillan, 2004).

9 Collective security has produced a voluminous literature. See, for example, Nicholas Tsagourias and Nigel D. White, *Collective Security – Theory, Law and Practice* (Cambridge: Cambridge University Press, 2013), 12–20.

10 Inis L. Claude, Jr, *Swords into Ploughshares: The Problems and Progress of International Organisation* (New York: Random House, 1956), 223.

11 Mark Mazower, *No Enchanted Palace* (Princeton, N.J.: Princeton University Press, 2008), 14.

12 Patricia Clavin, *Securing the World Economy: The Reinvention of the League of Nations 1920–1946* (Oxford: Oxford University Press, 2013), 7.

13 Martin D. Dubin, "Toward the Bruce Report: The Economic and Social Programs of the League of Nations in the Avenol Era," in *United Nations, The League of Nations in Retrospect* (Berlin: Walter De Gruyter Inc, 1983), 43. See also James Barros, *Betrayal from Within: Joseph Avenol, Secretary-General of the League of Nations, 1933–1940* (New Haven, Conn.: Yale University Press, 1969).

14 Franklin D. Roosevelt, "Our Foreign Policy – A Democratic View," *Foreign Affairs* VI (July 1928): 577.

15 Michael Howard, "The United Nations: From War Fighting to Peace Planning," in *The Dumbarton Oaks Conversations and the United Nations, 1944–1994*, ed. Ernest R. May and Angeliki E. Laiou (Washington, DC: Dumbarton Oaks Research Library and Collections, 1998), 2.

16 Mazower, *No Enchanted Palace*, 16.

17 David Mayers, "John G. Winant 1941–45," in *The Embassy in Grosvenor Square: American Ambassadors to the United Kingdom 1938–2008*, ed. Alison Holmes and J. Simon Rofe (Basingstoke: Palgrave Macmillan, 2012). The interwar and postwar International Labour Organization is considered in Norman A. Bowen, "The Long Shadow of UN Reform: The Case of the Specialized Agencies," paper presented at the International Studies Association Annual Conference, March 2008.

18 Justus D. Doenecke, *Nothing Less Than War: A New History of America's Entry into World War I* (Lexington: University Press of Kentucky, 2011), 37, 86.

19 Michael G. Carew, *The Impact of the First World War on U.S. Policymakers: American Strategic and Foreign Policy Formulation, 1938–1942* (Lanham, Md.: Lexington Books, 2014).

20 Andrew Johnstone, "Isolationism and Internationalism in American Foreign Relations," *Journal of Transatlantic Studies* 9, no. 1 (2011): 7–22; J. Simon Rofe, "Isolationism and Internationalism in Transatlantic Affairs," *Journal of Transatlantic Studies* 9, no. 1 (2011): 1–6. The term "isolation" is far from accurate in its literal meaning; subsequently there is a worthy canon of literature to be consulted that should begin with Justus Doenecke, *Storm on the Horizon: The Challenge to American Interventionism 1939–1941* (Lanham, Md.: Rowman & Littlefield, 2000). The classic text on the subject is Wayne S. Cole, *Roosevelt and the Isolationists 1932–1945* (Lincoln: University of Nebraska Press, 1983), which follows Robert A. Divine, *The Illusion of Neutrality* (Chicago, Ill.: University of Chicago Press, 1962); and Manfred Jonas, *Isolationism in American 1935–1941* (Ithaca, NY: Cornell University Press, 1966).

21 Clavin, *Securing the World Economy*, 269; Carew, *The Impact of the First World War on U.S. Policymakers.*

22 Address at Chautauqua, NY, 14 August 1936, *Public Papers and Addresses of Franklin D. Roosevelt 1936*, ed. Samuel L. Rosenman (London: Macmillan, 1936).

23 Paper in the author's possession by Arthur Schlesinger, Jr., prepared for "In the Shadow of FDR: How Roosevelt's Wartime Leadership Shaped the Postwar World," 22–25 September 2005, Hyde Park, New York.

24 Roosevelt, "Our Foreign Policy," 580–81.

25 Mary Stuckey's recent scholarship looking to the Good Neighbor's broader implications beyond Latin America is relevant here. Mary Stuckey, *The Good Neighbor: Franklin D. Roosevelt and the Rhetoric of American Power* (East Lansing: Michigan State University Press, 2013). Also relevant in the links between Roosevelt's thinking on domestic, regional, and international planes is Elizabeth Borgwardt, *A New Deal for the World: America's Vision for Human Rights* (Cambridge, Mass.: Harvard University Press, 2005), and Leon Gordenker's argument that the parallels between the postwar planning and "New Deal strategies and constructions are too striking to be pushed aside," and "[t]he post-war plans, like those of the New Deal, were driven by the general assumption that coping with social problems and maintaining a fair society required the attention of government." Leon Gordenker, "American Post-war Planning: Policy Elites and the New Deal," in *The Roosevelt Years – New Perspectives on American History 1933–1945*, ed. Robert Garson and Stuart Kidd (Edinburgh: Edinburgh University Press, 1999), 182–83. The former's cover bears mention as it has three Boy Scouts standing in front of the US Capitol holding a poster stating "The United Nations Fight For Freedom," which vividly illustrates the cross-pollination of the United Nations in US political thinking.

26 Susanna Hast, *Spheres of Influence in International Relations* (Farnham: Ashgate Publishing Limited, 2014), viii, 1.

27 Frank Costigliola argues that Roosevelt was mindful of maintaining the need for postwar order and settled in private upon the concept of the "Three Policemen" while promoting a universal international organization. Roosevelt "wanted most of the power in the United Nations organisation to reside not in the General Assembly but rather in the Security Council, run by the big powers." There "The Three (or Four [to include China]) Policemen would guard strategic locations, contain Germany and Japan,

discipline small nations, promote global prosperity, and, in the post-Churchill era, shepherd colonies toward gradual independence." Frank Costigliola, *Roosevelt's Lost Alliances: How Personal Politics Helped Start the Cold War* (Princeton, N.J.: Princeton University Press, 2012), 211.

28 Memorandum for the President, 11 August 1943, box 189, Postwar Foreign Policy Files, 1940–43, Sumner Welles Papers, Franklin D. Roosevelt Library, Hyde Park, New York.

29 In addition to Clavin, *Securing the World Economy*, and Mazower, *Governing the World*, recent works include: Zara Steiner, *The Triumph of the Dark: European International History 1933–1939* (Oxford: Oxford University Press, 2011); Daniel Gorman, *The Emergence of International Society in the 1920s* (Cambridge: Cambridge University Press, 2012); Justin Hart, *Empire of Ideas: The Origins of Public Diplomacy and the Transformation of US Foreign Policy* (New York: Oxford University Press, 2013); Barbara J. Keys, *Globalizing Sport: National Rivalry and International Community in the 1930s* (Cambridge, Mass.: Harvard University Press, 2013); and Katharina Rietzler, "Before the Cultural Cold Wars: American Philanthropy and Cultural Diplomacy in the Interwar Years," *Historical Research* 84, no. 223 (2011): 148–64, and "Of Highways, Turntables and Mirror Mazes: Metaphors of Americanization in the History of American Philanthropy," *Diplomacy and Statecraft* 24, no. 1 (2013): 117–33.

30 A recent special edition of *Global Society* 28, no. 1 (2014), edited by Inderjeet Parmar and Katharina Rietzler, is worth consulting, particularly the following articles: Andrew Johnstone, "Shaping Our Post-war Foreign Policy: The Carnegie Endowment for International Peace and the Promotion of the United Nations Organisation during World War II"; David Ekbladh, "The Interwar Foundations of Security Studies: Edward Mead Earle, the Carnegie Corporation and the Depression-Era Origins of a Field"; and Katharina Rietzler, "Fortunes of a Profession: American Foundations and International Law, 1910–39."

31 Arthur Sweetser, "Approaches to Postwar International Organization," Preliminary Draft (PB 30), 17 September 1941, *Studies of American Interests in the War and Peace* (Washington, DC: Council on Foreign Relations, 1946).

32 See Thomas G. Weiss, Tatiana Carayannis, and Richard Jolly, "The 'Third' United Nations," *Global Governance* 15, no. 1 (2009): 123–42.

33 Gordenker, "American Post-war Planning," 174.

34 The Bruce Report, *The Development of International Co-operation in Economic and Social Affairs* (Geneva: League of Nations, 1939).

35 Dubin, "Toward the Bruce Report," 43.

36 David Lee, *Stanley Melbourne Bruce: Australian Internationalist* (London: Continuum, 2010), 188.

37 "Bruce, Stanley Melbourne 1883–1967," *Australian Dictionary of Biography* vol. 7, (Melbourne: Melbourne University Press, 1979), available at: adb.anu.edu.au/biography/bruce-stanley-melbourne-5400 (accessed 26 April 2014).

38 Unpublished aide-memoire, 13 March 1940, file 242490, The Papers of Stanley Melbourne Bruce, National Archives of Australia, Canberra.

39 "The Peace Settlement. Which is the more Practical – A Cooperative or an Enforced Peace Settlement?" 13–14. Attached to a record of conversation

between Welles and Bruce, London, 12 March 1940 ("The Welles Report"), box 6, The Franklin D. Roosevelt Papers: The President's Secretary's File, Franklin D. Roosevelt Presidential Library, Hyde Park, New York. In July 1941, Bruce wrote a letter of introduction to Welles for McDougall who was Australia's representative at the Wheat Conference in Washington. Bruce referred to their conversations as having covered "some of the economic and social problems which will confront us after the war." Letter from Bruce to Welles, 3 July 1941, M104 9/1, file 242508, The Papers of Stanley Melbourne Bruce, National Archives of Australia, Canberra.

40 "Diary of Trip to Europe with Sumner Welles," by Jay Pierrepont Moffat, 27–28, The Jay Pierrepont Moffat Papers, Houghton Library, Harvard, Mass.

41 Letter from McDougall to Pasvolsky on 24 July 1940. The Papers of Leo Pasvolsky, The Library of Congress Manuscripts Division, Washington, DC.

42 Norman A. Bowen, "The Long Shadow of UN Reform: The Case of the Specialized Agencies," paper presented at the International Studies Association Annual Conference March 2008.

43 "Memorandum: The Situation in Europe and Our Position with Respect Thereto, 18 January 1937," Leo Pasvolsky Papers, Manuscripts Division, Library of Congress, Washington, DC.

44 J. Simon Rofe, "Pre-war Post-war Planning: The Phoney War, the Roosevelt Administration, and the Case of the Advisory Committee on Problems of Foreign Relations," *Diplomacy and Statecraft* 23, no. 2 (2012): 254–79.

45 Memorandum Leo Pasvolsky, 16 February 1942, box 190, Postwar Foreign Policy Files, 1940–43, Sumner Welles Papers, Franklin D. Roosevelt Library, Hyde Park, New York.

46 Harley Notter, *Postwar Foreign Policy Preparation 1939–1945* (Washington, DC: US Government Printing Office, 1949), 24.

47 In London too, the postwar world was being considered. Winston Churchill, prior to becoming prime minister, had told the visiting Welles in March 1940: "As regards the peace settlement, [Churchill] had said that he looked to the establishment of some international body on the lines of the League of Nations, and also to the establishment of an international tribunal for dealing with disputes of a justiciable character. He had also said that he had advocated the establishment of an international air force." Winston Churchill's account of meeting with Mr Sumner Welles (US Undersecretary of State), War Cabinet, Conclusion 67 (40), 13 March 1940, FO 371 24406, The National Archives, Kew.

48 The former's membership was: Welles (chair) with members composed of Isiah Bowman, Benjamin Cohen, Green H. Hackworth, James T. Shotwell, Leo Pasvolsky, and Harley Notter.

49 Notter, *Postwar Foreign Policy Preparation*, 108; Minutes of Special Subcommittee on International Organization, 17 July 1942, box 190, Postwar Foreign Policy Files, 1940–43, Sumner Welles Papers, Franklin D. Roosevelt Library, Hyde Park, New York.

50 Notter to Welles, 27 August 1942, Agenda, box 189, Postwar Foreign Policy Files, 1940–43, Sumner Welles Papers, Franklin D. Roosevelt Library, Hyde Park, New York. The parenthetical reference to Woodrow Wilson suggests that his heritage was evident as early as 1942 in discussions of the postwar Charter.

51 Provisional Outline of International Organization, 26 October 1934, box 189, Postwar Foreign Policy Files, 1940–43, Sumner Welles Papers, Franklin D. Roosevelt Library, Hyde Park, New York.
52 Subcommittee on International Organization documents, 7 November 1942, box 189 Postwar Foreign Policy Files, 1940–43, Sumner Welles Papers, Franklin D. Roosevelt Library, Hyde Park, New York.
53 Notter, *Postwar Foreign Policy Preparation*, 109.
54 Unattributed comments, "The League Covenant Summary Analysis," 21 September 1943, Agenda, box 189, Postwar Foreign Policy Files, 1940–43, Sumner Welles Papers, Franklin D. Roosevelt Library, Hyde Park, New York.
55 Provisional Outline of International Organization, 26 October 1934, box 189, Postwar Foreign Policy Files, 1940–43, Sumner Welles Papers, Franklin D. Roosevelt Library, Hyde Park, New York.
56 Mazower, *Governing the World*, 194.
57 Tentative views of the Subcommittee on Political Problems, 7 March–8 August 1942, box 190, Postwar Foreign Policy Files, 1940–43, Sumner Welles Papers, Franklin D. Roosevelt Library, Hyde Park, New York.
58 Mazower, *Governing the World*, 194.
59 Quoted in Thomas G. Weiss, Tatiana Carayannis, Louise Emmerij, and Richard Jolly, *UN Voices: The Struggle for Development and Social Justice* (Bloomington: Indiana University Press, 2005), 412–13.

2   The UN and public diplomacy

Communicating the post-national message[1]

Giles Scott-Smith

- **Origins: the wartime UNIO**
- **The role of the DPI in the postwar world: a contested space**
- **The MDGs: redefining the DPI**
- **Conclusion**

> The Department of Public Information is dedicated to communicating the ideals and work of the United Nations to the world; to interacting and partnering with diverse audiences; and to building support for peace, development and human rights for all. *Inform. Engage. Act.*[2]

> In few fields could there be more problems in working together than in that of information.[3]

The Charter of the United Nations declares that the organization rests upon "the principle of the sovereign equality of all its Members" and is bound by the restriction that it shall not "intervene in matters which are essentially within the domestic jurisdiction of any state." Yet its Charter has also simultaneously sought to bind state behavior to "fundamental human rights," "social progress," and "better standards of life in larger freedom." Its design, in other words, was both to maintain and modify the international system of states, a somewhat contradictory goal that has hampered the UN from the beginning. In this situation a coherent and effective public information policy is both chronically hampered but also essential. It is needed not only for defending and promoting the UN's role in global governance, but also, more proactively, for persuading state authorities to comply with its aims and for reaching beyond those authorities to connect directly with the aspirations of global civil society. The UN therefore aims at different audiences: the member state authorities (including their UN delegations) and the "global public." Akira Iriye has spelled out this dilemma succinctly:

In contrast to the League of Nations, whose covenant never once mentioned "peoples," there was now greater emphasis on "peoples" whose well-being was to be considered a matter for international concern and solution. Although states and governments would be the primary agencies for defining economic policies or implementing social programs, ultimately the rights and interests of "peoples" would have to be safe-guarded through cooperative international action.[4]

This chapter considers the role of public information for the UN since its inception. It examines to what extent the UN's Department of Public Information (DPI) has moved beyond merely *informing* to actually *advocating* key causes.[5] It first looks at the origins, with the creation of the Information Board that promoted the new organization during World War II. It then considers the development of the DPI as the organ tasked with information provision, and the dilemma of how far this could actually involve advocacy of specific causes. The final section examines the reform of the DPI around the Millennium Development Goals (MDGs), which to some degree allowed the organization to conduct a successful information campaign without resolving the deficiencies of its apparatus.

While the DPI's mandate and organization have essentially changed little since 1945, the environment in which it operates has altered radically. First, the broad spectrum of UN agencies, with their array of specialist interests, necessarily complicates a fully centralized information operation. Second, the "personalization" of the UN in the form of the secretary-general has led to an increasing focus on that office and its spokesperson, yet how this is supposed to function alongside the DPI has never been fully resolved. Third, alongside member states and international secretariats, an associated network of nongovernmental organizations (NGOs) has become a vital component of global governance and to UN capabilities.[6] Fourth, the media landscape has changed dramatically, with the rise of digital technologies, the commercialization of information, and the diversification of news outlets. Attempting to have an impact on all fronts is therefore impossible, and the extent of current UN operations means that even a "smart diplomacy" approach that would attempt to coordinate agency information programs is hardly feasible.

The DPI currently operates through three subdivisions: Strategic Communications, News and Media, and Outreach. Additionally, the DPI's 63 Information Centers around the world provide the UN with a visible global presence, connectivity, and feedback on media impact.

Whereas the News and Media Division fulfills the role that the department has carried out since its inception—maintaining a flow of information to the global media—the Strategic Communications and the Outreach Divisions indicate how since the early 2000s the DPI has adopted a more active stance to target specific issues and mobilize support for them via institutional partners in global civil society. This noticeable shift from public information to public diplomacy occurred under Kofi Annan's leadership as secretary-general, as part of a post-Cold War revamping of the UN's mission. The capability to act in this way always existed; what was lacking was political will. As one observer remarked already in 1953, the DPI could always "inject into the stream of communications information which may be strategically influential."[7]

Origins: the wartime UNIO

The UN Information Organization (UNIO) holds the distinction of being the first international agency of the UN network and the first to hold the United Nations label. Its origins reflect the multilateral enterprise of the UNO, there being a two-track development via its main offices in New York and London that eventually coincided at the end of World War II. The UN itself dates the UNIO's origins back to the Inter-Allied Information Committee and Center (IAIC) in New York in September 1940, "which functioned as a clearing house for the information services of the nations at war with the Axis powers."[8] This was an initiative of the British government, and the first director of the center, Michael Huxley, described its purpose in a letter to Secretary of State Cordell Hull: "To meet at frequent intervals as an advisory committee to coordinate the work of agencies concerned with the survey of the American press and the issuance of information in the interests of the Allied cause."[9]

In terms of audience, the United States was therefore the main target. Still officially neutral for the first 15 months of the committee's existence, the stance of US public opinion was obviously vital for British war aims, and every effort needed to be made to secure widespread support. Those nations operating information services in the United States could join the committee, and it was only in July 1942, following the formation of the Office of War Information (OWI) that June, that the United States itself became a member. In November 1942, 10 months after the Declaration by United Nations, the New York Information Center became the United Nations Information Office overseen by an Information Board, and all signatories of the declaration were then invited to join.

Leading this transition from the IAIC to a body framed around the goals of the United Nations was the American Arthur Sweetser, a former member of the League of Nations' Geneva executive who saw the shift as a major opportunity to "promote internationalism in the United States."[10] A similar office was opened in London in November 1943, and the only difference in membership between the two was the Philippines, which possessed no representative in Britain. By January 1945 an official resolution provided for the "formal constitution" of the UNIO, with offices in New York and Washington, DC.[11] The UNIO therefore preceded other UN agencies such as the Food and Agriculture Organization (FAO) and the United Nations Relief and Rehabilitation Administration (UNRRA), both dating from 1943.

The output of the IAIC between 1940 and 1942 demonstrates a clear aim to influence opinion on the war effort in the United States. A document from January 1943 confirms this, identifying three basic stages of development of the IAIC/UNIO. The first involved the coordination of separate national efforts to increase the understanding of their cause. Thus, from January 1941 the monthly *Inter-Allied Review* was issued as "a record of documents and statements regarding the fight of the Allies against aggression and for world freedom."[12] The second stage saw the creation of a reference library to provide information on the war effort to an increasingly involved American public. The third stage was marked by the entry of the United States into the war and a subsequent demand "for understanding of the common aims and objectives for which each and all were fighting." It was this that brought greater attention for planning on postwar reconstruction, in a notable shift from winning the war to preparing the peace—and, hence, to becoming a public opinion "pathfinder" for the future, postwar United Nations.[13] A mistrust of behind-the-scenes scheming and the failure of post-World War I designs for peace caused widespread hope that the United Nations would bring something more lasting. It was "the same story all around the world," demonstrating the inter-dependence of US and Allied interests.[14] The office's remit for action was therefore anything that emphasized Allied unity, mutual aid and interests, and "the importance of cooperation and joint action for winning not only the war, but also the peace."[15] Promoting the outlook of multilateral planning boards and institutions displaying a common cause became a priority in order to demonstrate the changing nature of international relations thanks to the nascent UN system. This approach also included the League of Nations, parts of which, such as the International Labour Organization, remained in existence in Geneva through the war.[16]

Although it operated out of two principal offices in New York and London, it was the US location that determined its overall direction and status as an institution, and for this reason the relations between the UNIO and the agencies of the US government are of special importance. In September 1942, a working agreement with the OWI that spells out this relationship fully was finalized. To meet Congressional demands, the agreement required that "the policy and program of the Inter-Allied Information Center shall be consistent with the policy and the program of the Office of War Information."[17] Since technically the IAIC had to work according to unanimity, this same approach applied to all of its member states, yet the implication that the organization could not function without US approval was clear.

Divergences in outlook did occur within the US government itself. An OWI pamphlet, *The United Nations Fight for the Four Freedoms*, was blocked from being distributed in India by the State Department because its call for equality effectively opposed British rule and could undermine the war effort. Paradoxically enough, from 1942 the British Ministry of Information used the United Nations label as a way to counter Indian demands for British withdrawal, insisting instead that the collective interest lay with first winning the war and then determining the passage of decolonization.[18] National interests and global aspirations therefore became convoluted in both the US and British policymaking environments. Following the Declaration by United Nations of 1 January 1942, fear of triggering resistance in the US Senate to any new international agreements meant that President Franklin D. Roosevelt was very reticent to discuss UN planning publicly during the following three years.[19] The room for maneuver for the UNIO was therefore from the beginning circumscribed by US national interest. Politically this had to be managed very carefully. US public opinion avidly picked up on the United Nations as a concept for winning the war and creating a better peace. The report *Postwar Trends in the United States* from mid-1943 included a survey of the American press that demonstrated widespread civilian and military support for the Four Freedoms and "active, effective cooperation with other nations after the war, even if such cooperation takes the form of a world federation in which the United States would merge some of its sovereign rights."[20] The value of the UN concept as a "psychological weapon" for propelling the war effort was clear, but there was also the danger that public demand for concrete results would outstrip political capabilities to reach agreement. For these reasons it was deemed necessary to produce a simple, easily reproducible symbol or emblem for the UN that could be used to highlight the cause and merits of this new form of international cooperation. The thinking behind this is worth quoting:

> A symbol would simplify a rather complex concept, reduce it to terms that would be easily understandable at almost any level of age or intelligence … In advertising this principle of linking separate projects into a major campaign by means of easily-recognized devices is commonly accepted. The principle applies with equal force to propaganda. Thus, a United Nations emblem would give added force and continuity to thousands of separate deeds, would identify them with the common cause.[21]

With confusion being caused by various US agencies choosing their own UN symbols, a collection of private groups within the United States did eventually decide on a basic UN flag by March 1943, consisting of four colored blocks representing the Four Freedoms on a pale background. Although it was only meant to be flown alongside national flags, it inevitably never gained complete acceptance either within the United States or elsewhere.[22] Nevertheless, the principle of a common symbol was a sound ploy for public relations—arguably, a similar strategy lies behind the adoption of the MDGs in the early twenty-first century.

By the end of 1944, the IAIC and the UNIO had collectively held more than 100 sessions, with subcommittees covering films, exhibitions, radio, the press, women's affairs, and postwar planning. The arrival of new UN agencies such as the UNRRA and the FAO necessitated the expansion of UNIO's task to show that the different elements of the UN system itself were working together. A publicity document chronicling the evolution of the United Nations referred to 74 separate top-level meetings between June 1941 and April 1945 covering the war effort and postwar planning.[23] The pitch was solidly along the lines that victory was *only* achievable because of the cooperation initiated by the United Nations. The UN role in the war effort in Europe is described thus:

> The coordinated military strategy of the United Nations that resulted in the great victorious campaigns of western and eastern Europe, was planned at Tehran and later at Yalta, by Marshal Stalin, Prime Minister Churchill and the late President Roosevelt. Acting on these plans, the Combined Chiefs of Staff set in motion the mighty forces that ultimately linked up the Allied armies' offensive in the west with that of the triumphant Red Army in the east.[24]

Differences of opinion among the Allies were occasionally acknowledged in the publicity material, and the divergence of opinion between the Soviet Union, the United States, and the United Kingdom on postwar arrangements for Europe could hardly be ignored. Obviously, all attention was therefore given to the many examples of constructive cooperation, in order to overshadow the disagreements. An early analysis by the Federal Communications Commission confirmed that "solidarity" was an appropriate keyword for the radio broadcasts of the allied nations, and particularly in terms of the relationship between Russia and the other Allies. Great efforts were made to insist on a common military, political, and moral front, to the extent that "praise of Russia occurs with such frequency in the United Nations' broadcasts as to warrant specific mention as a recurring and important theme in itself." Disagreements primarily existed in relation to Australian, Chinese, and Dutch East Indies criticism of the Pacific War being given secondary status in comparison with Europe, and Britain's poor position in the region as a result. These criticisms were not ignored, with the British Broadcasting Corporation (BBC) countering with details of the UK war effort and a general aim to resist the potential appeal of fascist propaganda dividing the Allies among themselves.[25]

What conclusions can be drawn from the wartime IAIC/UNIO formula? First, coordinating information output during a global war was a unique environment that necessarily separates it from anything undertaken by the DPI since. Second, there was the need to maintain allied cohesion and not give the enemy any source of entry to cause damaging division. The overarching message—win the war and create a durable peace and a better life for all—resonated powerfully amongst the Allied publics and all those who were resisting the Axis powers. Third, this message would have a greater impact if it was projected in the simplest of terms. The Four Freedoms were ideal in this respect, projecting aspirations that were universally appealing. The attempt to create a common UN symbol as a mark of the ubiquity of UN activity was a similar move. Fourth, there was the special focus on the United States as the decisive public to be won over. Throughout the war, the IAIC/UNIO organization was primarily directed toward the US media landscape, and positive relations with the US government were crucial for their operations. Ironically, as it turned out, US public opinion was largely ahead of the upper levels of the Roosevelt administration in wanting to pursue the UN ideal fully. Fifth, as the war progressed, there was the deliberate aim to emphasize the collective effort of the United Nations toward goals of universal consequence. It was a global war for a just cause, and it would be a global peace in the same vein.

Common interests should prevail over national interests. Last, there was the recognition of interdependence—all nations needed to appreciate the greater value of collective action, since acting alone or expressing isolationist tendencies would not deliver improvements for their citizens.

What elements of this wartime formula are still relevant today? These can be summed up as follows: a determination to project goals for a future, better world; the need for collective responsibility in achieving them; the recognition that interdependence prevented alternative national solutions in isolation of each other; the possibility of an effective *supranational* public diplomacy, wherein the message and the advocacy is not wholly determined by and not reducible to simple national interest; the recognition that, similar to the League of Nations, positive public opinion was vital for creating the conditions for the UN's overall success.[26] How these elements faired as UN membership grew within a rapidly changing post-World War II environment is covered below.

The role of the DPI in the postwar world: a contested space

In March 1945 a UNIO future planning memorandum laid out the postwar purpose of UN public information. "The widest possible dissemination of information among the peoples of the world" was vital for establishing a peaceful postwar order, yet at the same time the development of communications, the diversity of outlets and media, and the complexities of an increasing number of specialized agencies made such a task all the more difficult to manage. A postwar information component to ensure wide recognition of the UN's central role was therefore essential. During 1946–55 the UN invested around 12 percent of its annual budget in information programs, a significant figure and indicative that the organization from the start considered the promotion of its public profile, activities, and goals a vital part of its mission.[27] Yet from 1948 onward its mandate, budget, and operating principles were the subject of regular debate in the General Assembly and between the assembly and the UN Secretariat. At the root of this was the inevitable contest for supremacy between the member states and the secretary-general as to the limits of UN competencies. How this contest was conducted during the DPI's first 15 years is revealing for understanding the place of public information in the UN system.

The wartime UNIO was eventually absorbed into a Department of Public Information, formally established by General Assembly resolution 13 during its first session in 1946. The DPI, led by an assistant secretary-general, was assigned "to promote to the greatest possible extent an informed understanding of the work and purposes of the United Nations among the peoples of the world." To achieve this goal, the DPI "should primarily assist and rely upon the co-operation of the established governmental and non-governmental agencies of information," which referred to independent news outlets. It was thus intended to work through and in tandem with existing information outlets and not seek to bypass them with its own. Yet a further directive seemed a contradiction in that the DPI "should on its own initiative engage in positive informational activities that will supplement the services of existing agencies of information to the extent that these are insufficient to realize the purpose set forth above." Such an advocacy role could work successfully if all states agreed to move broadly in the same direction as the UN intended—or if the DPI took on the task of mobilizing public opinion in order that this would put pressure on governments by a different route. DPI staff benefit from the diplomatic privileges of all UN personnel, in that they "shall enjoy in the territory of each of its members such privileges and immunities as are necessary for the fulfillment of its purposes" (UN Charter Article 105), but it is not credible to assume that they would be able to proselytize UN goals in a member state that would regard those goals as detrimental to its national interest. Aside from this, the department "should not engage in 'propaganda'." As one of the first critiques of this mandate remarked some years later, the difference between public information and propaganda is barely identifiable "if propaganda be understood to consist of information fed to a public with the intention of having it adopt given views."[28]

This apolitical role for the UN's information wing is reflected in studies on the postwar DPI. Benjamin Alvaro Cohen, the first assistant secretary-general in charge of the department, published a cautious article on its activities that did little more than echo the official mandate, stressing it was "not a propaganda agency" and that it would only provide "factual information." Nevertheless, Cohen also expressed the transformational ambition that lay at the heart of the UN ideal:

> [I]t is essential for the United Nations to build up a direct audience. It is a collectivity, not merely a group of fifty-one separate nations. As a collectivity, it has its own responsibility to make its voice heard throughout the world. Unless it can develop and maintain permanent contact with world opinion it will be powerless in time of crisis. This is especially true since national stations

cannot always be relied on in the event of conflict between their respective countries and the Organization.[29]

Cohen, a Chilean diplomat with experience in the media, had been involved in the preparatory commission and was a popular figure. His presence was also significant for solidifying a Latin American bloc of support behind the DPI, which would be very useful as it faced increasing opposition from those looking to economize and curtail its activities in the ensuing years. Under Cohen's leadership the DPI steered a careful course, so that most of its output "simply reported on meetings and promoted the UN's activities in social, humanitarian, and economic realms ... Seeking to avoid controversy, the DPI sold the UN as a central force moving the world toward a more peaceful, prosperous future while avoiding any broader geopolitical or ideological context or debate."[30] However, the tensions between national interest and the proselytizing of an international organization based on supranational ideals, over which Cohen glided in his article, soon became the central bone of contention. While the DPI's budget was the principal target, it was this essential divide that fueled many of the arguments from behind the scenes.

These tensions came out in the annual debates on the DPI's role. Its mandate and activities were evaluated by the General Assembly's Administrative and Budgetary Committee (Fifth Committee), where the "economizers" (led by the United Kingdom and the Soviet Union) lined up against the "proselytizers" (led by the Latin Americans in support of Cohen), with the United States a relatively neutral observer. During 1950–52, the Fifth Committee attempted to force the DPI to produce a list of priorities in order to assess where cuts to its activities could be made, but this was successfully resisted. The department essentially resisted this request on the basis that it was doing the best it could on all fronts. By 1957 the stand-off on the department's role and budget led to the creation of a six-man expert committee to review the DPI. Although intended purely to look for efficiencies in order to reduce the budget, the Expert Committee instead sought out the "basic principles" upon which the DPI went about its work.

The report, submitted in March 1958, argued that the "mass approach" pursued until then should be replaced by "the selective approach of public relations." The main conclusion of this was that the UN should focus on four target groups to get its message across: national governmental information programs, mass media professionals, supportive NGOs, and educators.[31] This drew criticism from both Secretary-General Dag Hammarskjöld, who wanted to maintain the DPI's outlook that the global public was its target and not simply identifiable professionals, and from those who felt a public relations approach meant a shift from impartial information to partisan advocacy. Hammarskjöld was also prepared to face down the Fifth Committee by claiming the running of the DPI as his responsibility, which under the UN Charter it effectively was. The expert committee was therefore unable either to shift DPI priorities or solve its dilemma of being part of an international organization that relies on its member states to achieve anything. In the process it was exposed that the department did possess determined allies—not least among the press corps assigned to following the UN and the diplomatic corps assigned to the UN—who benefited from its services and were prepared to support its existing role.[32]

Some commentators saw only an unchanged situation. A decade after the expert committee's report and the ensuing debate, an overview of the DPI's activities still saw its role pretty much as Cohen had in 1946.[33] Others, such as the 1969 Jackson report on the UN and development, were more critical of the quality of information provision.[34] Resistance to "public relations" and the lack of any research capability also meant very little was done to assess how the UN was actually seen by the global public in whose name it claimed to be acting. It was only in 1972 that the first full assessment of information activities was published—in 1949 the DPI had been forced to abandon its first attempt to conduct a limited opinion survey, and for the next two decades the demands for budget restraint prevented any application of social scientific investigation on this front.[35] Yet from the early 1960s, a major seachange occurred, directly related to the influx of newly independent states as new UN members. In a superb overview of the consequences of this, Seth Center has described how from 1960—the year that the UN General Assembly passed by 89 to 0 (with 9 abstentions) the Declaration on the Granting of Independence to Colonial Countries and Peoples—the DPI was re-directed to concentrate on the interests of colonial and postcolonial peoples, first (in the 1960s) to accelerate the path to independence, and second (in the 1970s) to promote a New International Economic Order (NIEO) and a New World Information and Communication Order (NWICO). The program of action, compiled and passed by General Assembly resolution 2621 in December 1970, called on the DPI to highlight "the struggle being waged by colonial peoples and the national liberation movements," and by 1974, fed by the committee established to oversee the independence declaration, the DPI was issuing documents such as *The Struggle against Colonialism in Southern Africa* and directing its attention more toward the public in the developed world as the "target audience" that needed to be convinced.[36]

This campaign, orchestrated by the Non-Aligned Movement and the Group of 77 developing countries from within the UN, led to the formation of the Committee on Information in 1978 to oversee DPI activities from the General Assembly, in order better to push it in line with the demands of the NWICO. This placed the department in the firing line between the global South determined to push their agenda, and the North complaining of outright politicization. Remarkably, the DPI hung on to its impartial label, so that "it largely refused to stake out its own positions, demurring to the will of the General Assembly and its mandates."[37] The counterattack against the UN's Southern agenda by Northern member states in the 1980s, encapsulated by the withdrawal of funding for the UN Educational, Scientific and Cultural Organization (UNESCO) by the United States and United Kingdom and the repeated demands for a scaled-down bureaucracy thereafter, effectively derailed the UN as a platform for postcolonial radical reform and returned the DPI to its original "apolitical" moorings.

The importance of this episode is that it demonstrates how the DPI can become the tool of whichever coalition of UN member states takes up a particular cause. In this particular case, the coherence of the UN information program was determined by a set of special postcolonial interests. This openly challenged the role of the DPI as a "neutral" provider of information, while at the same time taking its advocacy function into new territory. Since 2000, the information function has again been redefined, but this time around the needs of a revived UN looking to promote its principal cause, the Millennium Development Goals.

The MDGs: redefining the DPI

The post-Cold War period was supposed to see a revival of the UN's fortunes, in particular as the disappearance of the East–West divide led many to hope that cooperation would be easier to achieve (e.g., in the Security Council). The rise of humanitarian intervention as a just cause through the 1990s—and the condemnation that resulted if this did not take place, as in the case of Rwanda—was evidence of a new phase in UN activism propelled by a changing global political landscape. Yet the perseverance of national interests, the inability to deal with "rogue" or collapsed state crises, and continuing arrears in national contributions for the UN budget (not least, from the United States) instead led from optimism to pessimism, or at least widespread skepticism as to the UN's capabilities and effectiveness. Running a successful information campaign in this environment is a tough task.

Under the leadership of Secretary-General Kofi Annan, the Millennium Development Goals became a means to tackle purpose and functioning of the UN's information task one more time. Set out at the Millennium Summit in 2000 and with the general target of a world without poverty by 2015, the MDGs represent a remarkable way to galvanize social, economic, and political action to meet the needs of a growing global population.[38] A litany of NGOs contributed to the cause, some especially created for the purpose such as the Millennium Promise Alliance, Inc., the Global Poverty Project, and Micah Challenge (an outgrowth of the debt-cancellation Jubilee 2000 campaign). As some commentators have claimed, Roosevelt's Four Freedoms speech and the subsequent announcement of the United Nations "was a crucial moment of collaboration in creating a new postwar order," and NGOs in alliance with governments were vital for forging milestones such as the Universal Declaration of Human Rights.[39] The mobilization of civil society has always been part of the strength of the UN as a moral force, able to project goals beyond the limitations of national interests.

Annan was appointed secretary-general in 1996, receiving US backing on the assumption that he would initiate a general overhaul of the UN organizational structure to reduce needless bureaucracy and costs, which Washington demanded in return for payment of over US$1 billion in outstanding dues. Keen to launch new campaigns and set an ambitious agenda, which he achieved not only with the MDGs but also the Global Compact and what would soon become the Responsibility to Protect, Annan set up a task force under World Bank official and public relations expert Mark Malloch Brown that in June 1997 delivered the report *Global Vision, Local Voice: A Strategic Communications Programme for the United Nations*. Arguing for the promotion of a comprehensive "culture of communication," the report emphasized that if the UN was going to act according to strategic goals, it required much better coordination and utilization of public information to make the organization more effective. This required a greater consolidation of communications management in the UN Secretariat (the offices connected directly with the secretary-general, including the DPI), and quicker adoption of the latest information technologies. Annan's ambitious agenda meant that information provision was a vital element: as he stated in March 1997, "because the United Nations relies on public support to implement its goals, the Organization's message must be transmitted to the peoples of the world with more vigour and purpose."[40]

The Millennium Summit of September 2000, with its final declaration and connected MDGs, provided a new impetus for the DPI. The

MDGs interlinked agency targets across the UN network, profiling a set of desirable, measurable, and attainable standards for poverty eradication, health care, and good governance that could be used to mobilize NGOs and put pressure on member state agendas. In this context, the DPI expanded and upgraded its methods: use of information technology to spread the message more broadly; greater focus on relations with news desks; strengthening the UN website; creating a UN news service for the 24-hour news cycle; providing 15-minute radio broadcasts in the UN's six official languages every day; and widening partnership networks with NGOs, universities, and business. The website, in particular, was a source of optimism, with daily "hits" from users rising from 16 million in 1996 to 488 million in 2000, the Iraq crisis of February 2003 would push website hits over 10 million within a single day for the first time. Library services were upgraded via provision of an online catalogue (UBISnet); daily live radio broadcasts from UN headquarters were introduced for the first time; and a donation from the Japanese public broadcaster NHK of high-definition cameras and television screens in the General Assembly hall enhanced media coverage. The *UN Chronicle*, the quarterly publication covering UN activities, shifted to a "twin-engined" format of simultaneous print and online release, and the annual reference compendium, the *Yearbook of the United Nations*, was made available in a CD-ROM. To enhance the use of the UN website and the Dag Hammarskjöld Library, training sessions for librarians and information officials from developing countries were also held in locations such as Abidjan, Beirut, and Islamabad.[41]

These moves, concentrated as they were around generating a greater digital presence and strengthening awareness of the importance of UN activities for people's daily lives, were definitely positive. Annan was seeking to reclaim the advocacy role of the UN, but in a way that would overcome the global North–South divide that had undermined the world organization in the NIEO era. Yet continuing problems remained despite the upgrade. The initial failure of the DPI to promote the MDGs indicated that the gap between information provision and advocacy remained large; it took the direct intervention of Malloch Brown in early 2001 to push the MDGs as a UN information priority. Coordination with other UN agencies was improved, exemplified by the integration of several DPI information centers with UN Development Programme (UNDP) field offices, ensuring a single message was being projected. Yet the Committee on Information noted in 2001 that even in the Secretariat itself there was a lack of "a strategic vision linking all the components."[42] In other words, there remained an organizational gap between the DPI and other services of the secretary-general—including the spokesperson who, due to the increasing personification of the UN in the secretary-general, was attracting the most media attention.

Neither was the DPI's mission absolutely clear, even after "at least seven periodic reviews and/or reappraisals of United Nations public information policies" since 1948. A new report in March 2002 that assessed Annan's reforms still concluded that "the fundamental problem ... relates to the prevailing ambiguity surrounding its mission (or 'aspiration'), as well as a lack of definition in the target audiences." The advice was that the DPI, with the Millennium Declaration as its "template," should focus more on propagating the content of *other* UN offices rather than producing its own. Too many diverse demands had led to a fragmentation of activities. Instead, budgetary constraints and a more stringent application of "performance management" techniques to measure impact would ideally lead to a leaner, meaner, more effective DPI.[43]

The ongoing restructuring in the wake of this report introduced in November 2002 the current set-up of Strategic Communications, Outreach, and News and Media. Strategic Communications was intended to overcome previous flaws by overseeing interagency coordination of information to enable the UN "to speak increasingly with one voice." To this end, the DPI became the secretariat of the newly formed UN Communications Group, linking staff from all the agencies, programs, and funds across the UN network. Rising costs meant that standard UN publications such as the quarterly *Chronicle* and the *Yearbook* would continue in print but would be made freely available on the web. Outreach channeled greater attention to educational programs, link-ups with NGOs, and the training of journalists and librarians. The network of information centers was reviewed, and resources shifted out of the developed world (35 percent of the costs of the network) to better-equipped "information hubs" in the global South. With the Millennium Declaration as the cause, the DPI was now directed to focus on "the eradication of poverty, conflict prevention, sustainable development, human rights, the HIV/AIDS epidemic, the battle against international terrorism and the needs of the African continent."[44] The list remained very broad, but the MDGs (with the exception of terrorism) were at least now providing the core of the department's mission.

Conclusion

It is worth considering the central themes of the IAIC/UNIO period in the context of the current MDG debate. The wartime experience exposed several necessary criteria for an effective information campaign: cohesion of vision, simplicity of message, victory through collective action, and the necessities of interdependence. These all remain crucial for the UN in the twenty-first century. The High-level Panel on the Post-2015 Development Agenda issued its report in 2013, identifying five "transformative shifts" (inclusiveness, sustainability, responsible growth, accountability, and partnership) that move beyond the original MDGs for a more all-inclusive second phase. Monitoring remains crucial for success:

> The MDGs brought together an inspirational vision with a set of concrete and time-bound goals and targets that could be monitored by robust statistical indicators. This was a great strength of the MDGs and, as time progressed, data coverage and availability have increased.[45]

The DPI was prevented from being effective in the postwar period due to disagreements over its purpose (1940s–50s), the global South's advocacy campaign (1960s–70s), and budgetary and staffing restraints (1980s–90s). The millennium program begun under Annan's leadership undoubtedly gave the UN a new sense of purpose. It also provided the perfect vehicle for revamping the DPI and clarifying its organizational structures and functional goals.

The MDGs provide the basis for a moral cause over and above any national prerogatives, with initiatives such as The World We Want, applying 2.0 media technology and crowd-sourcing, opening up new terrain for linking input, publicity, and activism.[46] The MDGs have now also been re-defined for the post-2015 era, with a strong focus on ending poverty.[47] The proposed Sustainable Development Goals (SDGs), with their universal outlook collapsing remaining North–South divisions, may prove more successful than the MDGs in obtaining widespread "social consensus."[48] Meanwhile, the fundamental problems associated with the DPI—and by extension the UN's public diplomacy efforts as a whole—still remain. An extensive survey conducted by the Office of Internal Oversight Services in 2011 found that coordination within the Secretariat "remained largely informal," that the DPI still lacked a sufficient mandate to coordinate public information successfully, and that there was widespread confusion over whether the DPI's under-secretary-general or the secretary-general's spokesperson occupied the primary position.[49]

One may well question whether comprehensive coordination across the UN spectrum could ever be an achievable aim, but an effective "central point" is needed to emphasize the UN's overall purpose and goals and function as the principal outlet for that message. Increasing competition between UN agencies for media attention has not helped matters either.[50] This was the clear conclusion of Malloch Brown, who recognized that only then could a productive "culture of communication" be instilled. The Annan/Malloch Brown reforms, and the introduction of new technologies, have improved the DPI's purpose and outlook even if its position in the UN's structural hierarchy remains opaque. The DPI's budget for 2014–15 was projected to be a sizeable US$186 million, with almost 38 percent going into strategic communications.[51] The UN is not alone with these dilemmas: national public diplomacy apparatuses also often suffer from bureaucratic divisions, intra-governmental competition, and a lack of integration with the policymaking echelons. Nonetheless, the UN, as an international organization, has been able since its inception to run an information campaign on a global scale that has not been bound by national interests. Despite obvious constraints, the DPI therefore represents a significant departure from the orthodox theory and practice of statist public diplomacy.[52]

Notes

1 I would like to thank Leon Gordenker and the other members of this research project for their comments and advice. Responsibility for the outcome, of course, rests with the author.
2 Mission Statement, Department of Public Information of the UNO, available at www.un.org/en/hq/dpi/about.shtml.
3 Secretary-General to the United Nations Information Board, Annual Report 1944, box 6, file 1, papers of the United Nations Information Office, UN Archives, New York (hereafter UN).
4 Akira Iriye, *Global Community: The Role of International Organizations in the Making of the Contemporary World* (Berkeley: University of California Press, 2002), 42.
5 On public diplomacy's key components, see Nicholas Cull, *The Cold War and the United States Information Agency* (Cambridge: Cambridge University Press, 2008), xv.
6 The notion of an NGO "Third UN" comes from Thomas G. Weiss, Tatiana Carayannis, and Richard Jolly, "The 'Third' United Nations," *Global Governance* 15, no. 1 (2009): 123–42, building on the two-UN model of Inis Claude, *Swords into Plowshares: The Problems and Prospects of International Organization* (New York: Random House, 1956).
7 Robert Cory, "Forging a Public Information Policy for the United Nations," *International Organization* 7, no. 2 (1953): 230.
8 See the overview of the archival holdings of the UNIO at archives.un.org/ARMS/Records-Predecessor-Organizations.
9 Secretary-General to the United Nations Information Board, Annual Report 1944, UN.

10 Nicolas J. Cull, *Selling War: The British Propaganda Campaign against American "Neutrality" in World War II* (Oxford: Oxford University Press, 1995), 193.

11 "Resolution providing for the Formal Constitution of the United Nations Information Organization in the United States of America," March 1945, folder: UNIO Annual Reports, box 6, UN. The resolution declared that the director of the OWI would convene the first meeting of the UNIO's official representatives to determine the organization's officers.

12 Secretary-General to the United Nations Information Board, Annual Report 1944, box 6, file 1, UN.

13 Dan Plesch, *America, Hitler and the UN* (London: I.B. Taurus, 2011), 36.

14 "A Tentative Outline of the Development of Policy of the U.N.I. Office since its Inception and Some Considerations for Future Development (Revised)," Annex 3/65a, 65th Meeting, United Nations Information Board, 5 January 1945, box 2, file 2, UN.

15 "Suggested Definition of Policy for the U.N.I. Office (Revised)," Annex 3/65b, 65th Meeting, United Nations Information Board, 5 January 1945, box 2, file 2, UN.

16 See *Post War Notes* 1, no. 1 (July 1944), which refers to the ongoing work of the League on "economic, financial, transit, social, health, opium, and other questions," as well as "preparing studies and reports on the lessons to be drawn from the experience of the League since its inception." Box 11, file 7, UN. The League's Secretariat did move to the United States, thanks to support from the Rockefeller Foundation. See Mark Mazower, *Governing the World: History of an Idea* (New York: Penguin, 2012), 192–93.

17 "Secretary General IAIC to IAIC representatives, 5 September 1942," box 2, miscellaneous, UN.

18 Alan Winkler, *The Politics of Propaganda: The Office of War Information 1942–1945* (New Haven, Conn.: Yale University Press, 1978), 84; Susan Brewer, *To Win the Peace: British Propaganda in the United States during World War II* (Ithaca, NY: Cornell University Press, 1997), 151–52.

19 Townesend Hoopes and Douglas Brinkley, *FDR and the Creation of the UN* (New Haven, Conn.: Yale University Press, 1997), 78, 123–24. Steven Casey's *Franklin D. Roosevelt, American Public Opinion, and the War against Nazi Germany* (Oxford: Oxford University Press, 2001) includes only a few references to the United Nations in terms of specific planning for postwar Germany.

20 "Postwar Trends in the United States July 10–July 31 1943," box 4, file 7, UN.

21 "A Suggested Information Technique for the United Nations," n.d. [early 1943?], box 6, folder: UN Information Board, UN.

22 See Plesch, *America, Hitler and the UN*, 50–51.

23 "United Nations and Allied Meetings and Conferences," April 1945, box 85, file 3, UN.

24 "United Nations' Contributions to the War in Europe," n.d. [July 1945], box 85, file 9, UN.

25 "The United Nations (December 1, 1941–March 1, 1942)," *FCC Quarterly Review*, box 90, file 4, UN; "Let Us Not Forget: Achievements of the United Nations in 1944," box 11, file 8, UN.

26 "The League's main force is publicity, in the sense of public discussion and public documents by which world opinion may judge the results. The

54   *Giles Scott-Smith*

League recognizes this. It opens its doors and makes information available ... It neither interprets news nor, in the journalistic understanding of the term, transmits it." Eric Drummond, *Ten Years of World Co-operation* (Geneva: Secretariat of the League of Nations, 1930), 402–3.

27 Cory, "Forging a Public Information Policy," 230. Some have disputed this: In 1960 Gordenker calculated that the amounts actually spent in 1949–57 ranged between 6 and 8 percent. See Leon Gordenker, "Policy-making and Secretariat Influence in the U.N. General Assembly: The Case of Public Information," *American Political Science Review* 54, no. 2 (1960): 371, n. 55.
28 See Gordenker, "Policy-making and Secretariat Influence in the U.N. General Assembly," 360.
29 Benjamin Cohen, "The U.N.'s Department of Public Information," *Public Opinion Quarterly* 10 (Summer 1946): 148.
30 Seth Center, "Supranational Public Diplomacy: The Evolution of the UN Department of Public Information and the Rise of Third World Advocacy," in *The United States and Public Diplomacy: New Directions in Cultural and International History*, ed. Brian Etheridge and Kenneth Osgood (Leiden: Martinus Nijhoff, 2010), 144.
31 Richard Swift, "The United Nations and its Public," *International Organization* 14, no. 1 (1960): 68.
32 Swift, "The United Nations and its Public," 84–91; and Gordenker, "Policy-Making and Secretariat Influence," 368–73. See *The New York Times*, 20 October 1958, for a defense of the DPI's role.
33 Marcial Tamayo, "The United Nations: A Rich Source of Information," in *The Diplomatic Persuaders: New Role of the Mass Media in International Relations*, ed. John Lee (New York: John Wiley, 1968), 181–96. For a more critical view from that period, see the work of Cohen's successor as assistant secretary, in Hernane Travares de Sa, *The Play within the Play: The Inside Story of the UN* (New York: Knopf, 1966).
34 See R.G.A. Jackson, *A Study of the Capacity of the United Nations Development System* (Geneva: UN, 1969).
35 See Swift, "The United Nations," 84–85. The first evaluation was published by Sander Szalai and Margaret Croke, *The United Nations and the News Media: A Survey of Public Information on the United Nations in the World Press, Radio, and Television* (New York: United Nations Institute for Training and Research, 1972).
36 Center, "Supranational Public Diplomacy," 146–55.
37 Center, "Supranational Public Diplomacy," 161.
38 The UN Development Programme's Human Development Index from the early 1990s was the forerunner of the MDGs, but at the time was not made central to the UN's mission.
39 Margaret Keck and Kathryn Sikkink, *Activists Beyond Borders: Advocacy Networks in International Politics* (Ithaca, NY: Cornell University Press, 1998), 84.
40 Thant Myint-U and Amy Scott, *The UN Secretariat: A Brief History (1945–2006)* (New York: International Peace Academy, 2007), 103–4; quote from "Reorientation of United Nations Activities in the Field of Public Information and Communications," Committee on Information, 23rd Session, UN document A/AC.198/2001/2, 1 March 2001.
41 Myint-U and Scott, *The UN Secretariat*.

42 Myint-U and Scott, *The UN Secretariat*, 11; "Integration of United Nations Information Centres with Field Offices of the United Nations Development Programme: A Case-by-case Review," Committee on Information, 22nd Session, UN document A/AC.198/2000/3, 6 March 2000.

43 "Reorientation of United Nations Activities in the Field of Public Information and Communications," Committee on Information, 24th Session, UN document A/AC.198/2002/2, 25 March 2002.

44 "Reorientation of United Nations Activities in the Field of Public Information and Communications," Committee on Information, 25th Session, UN document A/AC.198/2003/2, 7 March 2003.

45 *A New Global Partnership: Eradicate Poverty and Transform Economies through Sustainable Development*, Report of the High-level Panel of Eminent Persons on the Post-2015 Development Agenda, May 2013, available at www.post2015hlp.org/wp-content/uploads/2013/05/UN-Report.pdf.

46 See www.worldwewant2015.org.

47 The specific goal of ending poverty has so far dominated media coverage. See "New UN Goals Call for End to Extreme Poverty by 2030," *The Guardian*, 30 May 2013, available at www.theguardian.com/global-develop ment/2013/may/30/un-end-extreme-poverty-2030-goals; "UN Urged to Embrace 2030 Goal on Ending Extreme Poverty," *BBC News*, 30 May 2013, available at www.bbc.co.uk/news/uk-politics-22719812; "Towards the End of Poverty," *The Economist*, 1 June 2013, available at www.economist.com/news/leaders/21578665-nearly-1-billion-people-have-been-taken-out-extreme -poverty-20-years-world-should-aim?frsc=dg%7Cd.

48 Stanislav Saling, "Beyond MDGs: Branding the Sustainable Development Goals," *The Guardian*, 16 October 2013, available at www.theguardian.com/global-development-professionals-network/2013/oct/16/mdg-sustainable-dev elopment-goals.

49 "Review of the Organizational Framework of the Public Information Function of the Secretariat," Office of Internal Oversight Services, UN document A/66/180, 25 July 2011.

50 See Andrew Caddell, "Like Moths to a Flame: The News Media, the United Nations, and the Specialized Agencies," *Behind the Headlines* 59, no. 2 (2001–02), available at 2glspd2t2a9zr20ie1z7bx8zbb.wpengine.netdna-cdn.com/wp-content/uploads/2011/05/BTH_vol59_no2.pdf.

51 "Proposed Programme Budget for the Biennium 2014–15," UN General Assembly, 68th session, UN document A/68/6 Sect.28, 18 April 2013.

52 Research on this point is limited. See for instance, Michael Merlingen and Zenet Mujić, "Public Diplomacy and the OSCE in the Age of Post-International Politics," *Security Dialogue* 34, no. 3 (2003): 269–83.

3 Educators across borders

The Conference of Allied Ministers of Education, 1942–45

Miriam Intrator

- **Convening the Conference of Allied Ministers of Education**
- **The work of the CAME commissions**
- **The early postwar years and the United Nations**
- **Conclusion**

In his capacity as first director of the interwar International Institute for Intellectual Cooperation (IIIC), the cultural arm associated with the League of Nations, Julien Luchaire viewed himself as representing those who were neither diplomats nor economists, but who envisioned the construction of peace occurring in the minds of men. Luchaire described how others all over the world "were obsessed by the same dream."[1] Belief in that dream continued to drive individuals like Luchaire into and through the World War II years. The Conference of Allied Ministers of Education (CAME), convened in London in 1942 and the focus of this chapter, brought together a group of men and women who viewed education and culture as vital elements for healing the world from the horrors of war and building a more peaceful future.

It is worth recalling that for governments to pay any attention to such matters when Nazi victory looked likely demonstrated breathtaking self-confidence and practical vision. Their work culminated in the November 1945 establishment of the United Nations Educational, Scientific and Cultural Organization (UNESCO). The continuity of that shared dream is reflected in the most often-quoted line of UNESCO's Constitution which still headlines the organization's website today: "since wars begin in the minds of men, it is in the minds of men [and women] that the defences of peace must be constructed." This chapter outlines the initial convening of CAME, the work of the commissions responsible for its specific activities and programs within the wartime context, and the early postwar transition of CAME into UNESCO. It concludes by reflecting on potential present-day relevance of innovative ideas and activities that emerged out of CAME.

Tasked with reconstructing communities and societies based on focusing on the realms of culture and education and on reaching people on an individual basis, CAME's approach was not new to the World War II period. Indeed, CAME may be viewed as the inter-mediary body between the IIIC and UNESCO, though the connections are far from seamless. The IIIC, active from 1926 until 1939, did not have the time, resources, or reach to achieve a broad international impact and has largely been considered part of the failure of the League of Nations. Looking back, many at CAME also wanted to distance themselves from the perceived elitism of being identified by the word "intellectual."[2] Perhaps the greatest inspiration taken from the IIIC was that international cooperation in the realms of culture and education was essential to solving the overwhelming imbalance between resource supply and demand in the immediate postwar period, and to constructing a stable and peaceful world. At the first CAME meeting on 16 November 1942 (with the Nazis still winning at Stalin-grad), Malcolm Robertson, chairman of the British Council, stated his belief that "collaboration on common tasks and problems would lead to that educational fellowship which [...] would be the solution to many of the problems of the future."[3]

The primary forces driving CAME were anxiety about what impact the horrors of war and occupation were having on young people and the resultant conviction that the (re)education and de-Nazification of children and youth in all countries occupied by Germany should play a para-mount role in reconstruction and rehabilitation. In order to heal the world from fascism, CAME and then UNESCO sought to instill values that would open young people's minds to democratic ideals and render them less susceptible to militarist and other extremist politics, thus creating a more educated, tolerant, global society and peaceful future. A November 1946 report highlights how heavily World War II and its aftermath weighed on the nascent UNESCO: "The human and material losses and the war-born complexities of reconstruction are like great weights shackling the feet of the young Unesco, crippling its progress towards the goals of a better world. Until the weights are in some major way reduced, Unesco cannot run its best race."[4] To understand the estab-lishment of UNESCO and how its initial activities came to be char-acterized primarily by reconstruction and rehabilitation efforts, it is necessary to look back to how its roots evolved over the course of the war.

As this chapter demonstrates, the planning that enabled UNESCO to undertake a relatively rapid and effective postwar response was launched early in the war years. Indeed, CAME exemplifies Mark Mazower's argument that "the origins of the post war were to be found in the war years themselves."[5] According to Grayson Kefauver, American education specialist and delegate to CAME and UNESCO, "without the work of the Conference [CAME] it was unlikely that UNESCO would have been established so soon and so successfully."[6] The origins of CAME, and thus of UNESCO, emerged during the summer of 1942 in the offices of Rab Butler, member of Parliament and president of the British Board of Education, and Robertson of the British Council.

Convening the Conference of Allied Ministers of Education

During the summer of 1942, Butler and Robertson developed an idea to take advantage of the "unique opportunity afforded by the presence in Great Britain of so many Allied educational authorities for collaboration on educational questions affecting the Allied countries of Europe and the United Kingdom both during and after the war."[7] In October 1942, an invitation sent to the ministers of education of the Allied governments and National Councils in the United Kingdom announced Butler's hope "to confer with" them based on his belief "that it would be of value to have periodic meetings when educational questions affecting the Allied countries of Europe and the United Kingdom both during the war period and in the post-war period, could be discussed."[8]

The initial invitation suggested general points of inquiry that the Allied ministers might consider. Listed first, categorized under "The Present," came the study of British educational institutions, meaning that "accredited representatives of the Allied Departments of Education" could visit "any type of educational institution in the UK," and assistance, defined as "all possible support and advice" to Allied educational establishments founded in the UK during and as a result of the war. Listed second, categorized under "The Future" and introduced by the disclaimer that the organizers "fully realised that it is not possible to foresee in detail what the educational needs of our respective countries will be in the post-war period, but it is felt that there are various general problems which will affect all countries and on which a discussion and an exchange of views, even at this stage, will be profitable," came, "(i) the provision of books, especially text-books for schools, (ii) the provision of trained personnel, (iii) reports from unofficial organisations."[9] The unknown future represented by that second category was CAME's greatest preoccupation.

The first meeting occurred on 16 November 1942 and included representatives from Belgium, Czechoslovakia, France, Greece, the Netherlands,

Norway, Poland, Yugoslavia, and Great Britain. Through December 1945, CAME met 21 times (its various commissions and committees met many more), with participation growing steadily. Representatives of Luxembourg attended the conference's fourth meeting on 25 May 1943, as did observers from the United States and Soviet Union. The latter stopped sending participants to CAME's last two meetings in October and December 1945. At the fifth meeting in July 1943, CAME expanded beyond Europe with delegates and observers attending from Australia, Canada, China, India, New Zealand, and South Africa. Their arrival forced CAME to begin to take war damage in Asia and the East into increasing consideration, yet its focus, even as it transitioned into UNESCO, remained overwhelmingly on continental Europe. This geographical narrowness can be attributed both to CAME's European origins as well as to its geographical location and financial limitations. In the immediate aftermath of war, travel was expensive and complex, requiring time, people, and resources that UNESCO lacked. It was also difficult to obtain permission from various occupying powers, making it more feasible to focus initially on Europe.

After the fifth meeting, the US ambassador to the United Kingdom, John Gilbert Winant, wrote to the secretary of state reporting that discussions of "restructuring" CAME on a "broader basis" had included "general desire ... expressed for active participation of the United States, USSR and China"; all were already sending observers. The desire stemmed from the financial and material assistance they, and particularly the United States, would be able to contribute. As Winant wrote in a follow-up letter, "There is a general feeling that a satisfactory program of this character cannot be pushed through without assistance from the United States."[10] The United States began regularly sending observers at the next meeting, in October 1943, and officially joined CAME in mid-1944. Its commission consisted of key figures from the American educational arena, including Congressman J. William Fulbright, Librarian of Congress Archibald MacLeish, US Commissioner of Education John Studebaker, Stanford University's Dean of Education Grayson N. Kefauver, Ralph E. Turner from the Department of State, and Vassar College's Dean Mildred Thompson. The high-level delegation reflected those of other countries as well and is an indication of how seriously governments were taking concern with educational reconstruction. The impact of the official arrival of the Americans cannot be overstated, but it has been examined in detail elsewhere and is only briefly discussed here.[11]

The United States immediately encouraged a more clearly articulated plan and process, requesting "a memorandum indicating the end result toward which you are trying to move, the steps which you are taking and planning to take, and giving some indication of the justification for the various steps to be taken."[12] The goal of such a "compact and well-ordered analysis" was "to see the total process rather clearly, to avoid if possible taking preliminary steps in relationship to final objectives which are not in harmony with the total program of supply control and of planning for the procurement of essential materials for the badly devastated countries."[13] On one hand, the arrival of the Americans ramped up CAME's planning activities; on the other hand, it escalated existing intergovernmental tensions over everything from nomenclature to mission. The American delegation had very specific ideas and, given its generous budgetary contributions (upward of 50 percent), requirements regarding CAME's future scope and structure.

Among other things, the American delegation encouraged discussions begun in February 1944 regarding the establishment of a permanent body focused on culture and education. There was general agreement that this new organization should be associated with the United Nations, which should appear in its name "because it implied a broader basis," reflecting in part the non-European nations involved and demanding more inclusivity and attention.[14] The Australian delegate, for example, said that "it would not be possible for his Government to accept full membership of any organisation which did not include in its realm the territories of the Far East."[15] He was echoing the resistance of other non-European states to contribute to an organization without evidence that they would directly benefit. Nevertheless, throughout the CAME-to-UNESCO transition, there was virtually no debate over the primary mission: preparing for immediate postwar educational work. French philosopher Jacques Maritain addressed this surprising consensus, arguing that "different as [UNESCO] members are in their views, they all seem to believe *in doing the same things.*"[16]

Disagreements did arise, for example, over whether the focus would be on intellectual cooperation in a direct extension of the interwar IIIC as the French wanted, or on mass communication and education as the Anglo-American contingent wanted, or on whether or not science would be included in the organization's name. The founders of UNESCO attempted a conciliatory approach: headquartered in Paris, highly focused on mass communication, with English scientist Julian Huxley as first director-general and largely financed by the United States, they sought to incorporate the views of and assuage the concerns of these primary states, ultimately an impossible undertaking that also contributed to the fragmentation of mission and identity that continues to trouble the organization today.

Given CAME's concern with postwar reconstruction, becoming a UN agency was a delicate matter as the United Nations Relief and Rehabilitation Administration (UNRRA) had been established already in 1943. CAME's position was that "UNRRA would feed and clothe the people, and a parallel body must be started to go to the liberated countries, to re-create the schools, universities, etc., gather the students together and look after the rebuilding."[17] UNESCO's reconstruction and rehabilitation activities had, first, to be limited to the realms of education, science, and culture, and second, to be designed to integrate into broader, long-term development and improvement goals. UNESCO struggled from the outset to balance the short and long term:

> From an educational and cultural point of view, the Governments of the United Nations are facing a twofold international problem. One aspect of the problem is of a transitory nature and the other of a permanent character. The cold-blooded and considered destruction by the enemy countries of the cultural resources of great parts of the continents of Europe and Asia; the murder of teachers, artists, scientists and intellectual leaders; the burning of books; the pillaging and mutilation of works of art; the rifling of archives and the theft of scientific apparatus, have created conditions dangerous to civilization, and, therefore, to peace, not only in the countries and continents ravaged by the enemy powers, but throughout the entire world. To deprive any part of the inter-dependent modern world of the cultural resources, human and material, through which its children are trained and its people informed, is to destroy to that extent the common knowledge and the mutual understanding upon which the peace of the world and its security must rest.[18]

This organizational strategy ensured that UNESCO would not be confused for a relief agency, which it emphatically was not. At the same time, CAME argued that the feeding of people's bodies and minds was intricately interrelated and recommended that UNRRA consider providing meals to students during the school day: "Until the young are restored to good physical condition, they cannot learn well. They will not be able to concentrate or to attend properly; they will seem restless and disobedient; their memories will appear weak."[19] The two bodies communicated throughout their period of overlapping activity and UNESCO took over some of UNRRA's activities when the latter ceased operations.[20]

Ultimately, CAME was driven by its own specific interests: information gathering and sharing, re-equipping educational institutions, re-education and de-Nazification, restitution, and creating international standards and central clearing houses in order to ease the transnational sharing and exchange of information and resources. Eight commissions, each tasked with a specific realm of activity and formed over the course of the war years, addressed these interests:

1 Books Commission
   a) History Committee
   b) Inter-Allied Book Centre
2 Commission on Cultural Conventions
3 Science Commission
4 Audio-Visual Aids
5 Commission for the Protection and Restitution of Cultural Material
6 Basic Scholastic Equipment Commission
7 Commission for Special Problems in Liberated Countries
8 Committee on the Belgian Memorandum (de-Nazification)

The primary mission and plan of action of a selection of these commissions is discussed in the following section by highlighting some of their most innovative and effective ideas and projects. The selection reflects the fact that there was much overlap between certain commissions, and that some were far more active and productive than others.

The work of the CAME commissions

Re-education and de-Nazification constituted a central concern of all commissions from the outset, with CAME fearing the fascist propaganda infiltrating schools and media and poisoning young minds in occupied countries. Planning ways for "counteracting Nazi racial propaganda,"[21] CAME was sensitive to the reality that "de-nazification could not be achieved merely by setting up counter-propaganda, nor would it be wise merely to try destroying slogans by counter-slogans."[22]

Planning for the postwar in the midst of the ongoing war created a serious impediment: uncertainty, lack of information, and misinformation regarding the extent of damage and destruction and the resultant needs. Assumptions had to be made in order for progress to be achieved. Many leaned toward worst-case scenarios, assuming "that all institutions would be destroyed."[23] The Science Commission, for example:

> AGREED that lists should be prepared as follows: 1) That it should be assumed that Germany would devastate the occupied countries, and that the first problem would be to estimate the

immediate necessities for living and starting again. These would vary with the different countries. Each country would be able to indicate their individual requirements, and prepare a list on these lines. 2) That a second list should be prepared of equipment for reconstruction and teaching. 3) That a third list should be prepared at a later stage, covering requirements for university laboratories, research, etc.[24]

CAME's determination to empower individual countries to formulate their own priority needs, as in point one above, rather than to rely on whatever was available or that manufacturers chose to produce, further slowed its progress since accurate estimates were difficult if not impossible for the exiled ministers to calculate. While some were uncomfortable making assumptions regarding needs prior to liberation and the facts on the ground being known, others pushed for rapid action, urged on by the warning from industry that if orders were not placed early enough, production could be delayed by up to a year or more, an unacceptable outcome regarding equipment and materials perceived as essential to the immediate rehabilitation of education.

The Science Commission compromised, concluding that "the supplying authorities should be given some forecast, however rough, of the probable requirements of all countries."[25] Meanwhile, detailed analysis of precise needs would be collected on an ongoing basis allowing those rough estimates to be honed. Indeed, the gathering, analysis, compilation, and dissemination of information regarding damages and needs and supply and demand became the underlying activity of all CAME and UNESCO's reconstruction functions.

"The provision of books," "especially textbooks for schools," was a key item on the agenda of CAME's first meeting.[26] Within CAME's first month that initial concern significantly expanded:

[S]even categories of books believed "amongst those which will be in the most urgent demand: (i) Books to replace destroyed books in National or University Libraries. (ii) Books on learned subjects published during the period of occupation of the country concerned, so that the libraries may be brought fully to date and that the gap caused by the war years may be bridged. (iii) Textbooks for Universities other than those included under headings (i) and (ii). (iv) Textbooks for use in schools. [...] (v) General literature which will have been unobtainable in occupied countries during the war years, and for which there will obviously be an urgent demand. Books of this type would probably be needed in both the mother tongue of the country concerned and in foreign tongues. (vi) There will probably be outstanding books on the life and thought of the United Nations and on like subjects which the Allied Governments would consider should be made available. (vii) It is probable that a brief history of the war will be needed, written from the United Nations' angle.[27]

This ambitious list—though preliminary, given how early in the war it was drafted (1942)—coupled with the founding of the Books and Periodicals Commission during CAME's second meeting, illustrate the extent to which CAME was concerned from the outset about postwar book- and library-related issues. The commission directed most of its resources to its Inter-Allied Book Centre (IABC), the precursor to the International Clearing House for Publications (ICHP), one of the UNESCO Libraries Section's most significant contributions to facilitating the postwar sharing and exchange of books.[28] In 1944 CAME produced a pamphlet about the IABC, explaining its motivation: "A great task before us is the replenishment, on as large a scale as possible, in each of the allied countries, of national, university, public and other libraries, which are open freely to serious readers, and whose books have been destroyed. Unless this is done the development of the arts and sciences will suffer a serious check."[29]

Replenishment began with wartime book and periodical collection efforts. These were, necessarily, based primarily in the United States and United Kingdom and thus resulted in almost exclusively English-language materials. Although it was difficult, if not impossible, to ascertain what might be available in other countries, the commission was well aware that postwar demand would be for a broad diversity of languages, a point that was critical to its determination "to meet exactly stated needs" rather than only to distribute what was most easily or immediately available.[30] To begin, the commission recommended that CAME member nations collect, to the extent possible, copies of their wartime government documents and publications for postwar exchange. Its primary ongoing responsibility, however, was to gather, analyze, and disseminate details about book-related losses and needs and available stockpiles of publications in order to help guide the formulation and implementation of a rapid and effective postwar distribution.

Similarly focused on issues of supply and demand was the Science Commission, which was established at CAME's fifth meeting. At the commission's first meeting on 19 October 1943, it perceived the reconstruction and rehabilitation of science as a matter of national and international security insofar as, historically, most European countries had relied on German "scientific equipment, literature and education."[31] The commission was concerned with overcoming wartime losses, thefts, destruction, plunder, repurposing, and depreciation, and with the fact that "Germany had an absolute monopoly in Europe before the war, and will seek to recover this."[32] Members argued that "it is no use defeating Germany at war, if she is subsequently able to win at science."[33] Rather, Allied producers, and primarily the United States and Great Britain, had to take over and "provide the proper equipment at a reasonable price."[34] The commission argued this would also create jobs in Allied countries willing and able to become suppliers of vital scientific and industrial equipment.

There were two obstacles to this preferred solution. First, with predominantly German equipment traditionally utilized and illustrated in textbooks, manuals, and reference sources, other options were little known on the continent; the commission planned exhibitions, comprehensive inventory lists, and catalogs to introduce American and British products. Second, Allied manufacturers had to know what to produce and in what quantity. As previously mentioned, these unknowns made information gathering the first priority of the Science Commission as well: "at present confining its activities to collecting, digesting and supplying the Allied Governments with the information they need in the drawing up of their own individual lists of the urgent equipment they need for the year following the military period. […] It will not be possible to assess the magnitude of difficulty of the monitoring problem until this information has been collected."[35] Estimates based on (prewar) population numbers were dismissed as outdated and not accounting for countries' different priorities. As with books, CAME insisted that estimates be based upon what countries wanted and needed and not on availability or numbers and statistics generated and analyzed out of context by an external body: "it is highly desirable that each country should work out, and think about, its own requirements. We do not want a stereotypical world, but one in which each country can conduct science and scientific education according to its own particular genius."[36] The goal was for each country's identity and future vision for itself to guide reconstruction and rehabilitation, rather than trying to force one-size-fits-all solutions on very different needs and priorities.

By fall 1944, as CAME transitioned into UNESCO, the liberation of one country after another confirmed that the available financial and material resources would be utterly insufficient to meet the concrete reality, which often exceeded even the imagined worst-case scenarios of the overwhelming extent of postwar needs and demands. As a result,

CAME implemented the notion of "Minimum Essential Needs," defined by the Science Commission as "the bare needs for any particular schools or universities to begin teaching again,"[37] and guided by the principle that "the minimum essential needs of a country must depend on the extent of destruction which had occurred."[38] In a related development, CAME shifted from planning for the first 18 post-liberation months to the "Emergency Period," or first six months. With estimated losses and needs so overwhelming, focus also turned to prioritization: "The process by which normal life would be re-established within the countries had to be considered. It was a question of policy for the leadership of the country, and each country should be free to decide for itself."[39] The Science Commission divided the problem into three categories: "1) Scientific equipment to enable the people to live; 2) Scientific equipment and chemicals for reconstruction, teaching and applied research; 3) Academic research. The first consideration should be relief of the population in the occupied countries."[40] The information needed for prioritization was gathered by a variety of means, from surveys and questionnaires to on-the-ground observers.

In spring 1945, an Anglo-American Mission visited France, Switzerland, Italy, Greece, Austria, Czechoslovakia, Belgium, Holland, Denmark, Norway, Poland, and Sweden "to find out the needs of the countries of Europe for scientific equipment of all kinds." Their 1946 report priced "total world needs for essential scientific reconstruction" at £30–40 million "at least." With some irony, the mission pointed out that, looking forward, UNESCO's entire budget for scientific relief in 1947 was projected to only be £20,000.[41] This staggering discrepancy further highlights why the Science Commission, like the Books and Periodicals Commission, pushed so hard for the creation of centralized systems of information, materials, and expertise sharing and exchange; they could not foresee any other way to meet the extent of the need.

In addition to information gathering and resource distribution, re-education and de-Nazification were central concerns at CAME. As the full scope and extent of the war's impact on young people came to light, ranging from deportation to recruitment into spying and reporting on family and friends, CAME turned its attention beyond general educational reconstruction to consideration of how to avoid long-term damage to youth.[42] The Commission on the Belgian Memorandum first met on 23 March 1945. Through the commission, Belgium offered itself as "an experimental field," a re-education test case for CAME. While the commission's scope was narrow, concerned with re-educating youth between the ages of seven and 14 in the Eupen-Malmedy region of Belgium,[43] it believed "the results obtained in these districts may serve to throw light upon the general problems of denazification and of the promotion of democracy through the schools."[44] The Belgian minister described the situation:

[T]he Nazis applied their methods to convert Belgian youth into young Hitlerite Germans. These methods were not purely scholastic but more in the nature of recreation with games, parades, dancing, singing and so on, which has a great attraction for the children. It is necessary to lead them back to more normal methods of teaching without taking away all the attractive features of the German methods, which include physical culture, excursions and all kinds of audio-visual methods.[45]

In addition to emphasizing the need for "men *and* women" teachers at both the secondary and elementary levels, the commission requested any surviving "copies of the films, textbooks, wall charts, song books, etc., used by the Nazis." The idea was to study and potentially employ some of the same means and media the Nazis had used so successfully to spread their propaganda, but to achieve the opposite end: the spread of democratic values, tolerance, and peace.[46]

The ministers of Greece and Luxembourg seconded Belgium's experience as equally applicable in their respective countries. All had learned from the enemy's successes the effectiveness of different media and interactive activities.[47] Urged by Belgium, through its commissions on Audio-Visual Aids, Basic Scholastic Equipment, and for Special Problems in Liberated Countries, CAME increasingly advocated alternate means, methods, and tools of teaching, including toys, films, wall charts, broadcasts and other recordings, museums and exhibitions, theater, art supplies, games, physical education, lantern slides, as well as mobile units that would travel with film material, puppet shows, and other mobile media.[48]

The central mandate of the Commission for Special Problems in Liberated Countries was to address the needs of "children who had suffered mental and physical disabilities during the occupation of their countries."[49] Formed in January 1945, it began work on 1 April and submitted its final report in January 1946. The commission had a threefold goal: first, to explore "the educational and psychological problems which, of necessity, affect all children and young people in the liberated territories"; second, to "consider ways and means of re-establishing in the minds of children and young people a real understanding of the moral and ethical values current in democratic communities"; and third, to "take in hand the preparation of memoranda and pamphlets in which certain specialized problems will be dealt with—for example, problems connected with homeless children and young people; children of quislings and collaborationists."[50] An additional concern was the "enormous and still continuing growth of juvenile delinquency." The commission's greatest preoccupation, however, was the "certain categories of children [who] have been specially affected and need help urgently. Among these might be mentioned the homeless and the orphans; the war-mutilated; the children of collaborators, and the stateless children." In the case of Jewish youth who were "everywhere in a particularly painful situation," the commission worried about how to facilitate their emigration without neglecting their educational needs.[51] Despite its nine short months of activity, the commission's director, J.A. Lauwerys of the University of London's Institute of Education, concluded in his final report that "much work has been done and solid results achieved."[52] These results appear to have primarily taken the form of information gathered and interpreted through collaboration with psychologists, educationalists, and teachers.

Two of the most striking conclusions to emerge from the commission reveal much overlap with the Commission on the Belgian Memorandum: recognition that play, sport, and other creative and physical participatory activities allowed children and young people to be active agents in their own recovery, and demand that teachers experiment with new methods and activities in order to accommodate children not in physical or mental condition to withstand the demands of traditional classroom learning as well as to contend with the dearth of teaching materials.[53] Like the Belgian commission's desire to serve as example, Lauwerys argued:

> [M]any of these experiments […] will have an interest and importance extending beyond frontiers. Accounts of them should be brought together, analyzed by psychologists and educationists, and collated. The results should then be made available generally, by publishing the findings and circulating them among teachers, by facilitating visits of teachers and inspectors to places where particularly interesting work is being done, and by arranging special courses of training.[54]

Lauwerys recommended "play therapy in the recovery of mental health and in the fostering of general development" and dissuaded educators from harsh treatment, writing, "weakened children should not be punished, as they often are, for not paying attention." Rather, he argued, teachers had to adapt, doing more than just shortening classes, in order to accommodate special needs during the period of recovery. He further argued that given the extent and scope of damage to children, study and development of "adequate" teaching training "on a sound psychological foundation" was essential to teachers being prepared to work with these students in the most effective ways possible.

When it came to juvenile delinquency, the issues were moral values, impact of the black market, and "fraud, pilfering, etc." Given its commitment to international coordination, Lauwerys argued that these were issues appropriate to be addressed by CAME as "the problems are everywhere almost identical. To repeat the same work over and over again in each country would be not only wasteful but would mean losing the advantage of sharing experience and the stimulus of co-operation." One solution that Lauwerys admired, based on work being done in France and Switzerland, was to create safe havens for youth, "children's villages" that provided young people, even those beyond normal schooling age, the space, time, and support to recuperate while participating in social and educational activities.

Lauwerys concluded his report with a positive spin on the myriad devastating problems that youth faced after the war, writing that CAME had "in the present situation of the children and youth of Europe, an opportunity that may never recur of laying securely the foundations of international solidarity."[55] Here again the longer-term goal of CAME is visible as it transitioned into UNESCO, looking not only to assist in reconstruction and rehabilitation but also in the construction of an enduring world peace via educational means. These activities raised the natural question of whether CAME would also act in enemy states. The response was that "as a non-political body it could not concern itself with the policy of re-educating enemy countries, but as it had special experience in the educational field, its services might be useful in an advisory capacity."[56] As with restitution, however, in the early postwar years this responsibility would fall instead primarily to the occupying Allied authorities.

Even early in the war, news of looting and plunder, of theft and destruction in the cultural and scientific realms, launched discussion at CAME regarding postwar recovery and restitution. The Commission for the Protection and Restitution of Cultural Material, formed during CAME's tenth meeting and often referred to as the Vaucher Commission after French chair Paul Vaucher, first met in April 1944. Vaucher suggested that the commission define its mission broadly: "finding the best way in which experts on cultural material of all kinds could co-operate with the military authorities on the protection and restitution of such material."[57] There was general agreement, on both the Vaucher and Science commissions, to minimize planning for restitution of scientific equipment, which they distinguished as a category from art, books, and other cultural materials. Instead, they argued, "by far the more important part in rehabilitating scientific institutions in Occupied countries will consist of the supply of new and modern scientific equipment."[58] The exception to this rule regarded scientific equipment "whose value is antiquarian or historical rather than practical," such as Newton's telescope, considered an *objet d'art*.[59]

Regarding the "Agneau Mystique" triptych by Van Eyck, the Wit Stwosz altarpiece in Krakow, the Michelangelo statue in Bruges, and other works that might be considered "of European as well as of national significance," it was agreed that "the Conference was the only existing forum for the discussion of cultural questions between Governments; and that it would be legitimate for the Conference to express its collective interest in matters of common cultural concern."[60] The notion of there being no other central forum of discussion or information gathering was a driving force behind the commission. To that end, it proposed compiling a "central photographic file of works of art known to have been looted by the Germans and as yet unrecovered."[61] Having such a single go-to informational resource would have been an invaluable tool for those seeking to recover and restitute displaced cultural materials in the early aftermath of the war. However, the commission was unable to gain authority from the Allied occupying powers to act as that central body, impartially gathering and disseminating information about lost and found items. Without that authority, it could neither build the photographic file nor fulfill its goal to facilitate communication and cooperation among the many parties charged with pursuing property recovery and restitution based on particular interests and previous ownership, an undertaking that remains incomplete and contested to this day.

The early postwar years and the United Nations

During CAME's eighth meeting on 4 February 1944, the idea to establish "an international education body after the war," or to extend the ideas behind CAME into a long-term, post-reconstruction body, began to be discussed in detail. In January 1945, CAME established a Drafting Committee on the Constitution of UNESCO. Its first task was to look back to the language, mission, and goals of the IIIC as a model of what should and should not be adopted in establishing UNESCO. It then turned to the present, passing a resolution in July 1945 stating, "this Conference welcomes the inclusion of educational and cultural co-operation which has formed the subject of its activities since 1942 within the scope of the Charter of the United Nations."[62] CAME had to ensure that the UN's nod to culture and education turned into productive action at UNESCO. As the war came to an end, UNESCO's first main undertaking was to ramp up the survey and assessment of damages, losses, and needs begun by CAME. In order for reconstruction to be efficient, effective, and successful, the world first required a clear idea of what was needed, by whom, where, and how urgently, as well as of response efforts planned or underway:

> How can Unesco help? First, we need desperately continuous and accurate information about the needs of the country. The needs of various countries today are not what they were six months ago … In the second place we need, and need desperately, continuous and accurate information about what the various nations are doing. This is a co-ordinating function that only such an organisation as Unesco can perform.[63]

This coordination work served as the basis for UNESCO's reconstruction and rehabilitation program between 1945 and 1951, a program that ended before most war-impacted countries felt reconstruction was complete. Its demise stemmed from a variety of factors ranging from the escalation of the Cold War and McCarthyism in the United States that targeted individuals and programs within UNESCO, to declining support from international donors which felt that they had given enough to reconstruction, to the expansion of UNESCO's scope and mission based on the rapid and constant addition of new member states that pushed to prioritize development and expansion over reconstruction and rehabilitation.

Conclusion

Despite their best intentions, the IIIC was no more able to prevent plunder and destruction during World War II than UNESCO's cultural heritage protection policies were able to prevent the Taliban from destroying the Bamiyan Buddhas in 2001. The continued targeting of cultural institutions for destructive acts and the familiarity of UNICEF as the current UN body concerned with education mean that today UNESCO is known primarily for naming World Heritage Sites and its celebrity cultural ambassadors. From the outset UNESCO has struggled with defining and articulating its mission and identity in a manner coherent to its global audience, but there are a number of reasons for the shift of attention away from it. UNESCO expanded rapidly and dramatically after its 1945 establishment and was quickly overcome by tensions between the interests and demands of newly decolonized countries versus those of their former colonizers, most of which were also UNESCO founding members. Additionally, after 1950, with reconstruction no longer a central unifying theme, UNESCO quickly found itself spread very thin—programmatically, geographically, and financially—accompanied by increasing bureaucratic paralysis and exacerbating intergovernmental tensions within its supposedly neutral, apolitical forum.

Nevertheless, this story does not have to be one of inevitable failure and despair. Inspiration can be gleaned from UNESCO's early history and from CAME and the IIIC before it. The idea that international cooperation, including in the realms of education, science, and culture, could contribute to increasing tolerance and stability is perhaps more relevant today than ever before. The impediment has always been and continues to be the unwillingness or inability of competing groups and participating states to embrace fully—through actions and not just words—international collaboration in favor of, or indeed as a vital element of, furthering their own individual agendas.

Central clearing houses offer one potential starting place, whereby each group pursues its own needs via a centralized forum in which open communication, sharing, and exchange are essential to any single party fulfilling its needs. This idea is equally relevant when it comes to humanitarianism: central clearing houses could help minimize confusion over the almost countless number of humanitarian organizations active today, many of which have similar if not identical missions. If even some would aggregate their donations and purchases to central locations, recipients could consult comprehensive inventories and select the precise materials that they require, as done postwar by CAME's Books Commission and Science Commission, thus reducing redundancy and waste in spending and resources. Such a system minimizes delivery costs and complications for the donor (as well as, admittedly, acknowledgment) and empowers recipients to be active agents in obtaining needed materials.

The Commission for the Protection and Restitution of Cultural Material provides another powerful example. There is still no centralized source logging the millions of items looted, displaced, and still lost during World War II, nor the countless others that have disappeared as a result of armed conflicts since. As previously discussed, the commission's idea to maintain a central photographic file of stolen works could today be an open-access virtual database complete with photographs, 3-D imaging, descriptive text, and interactive maps of last known locations. It is worth reflecting upon the value that a single centralized documentation center would have to those who have lost items, to investigators charged with searching for these items, and to those who come into possession of items that they suspect of being stolen or of having questionable provenance.

Central clearing houses and restitution are big picture examples. The Commission on Basic Scholastic Equipment offers a different perspective. During the Emergency Period, or the first six months after liberation, its goals were: "(a) To enable children to resume their classes immediately by supplying them with paper, pencils, penholders, etc.; (b) Supplying teachers with tools and didactic material; (c) Supplying maintenance equipment for the cleaning of premises."[64] This level of detail with which CAME was concerned, down to ensuring that schools had cleaning supplies in order to maintain healthy and bright classrooms, illustrates how it viewed even the most nitty-gritty nuts and bolts as significant to the larger picture of effectively educating young people. That concrete view extends to CAME's commitment to empowering individuals, institutions, and countries with the agency to articulate and pursue their own needs rather than to accept passively whatever assistance might be funneled their way by external deciding bodies. Whether it was creating means for libraries to seek out the specific texts that they needed or providing creative outlets to allow children to participate actively in their own healing, empowerment emerged at CAME as much out of necessity—financial, material, and personnel resources were utterly insufficient in the face of the enormous postwar needs—as out of the fundamental belief that it was critical to reach individual people's minds in order to create a more tolerant world and a lasting peace.

Notes

1 Julien Luchaire, *Confession d'un français moyen I. 1876–1914* (Marseille: Le Sagittaire, 1943), 2–3.
2 For more about how tensions over the concept of "intellectual cooperation" manifested, see Chloé Maurel, *Histoire de l'UNESCO: Les trente premières années. 1945–1974* (Paris: L'Harmattan, 2010); Denis Mylonas, *La genèse de l'Unesco: La Conférence des Ministres alliés de l'Education (1942–1945)* (Bruxelles: Etablissements Emile Bruylant, 1976); William R. Pendergast, "UNESCO and French Cultural Relations 1945–70," *International Organization* 30, no. 3 (1976): 454–83.
3 British Council, Draft Report of a Conference, 16 November 1942. UNESCO Archives, CAME Vol. I. Unless noted otherwise all archival material quoted herein is from the UNESCO Archives, Paris.

4 Report of the Technical Sub-Committee to the Preparatory Commission, 15 November 1946, 1. General Conference First Session Paris 1946, Documents.
5 Mark Mazower, "Reconstruction: The Historiographical Issues," *Past and Present* 210 Supplement 6 (2011): 22.
6 Draft report of the 21st meeting, 5 December 1945, CAME vol. I.
7 British Council, Draft Report, 16 November 1942, CAME vol. I.
8 Robertson to Ministers, 28 October 1942, CAME box I.
9 CAME vol. I.
10 Winant to Secretary of State, 4 September 1943. Participation of United States in the Conference of Allied Ministers of Education, London, 5–29 April 1944, and the proposed establishment of a United Nations organization for educational and cultural reconstruction, 965–80, United States Department of State, Foreign Relations of the United States Diplomatic Papers, 1944, General (1944), images.library.wisc.edu/FRUS/EFacs/1943v01 /reference/frus.frus1943v01.i0028.pdf.
11 See Maurel, *Histoire de l'UNESCO*; and Gail Archibald, *Les États-Unis et l'UNESCO 1944–1963: Les rêves peuvent-ils résister à la réalité des relations internationales?* (Paris: Publications de la Sorbonne, 1993).
12 Grayson Kefauver to J.G. Crowther, 19 June 1944, CAME box V.
13 Grayson Kefauver to J.G. Crowther, 19 June 1944, CAME box V.
14 Draft report of the Open Meeting, 12 April 1944, CAME vol. I.
15 CAME vol. I.
16 Emphasis in original. John Marshall Rockefeller Foundation, November 1947. Rockefeller Archive Center, RG 3 series 900, box 24, folder 191, 900 Program and Policy – Literature Aid 1945–55.
17 AME/D/75, Minutes of the 9th meeting, 2 May 1944, CAME box IV.
18 Joint Statement by the Ministers of Education and Special Representatives of the United States, undated, CAME vol. VII.
19 J.A. Lauwerys, "Foreword," in *Report from the Director of the Commission of Enquiry*, January 1946, CAME vol. VIII.
20 Between 1946 and 1948 the two organizations slowly negotiated an agreement that UNESCO would take responsibility for some of UNRRA's education-related endeavors when it became inactive in 1948.
21 Draft report of the 16th meeting, 7 March 1945, CAME vol. I.
22 Commission on Belgian Memorandum, CAME box I.
23 Notes on a discussion between Dr. Devik, Dr. Tosic, and Mr. Crowther, 1 June 1944. CAME box V.
24 Minutes of 2nd Commission Meeting, 23 November 1943, CAME box V.
25 Minutes of 13th Commission Meeting, 8 August 1944, CAME box V.
26 Draft report of CAME first meeting, 16 November 1942. The National Archives of the UK: Public Records Office, ED 42/2 Conference of Allied Ministers of Education: Plenary Sessions: Reports, Agenda, Memoranda, Notes, Finance, Publicity.
27 AME/B/1 Paper C, Supply of books in the postwar period to countries now occupied by the enemy, 31 December 1942, CAME, vol. IV, part I.
28 Also important was the American Book Center, established in Washington, DC, in 1948.
29 "Restoration of Libraries," Conference of the Allied Ministers of Education, Inter-Allied Book Centre. Polish Institute and Sikorski Museum, London, A.19.II/32, Ministry of Religious Affairs and Education, CAME, 1942–45.

30 Carl M. White and P.S.J. Welsford, "The Inter-Allied Book Centre in London," *The Library Quarterly* 16, no. 1 (1946): 60.
31 AME/A/99, Confidential, Science Commission, Matters of Broad Principle Arising Out of its Work, CAME box III.
32 Confidential memorandum, 15 August 1944, CAME box 2.
33 AME/D/46, Report by Mr. Crowther on Progress, undated, CAME box V.
34 AME/D/46, Report by Mr. Crowther on Progress, undated, CAME box V.
35 Request to Conference for the agreement of Allied Governments, CAME box IV.
36 AME/D/46, Report by Mr. Crowther on Progress, undated, CAME box V.
37 Minutes of 15th Commission Meeting, 26 September 1944, CAME box V.
38 Minutes of 15th Commission Meeting, 26 September 1944, CAME box V.
39 Minutes of 11th Commission Meeting, 13 June 1944, CAME box V.
40 Minutes of 2nd Commission Meeting, 23 November 1943, CAME box V.
41 The Needs of European Countries for Scientific Instruments and Laboratory Equipment, to Mr. Drzewieski, 22 November 1946, CAME box V.
42 Tara Zahra, *The Lost Children: Reconstructing Europe's Families after World War II* (Cambridge, Mass.: Harvard University Press, 2011).
43 Commission on Belgian Memorandum, undated, CAME vol. VIII.
44 Lauwerys, "Foreword."
45 Draft report of the 16th meeting, 7 March 1945, CAME vol. I.
46 Emphasis in original. Commission on Belgian Memorandum, undated, CAME vol. VIII.
47 AME/G/3, Memorandum by Dr. Otto Neurath, undated. CAME, vol. VIII.
48 Commission on Belgian Memorandum, undated, CAME vol. VIII.
49 CAME vol. III Commissions.
50 J.A. Lauwerys, Note from the Director of the Commission of Enquiry on Special Educational Problems in Liberated Countries, undated, CAME vol. VIII.
51 Lauwerys, "Foreword."
52 Lauwerys, "Foreword."
53 AME/G/2, Commission on the Belgian Memorandum, Puppet Theatre, CAME box III.
54 Lauwerys, "Foreword."
55 Lauwerys, "Foreword."
56 Executive Bureau, Draft report of the 12th meeting, 29 March 1944, CAME vol. I.
57 Draft report of the first meeting, 25 April 1944, CAME vol. IX.
58 AME/A/40, Report on the Work of the Commission on Scientific and Laboratory Equipment, 4 February 1944, CAME box V.
59 Addition to Explanatory Note, AME/B/48a, CAME box IV.
60 Draft report of the 14th meeting, 18 October 1944, CAME vol. I.
61 James S. Plaut to Denys Sutton, 15 January 1946, CAME box III.
62 Draft report of the 19th meeting, 12 July 1945, CAME vol. I.
63 Mr. Brumbach, Commission on Reconstruction and Rehabilitation, Provisional Verbatim Record of the Second Meeting, 25 November 1946, 17. General Conference, 1 Session, Paris 1946.
64 AME/A/72, Basic Scholastic Equipment Commission, Summary of Activities, CAME vol. III.

II

Human security

4 Building on the 1943–48 United Nations War Crimes Commission

Dan Plesch

- **Legal and political amnesia**
- **Chinese and Indian leadership**
- **A global system of complementary justice**
- **The development of key international legal principles**
- **Conclusion**

A renaissance in international criminal justice drawn from lost lessons of World War II can empower the international community of states today.[1] The seemingly unstoppable war crimes in Africa and the Middle East and the turgid performance of the International Criminal Court (ICC) invite a defeatist response. Barbarism triumphs in the face of ineffectual justice. The lessons of this chapter are partly that the United Nations at war achieved far more in this area than is remembered, but more importantly that especially at a time when Nazi victory seemed almost certain, the Allies put legal justice among their war aims. Faced with comparatively minor adversaries today, those who advocate abandoning international criminal justice are at best encouraging simple defeatism and at worst encouraging would-be perpetrators.

The four-country Nuremberg International Military Tribunal considered 24 cases. In contrast, cases involving 30,000 individuals were approved for prosecution at a score of national civil and military tribunals by the 17-country UN War Crimes Commission (UNWCC) in the period 1943–48. The commission's member states submitted thousands of cases to the UNWCC, and when their charges were approved, they acted to pursue prosecutions in their own jurisdictions, which happened in countries as far apart as China and Norway.

This body of legal practice changes the paradigm of international criminal justice.[2] The breadth and depth of the UNWCC's work provides a far stronger basis in political practice and law than has been the general assumption for decades. The UNWCC should be considered as a massive platform on which to build international criminal justice compared to the narrower ones of Nuremberg and Tokyo.

This chapter summarizes the work of the United Nations War Crimes Commission and its associated courts and tribunals, but emphasizes the commission's potential to contribute to international criminal justice in the twenty-first century. The discussion of the UNWCC's contribution begins with the issue of whether international criminal justice should be seen as a Western creation and highlights Chinese and Indian contributions. It then details the global system of international criminal justice created in the mid-1940s and the lessons for the key contemporary debate on the relationship between the ICC and local jurisdictions, be they in Libya or under the auspices of a regional body such as the Arab League or African Union. Several specific issues are then analyzed: the crimes of aggression; the defense of superior orders; collective responsibility for crimes from being part of a group; and the prosecution of gender-based violence. The chapter concludes by outlining a research agenda on both the specific politico-legal issues and on the wider question of why experience of such value has been neglected by so many for so long.

Legal and political amnesia

Before launching into this analysis, it is worth pondering a question that only becomes clear as a result of probing the past: "Why was the UNWCC neglected for so long?" Then as now some states were hostile to the idea of war crimes trials. In the United States, an interagency conflict slowed the UNWCC's creation, limited its scope, and led to its premature closure. Chris Simpson[3] and Graham Cox[4] provide illuminating accounts of the opposition by die-hard realist opponents of war crimes trials to the leadership of President Franklin D. Roosevelt and of his Ambassador Herbert Pell. As a former congressman and US ambassador to Portugal and Hungary, Pell came from a similar class background as FDR and was a vocal opponent of racial discrimination in the United States. As a diplomat in Hungary during the war, he had the then rare experience for an American of seeing the impact of fascism first hand.

Cox makes a compelling argument that absent the public campaign by Pell after his dismissal, it is unlikely that Nuremburg would ever have happened. Supporters of the absolute right of states to govern their internal affairs combined with those who prioritized alliance with Germans against Soviet communism staunchly blocked efforts at retributive justice. However, the alliance of some sections of the US government and civil society with the leadership of smaller states led to progress. As Kerstin von Lingen[5] has reminded us, in the early 1940s it was the exiled governments of states under Nazi control—notably Belgium, Czechoslovakia, and Poland—that (along with China) combined with legal scholars and nongovernmental organizations (NGOs), including Jewish ones, to keep the issue of war crimes on the US and UK agendas.

Contemporary jurists including Justice Jackson and David Maxwell Fife were clear that the UNWCC played an important judicial role and helped develop the London Charter for Nuremburg. The commission's members included such leading international jurists and diplomats as René Cassin, Marcel de Baer, Bohuslav Ecer, André Gros, Cecil Hurst, Wellington Koo, Herbert Pell, and Lord Wright.

The UNWCC's mostly secret work was overshadowed by the resources and publicity accorded to the trials at Nuremberg. Subsequently, the US priority of rebuilding Germany required the closure of the commission and its files. A story became prevalent that its ineffectiveness meant that it warranted little more than a footnote in accounts of the development of international criminal justice.

Part of the background work to this research project resulted in 2011 in the UN agreeing to de-restrict partially the UNWCC's minutes and then the Prosecutor's Office of the ICC placing a good deal of this material online, helped by roughly parallel processes of digitization in the archives of the Australian, British, and US governments among others. In 2014, the US Holocaust Memorial Museum obtained a full copy of the until-then restricted sections of the archive, notably the 36,000 pre-trial dossiers sent to the commission by its member states.[6]

The UNWCC was created on the initiative of victim states to provide a global system of complementary justice to reinforce and legitimate the actions of these countries after liberation and to act as a warning to perpetrators and a glimmer of hope to victims that justice would be done. This alone is a useful example for our own time. Moreover, with respect to contemporary debates, a number of precedents stand out and can be headlined. Rape was prosecuted routinely. Legal responsibility was attributed routinely to those with collective or command responsibility and low-level functions. A uniform system of facts and evidence collection was developed and implemented. Torture, including waterboarding and stress positions, was prosecuted in a considerable number of cases. Prosecutions took place in the states where they occurred and were pursued with urgency and economy. The commission's minutes show multilateral debates and decisions about such contemporary headlines as collective responsibility, the mandate of an international criminal court, and the crime of aggression.

In brief, the political debates of the 1940s resonate today. The state-interest pragmatists in Washington and London were opposed to any legal process resembling Nuremburg. How would we fare today without Nuremberg? As Herbert Pell alleged at the time, there was no evident political will in Washington for the International Military Tribunal (IMT) that was established eventually at Nuremberg as late as May 1945. It was only a coalition of small states, civil society, and leading actors, notably President Roosevelt, that saw the creation of any war crimes processes. Resistance by traditionalist lawyers to legal innovation was a problem at the core of the UNWCC's work but the national representatives pioneered constructive innovation.

Before surveying the commission's value for our own time, it is important to specify a few caveats. Some of the conventions of the time, notably the use of the death penalty, are not practices that fit with twenty-first-century practice. The commission's remit was limited and could only support prosecutions of enemy personnel for offences committed against the United Nations during World War II. It had no role in respect of actions by personnel of its own members. It also sought jurisdiction over crimes committed by the Germans against their own people, notably the Jews; however, this unsuccessful pressure still contributed to the adoption at Nuremburg of crimes against humanity, a term used in formal debate in the UNWCC more than a year earlier, in the spring of 1944.

Chinese and Indian leadership

There is a tendency to view international criminal law, indeed international human rights in general, as a Western or even an Anglo-American invention. The records of the 1940s show a very different picture. Of the big four powers, it was China that was the first to adhere to the seminal declaration of January 1942 on the "Punishment for War Crimes" by the exiled governments in London—some months before Washington, London, and Moscow.

China went on to become a founding and prominent member of the UNWCC. It proposed and created in Chunking a sub-commission for the Far East that indicted thousands of Japanese for crimes in China. Chinese representatives proposed that the use of narcotics to subdue a population be a war crime and helped lead the effort to create a crime of aggression or crimes against peace. The Chinese role in developing the UNWCC and then applying it in its conflict with Japan has been the subject of a number of recent studies that confound the notion of international criminal law as a Western concoction.[7]

The representatives of the Imperial government of India sat alongside their British and Dominion colleagues on the UNWCC in London and in China, often taking different positions from the British. It appears that an Indian official, Niharendu Dutt-Majumdar, in the London meetings wrote the first main draft of a proposal for joint military tribunals. This form of justice is best known today under the titles of concentration camps where trials were held: the British at Belsen and the Americans at Dachau. The commission, thwarted by both Whitehall (the Foreign Office) and Foggy Bottom (the State Department), was unable to get support for a permanent UN criminal court. The proposal for military tribunals under the authority of commanders, including Dwight Eisenhower in Europe and Douglas MacArthur in Southeast Asia, was drafted by Dutt and appears to have been adopted and put into effect in a dozen or more tribunals. Certainly no other source of this system is clear.

Chinese and Indian judges were also active in tribunals across the Pacific and mainland China. The debate on Asian involvement in the post-World War II trials usually goes no further than the rejection of the crime of aggression as imperial hypocrisy by the Indian judge Radhabinod Pahl at the Tokyo trial. Yet from the earliest moments, the ideas and practices of international criminal justice that exist today had significant and at times leading input from the representatives of non-Western states. The leading role of China in developing the crime of aggression provides overriding empirical contradiction to the views of a single Indian judge at Tokyo. Scholars who rely exclusively on Pahl to support their arguments might explain why they overlook the position of the Chinese government, when it has been a matter of public record these last seven decades. China's experiences with aggression were far more severe than India's, but the Chinese nationalist government used the experience of World War II to draw a line against further aggression—in parallel with its successful efforts to overturn the unequal treaties governing many Western concessions in China.

A global system of complementary justice

The lack of a system of complementary justice in which international bodies support national legal efforts is one of the key problems in twenty-first-century international criminal justice. Yet where a state is struggling to implement its own legal measures there is no global system of support. The varied circumstances of Cambodia, Rwanda, and Libya illustrate the difficulties. While the ad hoc tribunals created in response to events in Africa and the Balkans set important precedents, they have limited mandates and are coming to the end of their lives.[8] Although the ICC exists to prosecute cases when national legal systems fail to prosecute and has a mandate to develop a system, it has thus far failed to do so.

The UNWCC was created by its member states to provide international legitimacy through legal, political, and administrative support for trials that they wished to conduct themselves. The great power decisions in Moscow of November 1943 mandated that, aside from the Nazi leadership, war criminals would face justice in the territories where they had committed their crimes. In contrast, today's criminal trials are conducted in the Netherlands even when the accused are not from the highest levels of government. The Hague is remote, both geographically and culturally, from the site of the crimes. The "gacaca" trials in Rwanda according to national practice echo the intent of Allied practice in World War II.[9] A reading of the debates among commissioners reveals vigorous arguments over points of law and evidence as they sought to develop best practice. There is little sense of a "kangaroo court" to just rubber stamp cases put before them.

The UNWCC provided legal and practical advice to national jurisdictions and legal legitimacy, even authority, to national legal processes that is a useful model for the twenty-first century. The process developed in 1944 was that a country would send to the commission charges to determine whether there was a case to answer—that is, on *prima facie* grounds—and after endorsement, a trial. By the commission's demise in 1948, this process was used across Europe and the Far East, with over 30,000 cases being considered, many against multiple defendants. On this basis, weak states today might bring cases to the ICC for validation of their own processes rather than simply handing them over to the ICC. Regional organizations such as the Arab League and the African Union—where currently an important push-back against the emphasis on African cases is obvious—might develop regional courts that similarly operate with the voluntary legitimation of the ICC.

States large and small considered it necessary and important to obtain international support for their national actions in the 1940s. This precedent should lend weight to legitimating such a relationship for our own era. The UNWCC member states were: Australia, Belgium, Canada, China, Czechoslovakia, Denmark, France, Greece, India, Luxembourg, the Netherlands, New Zealand, Norway, Poland, the United Kingdom, the United States, and Yugoslavia. The commission had three specific duties: to investigate and record the evidence of war crimes; to report to the governments concerned cases in which it appeared that adequate evidence existed to support a prosecution; and to make recommendations to member governments concerning questions of law and procedure as necessary for them to be able to fulfil their role of conducting trials.[10] The UNWCC had three committees that met weekly in the British Royal Courts of Justice in London to implement these mandates: Committee I, Facts and Evidence; Committee II, Enforcement; and Committee III, Legal Affairs.

Member states set up national offices within their governments to liaise with the commission, coordinate investigations, collect evidence, and create new legal structures to handle war crimes where necessary.[11] All national offices reported directly to the main UNWCC headquarters in London as they conducted investigations and constructed lists of suspected war criminals for review from 1944 to the end of 1947. A National Offices Conference was held in London in May and June 1945,[12] which discussed policy and practice for the pursuit and trial of war criminals, and its papers include a number of municipal statutes for war crimes trials.

The UNWCC conducted the only comparative analysis of the different national practices to take place during this time in a report to the UN Economic and Social Council (ECOSOC) in 1948.[13] Until recently, virtually no additional research on the work of the many national offices had been conducted over the last seven decades.[14]

In addition to setting up national offices, some Western European governments in exile in London created enabling legislation for war crimes courts. For example, by August 1943 Belgium and the Netherlands had passed laws creating courts to try war crimes in their own countries following liberation.[15] Through its committee structure, the UNWCC supported the national offices in conducting their investigations and also investigated some cases on its own by maintaining a small staff team that also liaised with governments through the national offices.[16] The UNWCC was ultimately responsible for issuing *prima facie* decisions on the cases brought to it by the national offices that resulted from their investigation efforts.[17] The United Kingdom provided facilities for the commission, but the staff was international and all member states contributed to its funding on the same basis as had been agreed for UNRRA, although the United States and United Kingdom limited the budget to around $60,000 (1940s prices) a year.[18]

Where national prosecutions resulted, states were encouraged to send trial reports to be recorded by Committee I. This process was incomplete at the time of the UNWCC's hasty closure in 1948, with many countries being unable to complete and process their reports in time to be included in the commission's publications. Nevertheless, over 2,000 trials were recorded at this point.

The efforts by the national offices and Committee I were complemented by the enforcement work of Committee II, which was led by former US Congressman Herbert Pell.[19] In short order in the spring of 1944, it developed mechanisms for a war crimes office in the territory of defeated enemies,[20] which contributed to the creation of the Central Register of War Criminals and Security Suspects (or CROWCASS) under the command of General Eisenhower, Supreme Commander Allied Expeditionary Force.[21] Other initiatives include a detailed proposal for mixed military tribunals under the major Allied commands that was later adopted[22] by many states, with strong Indian leadership in the drafting. In the specific case of the United Kingdom, the discussions within the UNWCC on how to bring accused war criminals to trial "ultimately resulted" in the issuing of the Royal Warrant and the creation of the British War Crimes Executive in July 1945.[23]

Committee III received complex legal questions from the different participating countries in order to generate debate and ultimately arrive at decisions and recommendations for the practice of the national offices.

Figure 4.1 The UNWCC committee and sub-commission structure

In addition to the national investigations and trials, the UNWCC helped design and initiate the establishment of military tribunals to address situations involving particularly complex crimes. Crimes addressed by military tribunals included incidents that did not have specific geographic locations and crimes committed against Allied nationals in Germany and across parts of the Far East under various forms of colonial administration.[24] The military authorities were primarily from the United States and United Kingdom and were also responsible for aiding their respective nations in investigations and holding trials. The integration of military authorities was also in part so that trials could be conducted "without waiting for the initiative of any one Government on the matter."[25] Collectively, Allied military authorities conducted a large number of trials around Europe and the Far East.[26]

The development of key international legal principles

The details of the national investigations and trials provide significant insight into the work of the UNWCC and the responsibility of its members in developing key aspects of public international criminal law. Indeed, the UNWCC's accomplishments also involve its work on specific issues, many of which remain contentious today. This section briefly summarizes some of the pertinent findings from five primary issues that the commission included in its investigations and trials, and which were important precedents for contemporary public international law: the crime of aggression; the defense of superior orders; fair trials; collective responsibility; and sexual and gender-based violence.

Aggression

The issue of the crime of aggression was present in the commission's debates from the very outset. The members recorded in the authoritative *History of the UNWCC* that "[b]y far the most important issue of substantive law to be studied by the Commission and its Legal Committee was the question of whether aggressive war amounted to a criminal act."[27] Faced with thorny questions related to the underdeveloped and highly contentious topic in the complex context of World War II, the commission sought legal ground in the Kellogg-Briand Pact of 1928. The first two articles of the pact sought to address the concept of aggressive war, explicitly stating that the contracting parties "condemn recourse to war for the solution of international controversies" and agree that settlement and solution for all disputes and conflicts should be sought only through pacific means.

The *History of the UNWCC* makes the case that in the context of World War II, "there are clear precedents for the rule that it is an unlawful act to start and wage an aggressive war. It has indeed been long held by humanity that he who does such a thing is guilty of a supreme offense."[28] Despite the seemingly clear legal support for the launching and waging of a war of aggression being against international law, the politics of the time limited the advancement of this principle just as it does today; it was not until after the London Charter was concluded in August 1945 that the principle of aggressive war was endorsed by the commission.[29]

However, the August 1946 trial of Takashi Sakai, conducted by the UNWCC-supported Chinese War Crimes Military Tribunal in Nanking, is evidence of the commission's support for the concept on legal grounds. The Japanese military commander was charged with crimes against peace and crimes against humanity. His incitement of numerous aggressive acts of atrocity against Chinese civilians is directly referenced in the trial report. He was found guilty "of participating in the war of aggression" and sentenced to death.[30]

Following the debate within the commission and the Sakai trial, Wright stated that "I am quite satisfied that in the future, even though other forces may temporarily and on occasion prevail, the nations of the world will not let the principle go."[31] However, it is clear that issues surrounding the crime of aggression continue to be contested, which is most clearly demonstrated by the ambiguous nature of the conclusions of the Kampala conference in 2010 that presented the ICC with the opportunity to incorporate the concept into the Rome Statute. While an historic agreement was reached on the adoption of a definition of the concept,[32] the ICC will not be able to enforce the crime until 2017 at the earliest.

Sakai's trial does not provide an indisputable precedent on the crime of aggression; however, it does represent support for the adoption of the principle. Additional precedents may be found in the national legislation for war crimes tribunals and in national practice. A question for further historical research is whether China pursued additional cases on the basis of the charge of making aggressive war or crimes against peace. Both the Yugoslav and Greek courts were empowered to pursue these types of cases.[33] The London Charter for the IMT influenced the subsequent provisions of US military tribunals and regulations in the Pacific and China, although it is not clear whether these provisions were enacted.[34] These Balkan and Asian examples of municipal practice indicate a wider application of crimes against peace than is usually assumed.

It is also worth noting that the UNWCC made routine use of "genocide" as a category of offense well before the 1948 Convention on the

Prevention and Punishment of the Crime of Genocide.[35] While further research is needed, it appears to have developed partly from a Polish proposal of "de-nationalization" as a crime in representations to the commission in 1944.

Superior orders

The question of the validity of the defense of superior orders was also debated throughout the duration of the UNWCC, the members of which unanimously agreed that "the mere fact of having acted in obedience to the orders of a superior does not of itself relieve a person who has committed a war crime from responsibility."[36] However, it did not seek to impose this view on its members. Many individuals accused in national trials pleaded the defense of superior orders. They were often anticipated by commission members and highlighted in numerous debates seeking to address "the extent to which persons pledged by law to obey orders of their superiors, in particular those issued by heads of State and Governments, were to be held personally responsible for acts committed by them in subordinate positions."[37] The issue was viewed as significant enough that Committee III appointed a small subcommittee to address the issue and reach solutions.

Historical disagreements about the issue complicated the commission's efforts to clarify the principle. There is at least one circumstance at the Leipzig trials of the acquittal of an officer of sinking a hospital ship on the grounds that he had obeyed orders from a superior. German law at that time held that such a defense was valid.[38] After numerous debates, the official statement of the commission was, "civil and military authorities cannot be relieved from responsibility by the mere fact that a higher authority might have been convicted of the same offence. It will be for the court to decide whether a plea of superior orders is sufficient to acquit the person charged from responsibility."[39] Along these lines, one of the key issues that the UNWCC addressed was the legal conundrum presented by traditional standards of immunity for state officials and their ubiquitous practice of issuing orders to subordinates to engage in illegal actions. This contention is echoed in the commission's report to ECOSOC in 1948.[40] This report also discusses criminal liability for keeping watch while a crime is committed, passing on orders, participating in lynching, as well as instigating crime and common design.[41] Ultimately, Wright expressed in his introduction to the official history that "I think it can now be taken as settled that [the] plea is not a sufficient defence but that it may have effect by way of extenuation."[42]

Fair trials

Among the telling criticisms leveled at modern international criminal trials is that despite their long duration and enormous costs, the issue of fairness remains. The trials supported by the UNWCC rarely lasted more than a few days, and yet both contemporary and recent reviews of the practice are far from condemnatory of the quality of fairness in the trials of the 1940s.

Even in the aftermath of World War II, the interim study made by the UNWCC of trials completed by 1948 indicated that one in five of those tried was acquitted.[43] This result is in itself strong evidence that the system of justice supported by the UNWCC cannot be considered a system of show trials only supporting victor's justice. The commission reported that the "basic elements of a fair trial" for the accused were emphasized in national trials. Mark Ellis noted that in relation to the trials held by the Allied nations, the UNWCC reported that:

> The rules relating to evidence and procedure which are applied in trials by courts of the various countries ... when viewed as a whole, are seen to represent an attempt to secure to the accused his right to a fair trial while ensuring that the guilty shall not escape punishment because of legal technicalities.[44]

Ellis cites the perception of a Japanese general who was concerned about the fairness of the court but subsequently "began to feel more at ease with the President and the members of the Court because of the way the trial has been conducted,"[45] a view supported by Suzannah Linton, who states that the British military courts in Hong Kong offered a "broadly fair trial in difficult circumstances."[46] Thus, modern attempts to reduce the time and procedural processes of trials should not be assumed to be necessarily reducing the fairness of the trials.

The relationship between national trials and the global judicial body of the International Criminal Court is one of the more troubling contemporary issues. The ICC has sought in some instances to take over cases from the national authorities against their wishes, as in Libya, and has been criticized for an overemphasis on crimes alleged to have occurred in Africa. Meanwhile, the continuing bloodletting in Syria has received little attention from the ICC. As yet there has been little sign of the ICC developing a role in providing advice and support to empower local systems, a key principle of the UNWCC.

Therefore, it is intriguing that there was such extensive debate on this issue of complementarity between international and national jurisdictions in the 1940s. As Ellis discusses, the overriding practice of that era was that accused criminals faced trial in the invaded territories where the crimes had occurred, except in the cases of the top leadership.

Some disillusionment with the baroque practices of the ICC and the winding down of the ad hoc tribunals created for events in the Great Lakes region of Africa and the Balkans has led to renewed interest in the role of national courts in applying international criminal legal standards. As Carsten Stahn has explored in detail, here too the UNWCC provides such a powerful example that he urges the creation of another iteration of the UNWCC for the modern era. He argues that the UNWCC offers "an alternative to the centralized and situation-specific enforcement model under the umbrella of United Nations (UN) peace maintenance. The Commission represents a cooperative approach to justice and sovereignty … in terms of cooperation between major powers and use of international expertise and advice in criminal proceedings, international criminal justice is still in search of a modern UNWCC 2.0."[47]

Collective responsibility

The historical precedent argument is developed further by Kip Hale and Donna Cline in respect to bringing charges for group responsibility for international crimes.[48] They have explored a number of recent cases and legal practices and conclude that there is much to be learned from the UNWCC-supported trials, especially because some of them have already been used to support modern trials.[49] "Most importantly, these [World War II] cases are perfect examples of how the newly released trove of UNWCC archival material can have a significant impact on the work of today's judges, legal scholars, and practitioners who are seeking further clarification on Joint Criminal Enterprise or other legal issues."[50] To name but one now easily available source, in the ICC Legal Tools Database there are now hundreds of case files that can be used by practitioners and scholars seeking precedents in customary international law for new cases.

Hale and Cline also argue for the relevance of the UNWCC's effort to the interpretation of the collective responsibility provisions of the ICC Statute, which applies criminal responsibility to an individual for both co-perpetration and indirect perpetration. The ICC's language is similar to the UNWCC's recommendation that member states "commit for trial, either jointly or individually all those who, as members of these criminal gangs, have taken part in any way in the carrying out of crimes committed collectively by groups."[51] Hale and Cline urge that "ICC judges and practitioners would be well advised to research the

Commission's debate on this provision as well as investigate any national jurisdictions that applied this provision at trial. The interpretative and precedential value is manifest." They conclude that: "It is beyond question that the UNWCC is the most underutilized and under-analyzed institution in the field of international criminal law. This fact is all the more surprising given the trailblazing role it played in many critical issues, including collective responsibility." They continue by arguing that: "the sheer number of cases that the UNWCC supervised and supported provides a bounty of case law in a field starved of such; and the Commission gives contextual information important to understanding the Nuremberg Tribunal and post-World War II trials."[52]

These analysts contribute to an appreciation of how understanding the lost processes of the UNWCC can help today's efforts to re-energize the international system of criminal justice. The commission's work also offers reinforcement to the prosecution of horrific crimes. These are brought to the fore by Lutz Oette in his study of torture, and in an analysis of crimes of sexual violence that I conducted with Susana Sácouto and Chante Lasco.[53]

Sexual and gender-based violence

As documents relevant to UNWCC prosecutions become increasingly available for scrutiny, the varying ways in which the crimes of rape and enforced prostitution have been defined and prosecuted may offer useful guidance for contemporary tribunals faced with adjudicating similar atrocities. Indeed, the fact that these offenses were included in the list of war crimes agreed upon by UNWCC member states, and that charges for these crimes were brought by prosecutors in a wide range of jurisdictions, resulting in many successful convictions, provides important precedent for contemporary courts and tribunals facing *nullem crimen* challenges in sexual and gender-based violence (SGBV) cases. Moreover, the ways in which these jurisdictions defined SGBV offenses in their domestic or military codes—and, in particular, how they approached issues of consent and coercion—could offer important guidance to contemporary tribunals dealing with comparable issues. Similarly, the application of various modes of liability to crimes of sexual violence in UNWCC-supported cases provides contemporary tribunals with not only a better understanding of the roots of current concepts of criminal culpability but also important support for the proposition that the same standard of evidence should be used to hold perpetrators responsible in cases involving SGBV crimes as those involving other offenses. Finally, the UNWCC-supported cases indicate that, although only recently codified, the practice of protecting witnesses from degrading questions was observed as early as the post-World War II era, reinforcing rulings issued by contemporary tribunals that follow this practice and offering tribunals that have not yet codified such rules important precedent when dealing with this issue.

The importance of the UNWCC-supported cases for the prosecution of SGBV cases before contemporary tribunals cannot be overstated. For centuries, acts of sexual violence were viewed as "a detour, a deviation, or the acts of renegade soldiers ... pegged to private wrongs and ... [thus] not really the subject of international humanitarian law."[54] Indeed, such crimes were often perceived as "incidental" or "opportunistic" in relation to other "core" crimes.[55] Even when recognized as criminal, SGBV offences committed in the context of conflict or mass violence were often tacitly encouraged or tolerated, making it challenging for prosecutors to link the perpetrator with the crime. Not surprisingly, commentators have noted that while there have been significant improvements in the prosecution of SGBV crimes by contemporary tribunals, particularly in the last two decades,[56] these cases continue to be plagued by prosecutorial omissions and errors as well as by a tendency on the part of the judges to require that the prosecution meet higher evidentiary standards in these cases than in other types of cases.[57] That UNWCC member states investigated and prosecuted these crimes some seven decades ago, held both direct and indirect perpetrators responsible for such crimes and offered some level of protection to witnesses participating in these cases, is incredibly significant in light of this history.

In addition to the value of the UNWCC archives for tribunals prosecuting conflict-related SGBV cases today, the jurisprudence emerging from UNWCC-supported cases may also be relevant to contemporary policy debates. Indeed, the active role of states in pursuing crimes of sexual violence in the 1940s provides a more reinforced foundation for pursuing such crimes today than they may realize. Indeed, four permanent members of the UN Security Council—China, France, the United Kingdom, and the United States—were members of the UNWCC. They, and Russia (then the Soviet Union), were also party to the Hague Conventions, which were relied upon by many states to prosecute rape and forced prostitution. Similarly, a number of states that are members of the European Union—including Belgium, France, Greece, Italy, Poland, and the United Kingdom—endorsed rape and forced prostitution as war crimes in the 1940s. To the extent that the issue of sexual violence committed in the context of conflict or mass violence continues to be the subject of debate in UN and European Union forums, the valuable work carried out in the 1940s could be potentially of great legal significance.

Conclusion

The UNWCC should be considered a large and important historical source to reinforce the politics and law of international criminal justice. It provides a rich, varied and, until recently, largely unexploited foundation for holding the perpetrators of atrocities to legal account. After more than half a century of neglect, this lost wisdom born in the worst years of modern civilization can be of great practical import today.

The opportunity should not be lost so there are essential lessons to be learned about our approach to knowledge. The *UNWCC Law Reports* and *History of the UNWCC* were in the public domain since 1948 but were almost unused as research tools, and large parts, but not all, of the central records were in the national archives of member states and available for scrutiny.

In the documents still to be uncovered, undoubtedly more valuable materials will be discovered. The opportunity is there. In deciding whether to explore this avenue, it may help to ask ourselves whose ideas we are going to support. Will it be the narrow pragmatists who initially fought the creation of the UNWCC and international military tribunals, and who later succeeded at the end of the 1940s in halting the pursuit of international criminal justice? Or will it be the pioneers who strove to lay the foundations for such a system, often exiled to London from their native lands and forced to meet as the Nazis bombed? We may have a difficult task in rejuvenating international criminal justice today but not in comparison to the difficulties faced by those who created it in the first place. While they display a rare unity today in standing outside the International Criminal Court, it is salutary to remind China, India, and the United States that 70 years ago they played distinct and leading roles in launching a global system of international criminal justice.

Notes

1 The author wishes to acknowledge Shanti Sattler with whom much of the previous research for this article was conducted. Previously published articles are cited below.
2 Richard Goldstone, "Foreword: The United Nations War Crimes Commission Symposium," in *The United Nations War Crimes Commission: The Origins of International Criminal Justice*, ed. William Schabas, Carsten Stahn, Dan Plesch, Shanti Sattler, and Joseph Powderly, special double issue of *Criminal Law Forum* 25, nos. 1 & 2 (2014): 9–15.
3 Chris Simpson, "Shutting Down the United Nations War Crimes Commission," in *The United Nations War Crimes Commission*, 133–46.
4 Graham Cox "Seeking Justice for the Holocaust: Herbert C. Pell Versus the US State Department," in *The United Nations War Crimes Commission*, 77–110.

5 Kerstin von Lingen, "Setting the Path for the UNWCC: The Representation of European Exile Governments on the London International Assembly and the Commission for Penal Reconstruction and Development, 1941–44," in *The United Nations War Crimes Commission*, 45–76.

6 "UN War Crimes Archive 'Should Be Open to Public'," *The Guardian*, 26 February 2012, available at www.theguardian.com/law/2012/feb/26/un-war-crimes-archive; "More than 2,200 Documents from World War II War Crimes Archive are Online for the First Time," *Associated Press*, 3 August 2013, available at www.foxnews.com/world/2013/08/03/more-than-2200-document s-from-world-war-ii-war-crimes-archive-are-online-for/; "US Shoah Museum Gets War Crimes Archive," *Associated Press*, 3 November 2013, available at www.ynetnews.com/articles/0,7340,L-4448298,00.html.

7 Wen Wei Lai, "China, the Chinese Representative, and the Use of International Law to Counter Japanese Acts of Aggression: China's Standpoint on UNWCC Jurisdiction," in *The United Nations War Crimes Commission*, 111–32

8 Martin J. Burke and Thomas G. Weiss, "The Security Council and Ad Hoc Tribunals: Law and Politics, Peace and Justice," in *Security Council Resolutions and Global Legal Regimes*, ed. Trudy Fraser and Vesselin Popovksi (London: Routledge, 2014), 241–65.

9 Thousands of accused *génocidaires* were in Rwandan prisons by the late 1990s awaiting trial. To speed up the process the government used *gacaca*, a local form of arbitration. Village populations convene assemblies to settle property and marriage disputes with a solution acceptable to both parties. The *gacaca* courts for the genocide have operated since 2006 and seek to combine reconciliation and justice. Unlike traditional *gacaca*, they are formal institutions set up according to national law and can impose sentences of up to 30 years in prison. See, for example, Phil Clark, *The Gacaca Courts, Post-Genocide Justice and Reconciliation in Rwanda: Justice without Lawyers* (Cambridge: Cambridge University Press, 2010); and Eric Stover and Harvey Weinstein, eds., *My Neighbor, My Enemy: Justice and Community in the Aftermath of Mass Atrocity* (Cambridge: Cambridge University Press, 2004).

10 UN War Crimes Commission, *History of the UNWCC and the Development of the Laws of War* (London: UNWCC, 1948), note 4.

11 The Netherlands laws for the trial of war criminals were enacted in 1943 and the French in 1944.

12 Minutes and papers of the UNWCC National Offices Conference, 1945. Available from cisd@soas.ac.uk.

13 United Nations War Crimes Commission, *Information Concerning Human Rights Arising from Trials of War Criminals* (New York: UN Economic and Social Council, 1948), 125–45; and Appendix, UN document E/CN.14-AM9 (15 May 1948), available at www.unwcc.org/documents/.

14 The treasure trove of previously restricted UNWCC documentation, some of which was used for this chapter, is easy to consult at www.legal-tools.org/en/go-to-database/ltfolder/0_28425/#results. In the references below, precise URLs are not given for each document as legal tools sometimes change. However, the documents remain plainly ordered by type, such as minutes of the main commission and its committees and the commission's papers. The reference system for these archives is the one developed and used by the commission in its own index to its archives, which is also in the legal tools system.

15 UN document E/CN.14-AM9 (15 May 1948). For the Netherlands, see page 130 [Netherlands Extraordinary Penal Law Decree of 22 December 1943 (Statute Book D. 61) and the Decrees of 22 December 1943 (Statute Book D. 62)]. For Belgium, see page 291.

16 UNWCC, Internal Memo, 18 April 1945.

17 Some criticism of this has been that it was based on hearsay evidence, a matter discussed by the UNWCC itself. See UNWCC, *Information Concerning Human Rights Arising from Trials of War Criminals*, no. 1. It appears to us that the colloquial sense of "hearsay" as gossip has been used to denigrate the work of the UNWCC as a whole. Also see the UNARMS application package for the UNWCC.

18 "UNWCC Budget for the Fourth Fiscal Period 1 April 1947–31 March 1948, Statement A, Actual Expenditure for 1946–47, £15,137." Available from the author on request at cisd@soas.ac.uk.

19 See Cox "Seeking Justice for the Holocaust."

20 UNWCC 21st mtg, 3 (6 June 1944) and the accompanying UNWCC Doc. C24, as well as UNWCC 22nd mtg, 3 (13 June 1944) and the accompanying UNWCC Doc. C30.

21 UNWCC 32nd mtg, 2–7 (19 September 1944). Also see UNWCC Doc. C52(1), "Recommendation in Favour of the Establishment by Supreme Military Commanders of Mixed Military Tribunals for the Trial of War Criminals," 26 September 1944.

22 UNWCC 32nd mtg, 19 September 1944. The commission approved the adoption of a proposal for a United Nations War Crimes Court (see the accompanying UNWCC Doc. C49, Doc. C50 and Doc. C58 Explanatory Memorandum).

23 Memorandum from the Treasury Solicitor's Office for the Attorney General (1945), 1, 2, 4. UK National Archives TS26, 897, 27–33.

24 See the October 1945 *Trial of Kapitanleutnant Heinz Eck and Four Others*, accused of killing crew members of the Greek steamship *Peleus*, in a British Military Court for the Trial of War Criminals.

25 UNWCC, 33rd mtg, 33, 6 (26 September 1944).

26 The UNWCC's reliance on military authorities was in part due to the UNWCC's commitment to providing justice that was swift and effective. The meaning of this was debated among members throughout the existence of the UNWCC. The internal document "Recommendation in Favour of the Establishment by Supreme Military Commanders of Mixed Military Tribunals for the Trial of War Criminals" declared that the strategy would be used in part " ... so that no criminals escape trial and punishment because of the inability to effect a speedy trial" (UNWCC Doc. C52(1)). In hesitation, French representative M. Gros addressed this idea in a written statement submitted at the UNWCC's thirty-first meeting on 12 September 1944. His first point stated: "[a]lthough the notion of swift justice is found in manuals of military law, 'justice' is something that does not admit of qualifying adjectives." Also see UNWCC, *History of the UNWCC*, 5.

27 UNWCC, *History of the UNWCC*, 180.

28 UNWCC, *History of the UNWCC*, 17.

29 UNWCC, 77th mtg, see earlier discussions at the UNWCC Meetings M35, M36, M41.

30 *Trial of Takashi Sakai*, United Nations War Crimes Commission, XIV Law Reports of Trials of War Criminals 1, Case No. 83, Chinese War Crimes Military Tribunal of the Ministry of National Defence, Nanking, 29 August 1946.

31 UNWCC, *History of the UNWCC*, 10.

32 The Kampala conference defined the crime of aggression as "the planning, preparation, initiation or execution, by a person in a position effectively to exercise control over or to direct the political or military action of a State, of an act of aggression which, by its character, gravity and scale, constitutes a manifest violation of the Charter of the United Nations."

33 UNWCC, *Information Concerning Human Rights Arising from Trials of War Criminals*, no. 5, 288, 295–97.

34 UNWCC, *Information Concerning Human Rights Arising from Trials of War Criminals*, no. 5, 158.

35 Carsten Stahn, "Complementarity and Cooperative Justice Ahead of their Time? The United Nations War Crimes Commission, Fact-finding and Evidence," in *The United Nations War Crimes Commission*, 223–60.

36 *Report to the Governments on the Plea of Superior Orders*, UNWCC, Document C86, and Meeting M54, 2.

37 UNWCC, *History of the UNWCC*, 263.

38 See the case of Lieutenant-Commander Karl Neumann, commander of the submarine U 67, and the case of the sinking of the hospital ship *Dover Castle* on 26 May 1917.

39 UNWCC, *History of the UNWCC*, 138.

40 UNWCC, *Information Concerning Human Rights Arising from Trials of War Criminals*, UN document E/CN.14-AM9 (1948), 217–36.

41 UNWCC, *Information Concerning Human Rights Arising from Trials of War Criminals*, 212–16.

42 UNWCC, *History of the UNWCC*, 11.

43 UNWCC, *Law Reports of Trials of War Criminals*, vol. XV (London: His Majesty's Stationery Office, 1948), xi.

44 UNWCC, *Law Reports of Trials of War Criminals*, vol. XV, 190, 273.

45 Post Sentence Statement of the accused in *Trial of Sergeant Major Ito Junichi*, British Military Court in Hong Kong, case no. WO235/1107, transcript 214, slide 247 (as cited in Suzannah Linton, "Rediscovering the War Crimes Trials in Hong Kong 1946–48," *Melbourne Journal of International Law* 13, no. 2 (2012): 62).

46 Linton, "Rediscovering the War Crimes Trials in Hong Kong," 61.

47 Stahn, "Complementarity and Cooperative Justice," 223.

48 Kip Hale and Donna Cline, "Holding Collectives Accountable," in *The United Nations War Crimes Commission*, 261–90.

49 UNWCC Comm. doc. 151 (15 Oct. 1945) 1; *Tadić* (Appeals Judgment) (n. 24) para. 202.

50 UNWCC Comm. doc. 105(1) (n. 141).

51 UNWCC Comm. doc. 105(1) (n. 141).

52 Hale and Cline, "Holding Collectives Accountable," 290.

53 This section is based on Dan Plesch, Susana Sácouto, and Chante Lasco, "The Relevance of the United Nations War Crimes Commission to the Prosecution of Sexual and Gender-Based Crimes Today," in *The United Nations War Crimes Commission*, 349–91.

54 See P.V. Sellers, "Individual(s') Liability for Collective Sexual Violence," in *Gender and Human Rights*, ed. Karen Knop (Oxford: Oxford University Press, 2004): 153, 190; R. Rhonda, "Gender Crimes as War Crimes: Integrating Crimes Against Women into International Criminal Law," *McGill Law Journal* 46, no. 1 (2000): 217, 223 (noting that only after rape began being discussed as a "weapon of war" in the former Yugoslavia was it transformed "from private, off-duty, collateral, and inevitable excess to something that is public or 'political' in the traditional sense"); Press Release, Human Rights Watch, "Human Rights Watch Applauds Rwanda Rape Verdict," 1 September 1998, www.hrw.org/press98/sept/rrape902.htm. It noted that "[d]espite these legal precedents, rape has long been mischaracterized and dismissed by military and political leaders as a private crime, the ignoble act of the occasional soldier. Worse still, it has been accepted precisely because it is so commonplace. Longstanding discriminatory attitudes have viewed crimes against women as incidental or less serious violations." Lutz Oette, "From Calculated Cruelty to Casual Violence – The United Nations War Crimes Commission and the Prosecution of Torture and Ill-Treatment," *Criminal Law Forum* 25, nos. 1–2 (2014): 291–321.

55 See P.V. Sellers and K. Okuizumi, "International Prosecution of Sexual Assault," *Transnational Law and Contemporary Problems* 7, no. 1 (1997): 45, 61–62 (noting that "[s]exual assaults committed during armed conflict are often rationalized as the result of a perpetrator's lust, libidinal needs, or stress"); C. Eboe-Osuji, "Rape and Superior Responsibility: International Criminal Law in Need of Adjustment," International Criminal Court, Guest Lecture Series of the Office of the Prosecutor, 20 June 2005. It was argued that "the theory of individualistic opportunism proceeds ... from the ... modest premise that rape is a crime of opportunity which, during conflict, is frequently committed by arms-bearing men, indulging their libidos, under cover of the chaotic circumstances of armed conflict."

56 See C. Steains, "Gender Issues," in *The International Criminal Court: The Making of the Rome Statute*, ed. R.S. Lee (The Hague: Kluwer, 1999), 361–64. The article concludes that because earlier international law failed to do so, the Statute's inclusion of "a range of sexual violence crimes, in addition to rape, under crimes against humanity creates an important new precedent."

57 See, for instance, S. Sácouto and K. Cleary, "The Importance of Effective Investigation of Sexual Violence and Gender-Based Crimes at the International Criminal Court," *American University Journal of Gender, Social Policy and Law* 17, no. 2 (2009): 337–59. Indeed, despite evidence of the widespread use of rape in the Balkans conflict and during the Rwandan genocide, the record is quite mixed with respect to the ability of the ad hoc criminal tribunals for the former Yugoslavia (ICTY) and Rwanda (ICTR) to prosecute sexual violence successfully. For example, despite the widely acknowledged use of rape and sexual violence as an integral part of the genocide in Rwanda, 10 years into the Rwanda tribunal's history, only 10 percent of completed cases resulting in a sentence contained rape convictions and "[n]o rape charges were even brought by the Prosecutor's office in 70 per cent of ... adjudicated cases." B. Nowrojee, *"Your Justice is Too Slow": Will the ICTR Fail Rwanda's Rape Victims?* (Geneva: UN Research Institute for Social Development, 2005), 3.

5   UNRRA's operational genius and institutional design

Eli Karetny and Thomas G. Weiss

- **UNRRA, an overview**
- **Logistical genius**
- **Other key factors**
- **UNRRA's temporary status**
- **Conclusion**

The experience of the United Nations Relief and Rehabilitation Administration (UNRRA) contains lessons not only as the first operational UN organization but also as a testing ground for the very notions of robust multilateralism and internationalism.[1] This chapter explores the industrial-scale undertakings by some 12,000 international civil servants who assisted 11 million displaced persons in Germany alone, administered some $4 billion of assistance, coordinated the relief efforts of about 125 international private voluntary associations, and eased suffering in 23 war-torn societies of Europe and Asia. To contextualize the challenge and magnitude of the UNRRA experiment, a year of its operations would be at least $22 billion in current dollars, more than the approximately $18 billion in 2012 (the latest year for which data are available) of total humanitarian disbursements worldwide, public and private.[2] The range of activities—from massive food and drug distribution to gigantic civil-engineering projects—is impressive. The geographical spread—across war-ravaged Europe and Asia—in a world without today's communication and transportation technologies is humbling.[3]

UN founders sought to write the next chapter in the history of intergovernmental cooperation following the League of Nations. The second generation of intergovernmental organizations (IGOs) naturally looked to the first generation's experience, including some of the mental constructs and biases.[4] That era was a crucial stage in the evolution of humanitarian thinking and practice, a time described as a "way station between humanitarianism's past and future," when states became more involved in relief work in part because of strategic benefits.[5] Principles now regarded as central to humanitarian action—impartiality, neutrality, and independence—began in 1865 with the establishment of the International Committee of the Red Cross (ICRC).

World War I resulted in a dramatic growth in international humanitarian action, including the founding of Save the Children in 1919. The most substantial assistance came from the American Relief Administration (ARA), which operated from 1919 to 1923 under the leadership of future president Herbert Hoover. He understood that humanitarian assistance during the famine in Europe and Russia could help foster Western influence in what would in 1922 become the Soviet Union. Financed by the US government, the ARA operated as a private relief agency and was not a model for intergovernmental organizations, especially because of impressions about squandered resources and partiality.[6]

More relevant as a precedent was the League's establishment of the High Commission for Russian Refugees (1920–22), headed by Fridtjof Nansen—Norway's explorer, scientist, humanitarian, Nobel laureate. Strategic factors may have driven Western states to stress humanitarianism, but leaders and beneficiaries are central to the story of World War I and the Bolshevik Revolution. Nansen later expanded his mandate to include Armenian and then other continental populations through the High Commission for Refugees. After his death in 1930, the League's member states changed the name to the Nansen International Office for Refugees (1931–39).[7] As high commissioner, he enlarged the geographic range of relief efforts and negotiated a set of refugee rights, which included travel documents (the Nansen passport), education, and employment (the International Labour Organization helped refugees find work).

These precedents were building blocks in 1943 for UNRRA. Just as Nansen's efforts helped shape the early institutional attempts at international cooperation on refugees, UNRRA's relief work and organizational improvements were decisively affected by Robert G.A. Jackson. This chapter begins with a brief overview of UNRRA before exploring his contributions. Part of the explanation for UNRRA's performance involves more commonly accepted factors (US power and changing geostrategic interests), which are briefly discussed before examining another overlooked variable, the organization's unusual design.

UNRRA, an overview

George Woodbridge tells UNRRA's official history in three volumes published in 1950.[8] He discussed four key characteristics: the actual

"Work" of relief and rehabilitation; the intergovernmental machinery, or "Organization" of member states in the Governing Council and Central Committee; the "Administration" of international civil servants in headquarters and the field; and the "Concept" of multilateral cooperation guided by common interests. His perspective was that of governments or what some observers call the "First UN" of member states. His monumental work is the point of departure for anyone working on the topic—indeed, observers should wonder why there have been so few such documentary efforts for the work of intergovernmental bodies. Nonetheless, Woodbridge said too little about UNRRA staff (the "Second UN") and almost nothing about nongovernmental organizations (NGOs), academics, policy experts, the media, and the private sector (the "Third UN").[9]

According to the "Introduction" of the UNRRA Agreement, the United Nations determined that the population of liberated areas would immediately receive "aid and relief from their sufferings, food, clothing and shelter, aid in the prevention of pestilence and in the recovery of the health of the people."[10] Furthermore, "preparation and arrangements shall be made for the return of prisoners and exiles to their homes and for assistance in the resumption of urgently needed agricultural and industrial production and the restoration of essential services." However, the agreement recognized that UNRRA had to be flexible and experimental and also function for a limited time. This design helped achieve its primary objectives and laid the groundwork for future intergovernmental organizations, many already on various drawing boards.

UNRRA's end date was not predetermined, but operations were to cease after meeting wartime and postwar strategic and humanitarian needs. That UNRRA was not meant to last beyond the war and immediate postwar context in some ways enhanced its flexibility, ability to accomplish goals, and capacity to adapt. While many of its inputs and outputs were controversial, advocates and detractors alike would agree that its performance fell short of satisfying the longer-term hopes of those who saw it as a test for a more ambitious brand of international cooperation.

Key provisions in the agreement helped UNRRA manage four challenges that still confront today's intergovernmental organizations. The first three are treated in another essay,[11] which highlights how UNRRA managed complex tensions. The first was leadership and commitments, which focused on what Edward Luck called America's "mixed messages,"[12] the tension between US multilateral leadership and ambivalence toward the very concept of international organization. The second was strategic goals and humanitarian action; while wartime demands ensured respect for national sovereignty, they also promoted redefinitions of vital interests that sustained an unusual degree of international cooperation. The third consisted of oversight and colla-boration with NGOs because UNRRA orchestrated the activities of private voluntary agencies without over-centralization.

This chapter's main purpose is to explore a fourth tension, the impact of institutional design and structure. First, however, it investigates how Robert Jackson transformed UNRRA after early stumbling threatened to destroy it. Substantial analytical attention has been paid to the organization's political leadership in dealing with the US Congress—especially to lobbying by the first two directors-general, Herbert Lehman and Fiorello LaGuardia. Without demeaning their contributions or implying that UNRRA's relief workers at numerous levels were inconsequential, we emphasize UNRRA's operational leadership.

Logistical genius

Jackson's early wartime experience demonstrated and reinforced skills that would later serve him well as he took charge of a struggling UNRRA. A product of the Royal Australian Navy who transferred to the Royal Navy in 1937, "Jacko" rejected the view of most in the British government that Malta, despite its importance as a naval base, could not be defended against a sustained air attack. He was variously called "the master of logistics" and "the man who saved Malta."[13] According to Jackson's notes, the basic strategy required for Malta to withstand the Axis siege was that the "civilian population must be protected and provided with essentials" like food, fuel, and other basic commodities, which would be difficult to resupply after reserves had been depleted. Without the cooperation and support of the local population, "no defence would be possible." This experience prepared him for subsequent relief efforts in part because of the logistical challenges of coordinating limited supplies but also because of the entwined logics of humanitarian action and military strategy.

Barely in his thirties, Jackson later commanded the Middle East Supply Centre (MESC) in Cairo, which was tasked with stopping nonessential civilian imports that had been taking up vital shipping space, clogging the ports, and complicating unnecessarily the resupply of British forces. As director-general, Jackson ensured that the MESC performed its core functions of developing local production of food and materials through the cooperation of individual Middle Eastern governments, and that imports were obtained from the nearest source. The operation made certain that demand for civilian imports was restricted to essentials, assisted Middle Eastern governments in control and distribution so that imports were put to the best use, and provided a nexus for the exchange of information on problems of agricultural and industrial production and distribution. At MESC, Jackson's military logistical acumen for command organization was necessarily supplemented by honing his civilian administrative and diplomatic skills, which were then directly transferred to UNRRA—indeed, they were later on display during massive UN operations in Bangladesh and Cambodia.[14]

Jackson's transformative role in UNRRA is acknowledged, but analysts have paid insufficient attention to the actual mechanics of his leadership. Early difficulties related to personnel problems, supply challenges, and insufficient funding. Many viewed UNRRA's debut as a botched experiment, and so Jackson's reputation made him an obvious recruit to come to the rescue. He assumed operational leadership of UNRRA on 7 May 1945, the day of German surrender, and oversaw crucial organizational changes including the recruitment of international civil servants; a second 1 percent contribution from donors (especially difficult was a reluctant US Congress); the transition from military command (and a strategy for resource maximization) to a more humanitarian conception of self-government; the expanded understanding of rehabilitation (including psychological rehabilitation); and the reorganization of key elements of UNRRA's structure (including a shift toward increased centralization in some functions along with an increased emphasis on localization in other areas).

Jackson was asked to assess the nature of the problems that threatened people as well as the organization that was succoring them. After having submitted his report, he was named director of UNRRA's European Regional Office (ERO)—by far the most important theater, accounting for five-sixths of expenses.[15] UNRRA's dire situation was evident from his notes. It "is in a very dangerous condition," he wrote in the concluding statements of his first memo after coming on board, and "there is a great danger that the organization will collapse and become an international scandal."[16] While such a failure "would undoubtedly create chaotic conditions in those countries which now rely on UNRRA for their supplies, the political results would be even worse." Jackson understood the greatest challenge as restoring confidence in the very idea of multilateral cooperation. The knock-on effects of failure would be catastrophic: "should this, the first of the new international organizations fail, then people all over the world will most certainly lose confidence in the United Nations concept as a whole."[17]

His view that UNRRA was in danger of collapse was reinforced by Britain's chancellor of the exchequer, John Anderson, in a memorandum to US secretary of state Edward Stettinius. "The administration is in complete disorder," Anderson lamented, and "there is no system of authority or discipline, work is uncoordinated, there is a serious lack of good personnel in key positions, money is being uselessly squandered, there is no proper planning of major operations." Exacerbating matters was the "growing loss of American interest in UNRRA," which reflected the "marked tendency in America to think of the relief problem in national rather than international terms."[18] Washington's wavering commitment reflected historical ambivalence toward intergovernmental organizations of all stripes. Curiously, American efforts were central to founding and sustaining the organization but also to what many saw as UNRRA's premature death. Harnessing Washington's support for, and mollifying its resistance to, UNRRA remained a consistent challenge for Jackson as well as for the more political directors-general.

Some of his earliest notes highlight the measures necessary to make UNRRA effective. Of the six primary tasks, three required cooperation among great powers, namely the need to: "obtain efficient officials to direct the work of the organization"; "modify and streamline the international organization and administration"; and "ensure that UNRRA is given reasonably good allocations of available world supplies, especially transport." However, Jackson also recognized the centrality of economic and military calculations in promoting collaboration, which he hoped would eventually attract Moscow but absolutely necessitated at least Washington's and London's active support. UNRRA had to, he continued, "[o]btain an (even unofficial) Anglo-American understanding that further financial support will be forthcoming if UNRRA does a reasonably good job of work"; "ensure effective support from the British and American armies"; and "if possible, obtain Soviet support for the organization (and, if this is not forthcoming to go ahead regardless)."[19]

Given total authority as the deputy for operations by UNRRA's first director-general, Herbert Lehman, Jackson began his drastic reorganization by streamlining and centralizing authority.[20] He viewed Washington headquarters as inefficient, unfocused, and bloated; but it could usefully concentrate on overall policy development.[21] That office continued to have responsibility for providing supplies and shipping, because in the US capital were the Anglo-American Combined Boards—the US and UK joint wartime agency that aimed to maximize the utilization of productive resources, food, and raw materials; reduce the demands on shipping; and ensure both civilian and military needs. The Washington office also retained ultimate financial control. Missions were established from the start in all countries where UNRRA operated with the exception of Czechoslovakia and Poland, but Jackson pushed to have missions there as well as in Belarus and Ukraine in an effort to maintain Soviet support for UNRRA. As part of reorganizing the Washington office, Jackson insisted that full authority for controlling UNRRA's missions in Europe be delegated to the ERO in London, based in Portland Place alongside the British Broadcasting Corporation. This change streamlined decision making and vested authority in seasoned administrators closer to the actual location of operations. Jackson's notes emphasized the importance of improving UNRRA's public relations. Overly high early expectations along with operational failures and high-decibel criticism had led many, especially in the United States, to question UNRRA's value. Its weaknesses provided easy opportunities for those never reconciled to Roosevelt's internationalist project. Jackson understood the crucial importance of maintaining broad-gauged public support, which provided leverage when commitments by member governments wavered.

The ERO published an article in January 1946 detailing how a reorganized UNRRA would manage the transition from wartime to postwar operations. The principal donors—the United Kingdom, the United States, and Canada—had promised to make a second 1 percent contribution. The public was reminded that "in each country's contribution not more than ten percent is in foreign exchange … the contributions, like those of Lend-lease, were intended to be wheat, seeds, medicines, coal, sugar, motor lorries, wool, cotton, or, notably for Britain, shipping."[22] The sales pitch for humanitarian assistance was infused with economic calculations: relief and rehabilitation would help recipients and also benefit domestic producers.

The transition from military to civilian administration in the ashes of war was challenging and involved ongoing headaches. Yet as UNRRA took over responsibilities from Allied military forces in many liberated territories, Jackson's office reminded the public that UNRRA did more than run assembly centers and offer health and welfare services. It also "provides amenity supplies like cigarettes, chocolate, cobbler sets, sewing sets, toilet articles, and other goods which make all the difference between a transient camp and a tolerable community." Fostering a sense of community was part of UNRRA's publicized motto to "help people help themselves." This ethos was motivated by the logic of resource efficiency as much as democracy promotion, which was understood differently by Allied military forces and UNRRA field teams, who sometimes clashed about the trade-offs but often managed to work together.[23]

Jackson interpreted UNRRA's mandate as limited so that its goals were achievable. Rehabilitation came to be associated with psychological and economic empowerment through employment, job training, and community projects for displaced persons in self-governed assembly centers, where "UNRRA workers, by developing a complex liaison with the people of the centres, with Military Government, with the local burgomeisters, have 'made a little go a long way'."[24]

Although the end of hostilities freed-up access to military stockpiles, supply challenges and institutional turf battles persisted. The ERO pointed out that UNRRA was the "largest export undertaking the world has ever seen"[25]—and it still has that record. UNRRA's struggles were intensified due to the global shortage of basic supplies, but its greatest challenge came from the transportation bottlenecks and infrastructural destruction from the war. "All along the seaboard of liberated Europe the Germans left ports blocked or otherwise rendered useless, and docks and harbour installations destroyed." Exacerbating the problem of getting supplies away from the ports to needed areas were "blown-up bridges, torn-up railway tracks, vanished draft animals, and destroyed or stolen trucks [that] resulted in the complete breakdown of the inland transport system when supplies started to flow in."[26] Other setbacks complicated UNRRA's efforts: bad harvests, crop failures, disastrous droughts, and labor shortages from strikes in vital steel and coal industries as well as in railway and shipping systems. In September 1946 Jackson acknowledged publicly what he had emphasized repeatedly in his notes. Victory in Europe improved UNRRA's situation largely because "men of the desired caliber and experience" became available for key positions. It was only after the war ended that the staff could begin working "in a true spirit of international service."[27]

Jackson's efforts to revive UNRRA should be viewed through two lenses: ensuring that UNRRA could accomplish its primary tasks; and making sure that this operational experiment in international cooperation succeeded so that plans for future UN organizations would not be stillborn. Hence, Jackson emphasized UNRRA's limited mandate and duration, as well as his desire to obtain Soviet support albeit accompanied by his publicly enunciated willingness to proceed even without it.[28] In short, Jackson made UNRRA into a more professional, focused, and strategic humanitarian organization.

To fast forward, the growing tensions between Moscow and the West made UNRRA's work problematic because political pay-offs, not humanitarian needs, predominated. When it became clear that UNRRA could not survive the Cold War, Jackson knew that UNRRA would be replaced by the International Refugee Organization (IRO) and hoped for universal membership. He regretted that the State Department emphasized a bilateral instead of multilateral approach.[29] Accepting this policy shift and recognizing that the Cold War created a new strategic environment, Jackson and a visible segment of UNRRA's staff believed that their experience could and should inform the Marshall Plan, the IRO, and other fledgling UN bodies. UN organizations and the Marshall Plan's secretariat benefited from UNRRA's bureaucratic memory.

Other key factors

Jackson's hands-on leadership is an essential factor, but other variables are also crucial. They are detailed briefly to complete the picture before probing another underappreciated variable, institutional design. The other central factors include the value of people and ideas, the predominant United States, and the impact of the geostrategic environment.

Jackson began a no-holds-barred practice of replacing cronies, adventurers, and amateurs with qualified international civil servants. The results of his persistence underscore how much individuals at all levels matter for intergovernmental as for all organizations. As important as it was to recruit competent people made available by the war's end, jettisoning incompetent ones was perhaps more essential and required confronting the patronage practices of powerful political personalities.

Jackson's firing of numerous individuals infuriated key partners. He recounted an awkward exchange with John Gilbert Winant, the US ambassador in London, and Mrs. Churchill in the bunker of the Ministry of Defence, with an ill Winston Churchill within earshot.[30] "After we had tea," Jackson explains, "Gil said 'the reason why I asked you to come and talk with Mrs. Churchill is, the Prime Minister intends to fire you immediately'."[31] Asked why he had axed some 25 of Churchill's friends, Jackson said: "What I had done was without reference to any individual's friendships. All that I was concerned with was to make UNRRA efficient to do its job." "Anyone who had seen," Jackson continued, "the destruction wrought by the war—as undoubtedly Mr. Churchill had seen when he was in Greece—would want to see relief, rehabilitation and reconstruction started as soon as possible." Realizing that "perhaps the Prime Minister heard me," Jackson emphasized to Mrs. Churchill that "UNRRA only existed to help these people … it is not a matter of friendship, it's a matter of getting the job done."

Jackson kept his post, and future recruiting attracted individuals from a range of countries, ideally with a broad conception of interests.

Craig Murphy has noted that Allied officials, and especially those in UNRRA, moved directly from administrations in Asia and Africa into top positions in the newly established UN Secretariat.[32] "Working together in UNRRA were a number of people, particularly British and American, who were shortly afterwards to be appointed to key administrative posts in the United Nations," remembered Richard Symonds who worked in the UK colonial service and UNRRA before having a distinguished UN career. "With its shared background of mistakes as well as achievements, they were able to agree on common personnel, salary, pension, and other arrangements which have been an important element in holding together the UN system."[33]

US citizens had no "colonial" experience per se, but many shared Franklin Roosevelt's multilateral vision. "To be sure US officials supported international development in the 1940s for a number of strategic and economic reasons," Eric Helleiner concluded. "But they were also influenced by the ideology of the New Deal with its interests in social justice, poverty alleviation and interventionist economic policy."[34]

Roosevelt and other US officials viewed UNRRA as an international extension of the New Deal.[35] According to one historian, some officials "were offering 'lofty visions of democratic cooperation and equality' after the war," and Vice President Henry Wallace spoke of the New Deal being applied worldwide.[36] For UNRRA as for all intergovernmental organizations, ideas matter.[37] Elsewhere, we discuss how commitment to democratic principles, international cooperation, nondiscrimination, and operational flexibility aided in realizing UNRRA's strategic and humanitarian goals.[38] The idea that UNRRA could reflect an internationalized commitment to social justice through orchestrated governmental actions represented an improvement on the League of Nations' and Herbert Hoover's World War I approach through voluntary (mainly religious) agencies. International oversight increased accountability and coordination.

The most critical factor was sustained US government involvement. Given its preponderant military and economic power, Jackson worked to maintain Washington's support. American initiative under Roosevelt was crucial to UNRRA's getting off the ground and staying there. With Harry S. Truman's seismic shift to an America-centric anticommunism, the US commitment to UNRRA was replaced by a narrower multilateralism, the Marshall Plan. The State Department pointed to the growing tensions between East and West that signaled a dramatic change in the strategic environment. As such, Under Secretary of State William Clayton put it tersely: "the US must run this show."[39] Ironically, UNRRA would not have succeeded without enlightened US leadership. Washington nurtured an international organization that fostered US vital interests but without complete US domination. Washington's approach could be described as an earlier version of "leading from behind," getting other states to accept a broader understanding of their own interests and sharing the burdens of cooperation. Washington's calculations were that American aims and interests were best served by a multilateral relief organization whereas the Truman Doctrine necessitated distributing aid not on the basis of need but of political gain. American benevolence was no longer persuasive in Congress; political pay-offs were. "On both sides of the Iron Curtain," Jessica Reinisch summarizes, UNRRA "became a yardstick for how much priorities had shifted between 1943 and 1947."[40]

The puzzle remains why World War II's strategic moment was so brief, why multilateralism evaporated after the non-fascist world stood successfully together confronting common enemies, promoting shared visions, and pursuing mutual interests. The Cold War's onset immediately created a dramatically different strategic environment and a dramatically different and less cosmopolitan brand of US leadership. The clear message was that future assistance would be dictated by its major benefactor. The strategic moment signaled that a new multilateral organization for reconstruction was necessary, one based on carrots for siding with the West and sticks with the East. This brand of multilateralism reflected US perceived national interests, which required restricting possible partners and beneficiaries. While enormous challenges remained in the war's wake and the unfinished business of relief and rehabilitation, UNRRA's temporary status meant that it could be disbanded—its leftover funds in 1947 were distributed to several parts of the newly inaugurated UN system including the IRO, UNICEF, the UN Educational, Scientific and Cultural Organization, and the World Health Organization. Meanwhile, the United States funded the Marshall Plan.

UNRRA's decentralized structure enhanced flexibility and organizational learning, but when rehabilitation approached reconstruction, diffuse authority and improvised problem solving were obstacles to longer-term rebuilding, which required resources, planning, and accountability. Jackson understood that UNRRA was not permanent, but still it required shifting toward more centralized control over policy-making and increased local control over field operations. To accomplish its immediate goals and pave the way for longer-term needs, UNRRA collaborated with myriad partners: NGOs, for-profit producers, member governments, and an emerging international civil service.

Akira Iriye noted the importance of this array of actors and transnational perspectives because "migrants' well-being became the concern of international entities, most notably the United Nations Relief and Rehabilitation Agency."[41] As such, UNRRA had elements of "global governance" *avant le mot*.[42] Jackson believed that overreaching—one disappointed former official described staff as "fanatical internationalists" and "super idealists"[43]—could play into the hands of critics, and so UNRRA sought to strike a balance. Confronting political and operational challenges, the blend of strategic realism and humanitarianism facilitated a second US contribution despite a reluctant Congress; maintained Soviet support; and enhanced the legitimacy of global problem solving.

UNRRA's temporary status

UNRRA's limited duration facilitated some of Jackson's efforts. The organization's DNA included its flexible, adaptable, experimental, and temporary character. The value of this institutional design can perhaps be best appreciated by considering the arguments in favor of sunset legislation, which "subjects government laws and bodies to periodic review under threat of automatic cessation at a predetermined date unless the activity is reauthorized." It can promote accountability, innovation, and broad-based participation in lawmaking processes.[44] The earliest advocates for sunset provisions believed that periodic review would serve to hold legislators accountable, but even more importantly, Theodore Lowi argued that sunset provisions could encourage innovative legislation to replace ineffective programs and decrease the influence of special interests.[45] No consensus exists about the impact of sunset provisions on international organizations, mainly because member states have dismantled virtually no such institutions.

To the extent that sunset provisions envisage a limited-duration body, an argument can be made that they facilitate broad-based participation because diminished risks are associated with an initial buy-in. Moreover, they may accelerate negotiations and approval of such institutions when potential members are eager to be on the ground floor for an undertaking.

Opposing arguments emphasize that sunset clauses favor short-term rewards and hinder long-term investments because of heightened risks about future uncertainties. If so, they increase the cost of oversight and lobbying, and they lead to poorly crafted laws and institutions because "getting a statute enacted is much easier than getting it revised."[46] This problem is made worse because temporary laws can become permanent, as typically "temporary" international organizations do. The potential downside from inadequate long-term planning can be offset with experimentation and flexibility so that even temporary organiza-tions can improve in the short run through learning and adaptation, whether or not they become permanent. Unlike other UN agencies that became permanent but were temporary at that time—UNICEF and IRO (which later became the Office of the UN High Commissioner for Refugees)—UNRRA was shut down in 1947.

Limiting its mandate and duration made it easier for proponents to argue in favor of UNRRA's establishment. Despite the pressures of war and occupation, it provided relief and laid the groundwork for rehabi-litation. It was temporary *and* experimental. Limiting the size and scope of the experiment resulted, despite political and bureaucratic problems, in the delivery of massive life-saving relief before member states deci-ded to halt operations and begin transitions to other UN organizations and the Marshall Plan. The barriers to initial buy-in were manageable, which facilitated participation by great and small powers alike despite a host of concerns about open-ended commitments and insufficient voice in decision making. Short-term commitments alleviated donor concerns about providing weaker countries with leverage.

No commitment was more crucial than Washington's—responsible for three-quarters of the total budget—and UNRRA's limited time horizon and mandate were useful in decreasing the traction of argu-ments from detractors. Of course, not all came around, including Wil-liam Langer, the US senator from North Dakota, who complained that Jackson, "the man whom one must see if he wishes to see Mr. Lehman, does not come from Tennessee or the State of Montana or from Maine."[47] Yet the United States contributed 1 percent of gross domestic product (GDP) not once but twice during UNRRA's lifetime—with vigorous debate into which General Eisenhower had to intervene for UNRRA but without the kind of uproar that greets contemporary disbursements of US official development assistance that currently are barely 0.1 percent of GDP. Although the "strategic moment" was central to US support for UNRRA, the limited time horizon and circumscribed mandate helped diminish the opposition from Congress—in 1945 the House approved the second allocation by a vote of 327 to 29. Jackson's biographer notes that the legislature "finally agreed to contribute another one percent, on the assumption that UNRRA's work would end in March 1947."[48]

The theoretical distinction between international agreements with automatic sunset provisions and those with limited durations is less significant than the fact that both enhance flexibility by facilitating bargaining and overcoming concerns about path dependency. Analyses have focused mainly on trade, but a variety of other intergovernmental agreements contain flexibility clauses: the International Air Transport Association allows exit during a one-year period of renegotiation; the UN Framework Convention on Climate Change and the Kyoto Protocol permit withdrawal with a one-year notice; and the International Criminal Court contains an escape clause that permits temporary or permanent withdrawal within the first seven years after signing the Rome Treaty.

With no predetermined date to terminate or renegotiate UNRRA's Agreement, we have learning during a limited lifespan. Article I (c) of the Agreement states that UNRRA is to "study, formulate, and recommend for individual or joint action by any or all of the member governments measures with respect to such related matters, arising out of its experience." Article VIII details the amendment process, which anticipates the need for organizational changes, and Article X provides an escape clause for members to withdraw from the organization.

More research is required about the impact of flexibility enhancing clauses on multilateral organizations, but the UNRRA case suggests that international organizations with built-in flexibility may be equipped not only to meet their goals but also adapt quickly to changing external environments. In short, this experimental approach enables "the trial and error of different democratic institutions to determine how flexibility mechanisms induce institutional innovation."[49] Among the flexibility-enhancing devices that spur innovation, Jonathan Kuyper highlights a host of them but focuses on escape clauses and sunset provisions, neither of which technically UNRRA had. Nonetheless, the notion that flexibility and experimentation in the design of international organizations enhances the potential for problem solving and learning is directly applicable. He explains: "The greater the uncertainty surrounding the distribution of gains and losses from international agreement, the more likely the institution will contain flexibility-enhancing devices." The lack of analytical attention to such design questions is puzzling because virtually all international organizations continue once established—for instance, the UN Trusteeship Council still exists even though the last trustee graduated in 1994.

Escape clauses are one such device, but "to be effective, though, there must be some cost attached to their usage, otherwise states might use them every time there is an exogenous shock which threatens their gains." Escape clauses apply to previously negotiated concessions, which can be suspended without violating the terms of the agreement. UNRRA's Article X required a delay of six months from the entry into force of the Agreement before a government could give notice of withdrawal—and only 12 months after the notice and after meeting all financial and other obligations. This balance between flexibility and commitment seems apt because, as Kuyper explains, "too much flexibility and international agreements will become ineffectual; too little flexibility and states will renege or break the agreement when times get tough."

UNRRA offered appropriate doses of flexibility, which facilitated international cooperation in three ways. First, flexibility mechanisms made initial agreement more feasible—for instance, by striking a balance between repatriating and caring for displaced persons, UNRRA was able to get early Soviet cooperation. Second, these mechanisms alleviated concerns over complications resulting from path-dependent organizational development—exemplified by the nimble shift toward care and resettlement of the displaced who refused to be repatriated and forced UNRRA to reformulate strategic commitments in light of specific humanitarian needs. Third, by shortening time horizons, flexibility provisions shifted how contracting parties thought about the future and enabled a focus on specific goals—for example, convincing donors to make generous contributions in the face of domestic political pressures.

Theorists of neoliberal institutionalism expect to observe the value over the longer term of reduced transaction costs, increased trust, and better information. However, such longer-term considerations may make agreement more difficult at the outset if parties are hesitant. Kuyper argues that neoliberal institutionalists fail to consider adequately the bargaining phase in which institutional design has pride of place. As such, longer time horizons may actually lower the costs and raise the benefits for states to hold out, thereby making agreement more difficult. Yet flexibility mechanisms like periodic renegotiations, amendment processes, and withdrawal clauses can help assuage the possible downsides by making initial cooperation more feasible while still permitting bargaining.

Jackson complained from the beginning of his UNRRA tenure that there was no "settled policy for handling displaced persons after the first rush return movement" was completed by Allied armies, especially the US Army.[50] When UNRRA took over the responsibility for dealing with millions of displaced, Jackson observed that "UNRRA's task is now gradually beginning to become evident as we approach the hard core of 'non-repatriatables', i.e. the Poles, Czechs, Balks, and other nationalities, who it is said—do not wish to return to their homes."[51] After UNRRA took control of the camps, refugees who refused repatriation would first require care and then be granted safe travel elsewhere. Jackson's notes refer to "the beginning of the Nansen job," but he understood that UNRRA was temporary: "The governments concerned are now working out," he explained, "the long-term

international organization which will take over this job from us."
However, UNRRA first had immediate crises to confront.

Addressing the emergency needs of refugees could not be postponed
the way that such longer-run problems as development or education could.
Both strategic and humanitarian requirements were evident and pressing. Disease, famine, and despair threatened lives as well as postwar European stability. However, Jackson stressed that UNRRA was "considered
as a short-term incisive task, our main emphasis being devoted to the
delivery of relief supplies" through 1946. He narrowed the focus to primary objectives lest UNRRA's failure to achieve more ambitious goals
threatened to tarnish or even bring down the United Nations concept of
institutionalized multilateralism. "Far too many people," he regretted,
"had been thinking in terms of five, ten, twenty years, and so on, and
dreaming airy visions of Utopias which bore no resemblance to the
reality of Europe in 1945. All that matters is that at the present moment we
should make a reasonable and effective contribution."[52]

There also were, of course, problems resulting from UNRRA's limited
duration. For example, differences between member governments that
went beyond the scope of UNRRA's mandate could not be negotiated
or addressed by staff. It was impossible that any such organization
could confront, let alone overcome, the simmering and soon to be
boiling tensions between the West and the Soviet Union. Early on they were
managed, but at a cost. The legitimate complaint that forcibly repatriating Soviet nationals violated fundamental human rights could only
be finessed by highlighting the need to balance humanitarian and
strategic concerns and to foster international cooperation. But a limited
time horizon may have forced UNRRA to weigh short-term cooperation
too heavily against the UN's lasting commitment to human rights.

UNRRA's design vested authority in donor countries, and especially
the United States. Like all members, Washington could withdraw, but
it was the only country with the power effectively to close the organization by virtue of paying 75 percent of the budget along with an
economy strong enough to determine the nature of post-UNRRA
relief and reconstruction. Even the best-conceived development projects take longer than planners anticipate, and UNRRA's short leash
meant that while core industrial and agricultural infrastructure was
restored, it would not be part of longer-term projects and programs.

UNRRA was never going to be permanent, but was it killed pre-
maturely? The second US contribution was premised on all activities
being completed by the end of December 1946. The Cold War meant
that the battle for the future of multilateral cooperation was partially lost.
What would have happened if the UN system had been jump-started

by the infusion of $13 billion ($150 billion in current dollars) from the Marshall Plan? This counterfactual is worth asking, not least because the original Roosevelt plan envisaged UNRRA being replaced by US loans under Phase 3 of the Lend-Lease, and these being merged into the International Monetary Fund, World Bank, and the failed International Trade Organization. However, an affirmative reply is problematic not only because of the Truman Doctrine but also because virtually no UN organizations have gone out of business, although many have withered—a recent exception was the creation in 2010 of UN Women from four smaller organizations. States feel obliged to join IGOs (although they are not obligated to do so) for fear of "being left out," and once they join they almost never leave, and even more rarely do IGOs "die."[53] Would UN organizations be more accountable and transparent with fixed durations—for instance, like peace operations that are scrutinized before renewal?

In a 1983 interview, Jackson's response to why the United States was so hostile to UNRRA's continuation is instructive. The shift to anticommunism among key officials in the State Department was crucial at the Paris negotiations in June–July 1947 about post-UNRRA relief and the Marshall Plan. The US delegation—led by Clayton and Secretary of State James Byrnes—defeated the advocates of a broad-membership, international relief organization modeled on UNRRA. Jackson's explanation for Washington's categorical opposition was: "Because they felt we were strengthening Eastern Europe. And so Clayton and Byrnes just slaughtered Bevin and Cripps in Paris. And that was the end of UNRRA."[54] Disappointed that relief would now be channeled toward ideological partners and away from adversaries, Jackson nonetheless was keen to advise, even unofficially, so that UNRRA's lessons would inform the Marshall Plan. "After the Paris debacle," Jackson explained, "I had quite a lot to do, talking frequently to [Dean] Acheson and Clayton about post-UNRRA developments and that led on to General Marshall, who remains my hero of heroes." Why George Marshall was his hero, Jackson never says. Nor was there any indication as to whether Marshall, Acheson, or Clayton listened to his counsel. Nonetheless Jackson was "broken hearted at the blow to the practical application of the international United Nations concept of humanitarian operations."

He understood the strategic rationale for the Marshall Plan. "Clayton did not deny," Jackson notes, "that there was a political ingredient in the State Department's plan, although he placed it second to humanitarian considerations. He admitted that the Department might make the conditions on which relief would be granted so stringent that he anticipated that one or more of the potential recipients would reject the aid."[55] Whereas Jackson actively sought Soviet cooperation but was prepared to move ahead without it, post-UNRRA reconstruction contrived to exclude Moscow and its satellites.

Analysts can discount participants' evaluations of success and failure, but their passions are real. Before the First Session of the General Assembly on 11 November 1946, LaGuardia lamented: "It was one of the most beautiful things that came out of the war, for it was based on the concept of the brotherhood of man. UNRRA has been administered along those lines. It was a temporary organization. We have completed our assigned task, but the need still continues."[56] Philip Noel-Baker, the UK secretary of state for air at the time, recalled his disappointment: "We may take comfort in the thought that UNRRA, and these 'post-UNRRA' discussions, have certainly led to the 'Marshall' talks. Without them the 'Marshall' proposal would never have been heard of."[57] He continued, "Whatever regrets for non-achievement any of us may have, all those who ... have been associated with the administration of UNRRA itself, can look back with unmitigated pride and satisfaction on achievement of an historic kind. Without UNRRA we should have had disaster in many countries." Another "what if?" concerns the missed opportunities of improving East–West relations under UN auspices.

Conclusion

With two continents collectively on their knees and with the political complications of former allies at odds, Jackson's leadership and the impact of UNRRA's institutional design help explain how the organization achieved many of its goals but could not overcome Cold War politics. As Reinisch reminds us, UNRRA had the "near impossible twofold task of providing a new forum for international collaboration and rehabilitating a war-wrecked world."[58] It mitigated suffering among vulnerable populations in Europe and Asia and then turned over its remaining resources and sent its seasoned staff with their bureaucratic memories to newly created intergovernmental secretariats (of the West and of the United Nations). Its limited mandate and duration forced UNRRA to experiment and be flexible, which enhanced its ability to adapt to changing wartime and postwar circumstances before devolving responsibilities to successor agencies. As the first of the second generation (post-League of Nations) of intergovernmental organizations, UNRRA's contributions certainly amount to a glass at least half full.

Current and future international organizations should consider the potent lessons from UNRRA: Shared strategic goals made cooperation possible despite major geopolitical differences. The pursuit of legitimate national interests was not antithetical to broadening and redefining them to include more cosmopolitan interests. There was no substitute for qualified leadership, both political and operational. Enlightened American foreign policy reflecting Roosevelt's postwar vision helped pursue US interests and simultaneously enhance multilateral cooperation.

With regard to that most crucial lesson, at great costs Truman's visceral anticommunism arguably did not foster vital US interests. Moreover, it stunted the growth of the kind of robust multilateralism that could address what former UN secretary-general Kofi Annan calls a growing number of "problems without passports."[59]

Notes

1 Jessica Reinisch is the most authoritative contemporary source. See "'We Shall Rebuild a Powerful Nation': UNRRA, Internationalism and National Reconstruction in Poland," *Journal of Contemporary History* 43, no. 3 (2008): 371–404; "Internationalism in Relief: The Birth (and Death) of UNRRA," *Past and Present*, supplement 6 (2013): 258–89; and "'Auntie UNRRA' at the Crossroads," *Past and Present*, supplement 8 (2013): 70–97.
2 *Global Humanitarian Assistance Report 2013* (Somerset: UK Development Initiatives, 2013), 4.
3 Dan Plesch, *America, Hitler and the UN* (London: Tauris, 2011), 119–39.
4 Mark Mazower, *No Enchanted Palace: The End of Empire and the Ideological Origins of the United Nations* (Princeton, N.J.: Princeton University Press, 2009).
5 Michael Barnett and Thomas G. Weiss, *Humanitarianism Contested: Where Angels Fear to Tread* (New York: Routledge, 2011), 41–45, at 41.
6 Arthur Salter, *Allied Shipping Control* (Oxford: Oxford University Press, 1921), 221.
7 Peter Hoffman and Thomas G. Weiss, *Sword & Salve: Confronting New Wars and Humanitarian Crises* (Lanham, Md.: Rowman & Littlefield, 2006), 41–43; and Thomas G. Weiss, *Humanitarian Business* (Cambridge: Polity Press, 2013), 21.
8 George Woodbridge, *UNRRA: The History of the United Nations Relief and Rehabilitation Administration*, 3 volumes (New York: Columbia University Press, 1950).
9 Thomas G. Weiss, Tatiana Carayannis, and Richard Jolly, "The 'Third' United Nations," *Global Governance* 15, no. 1 (2009): 123–42.
10 Agreement for UNRRA, available at: www.ibiblio.org/pha/policy/1943/431109a.html.
11 Thomas G. Weiss and Eli Karetny, "UNRRA, Organizational Learning and Future Multilateral Cooperation," *Diplomatic History* (forthcoming).
12 Edward C. Luck, *Mixed Messages: American Politics and International Organization, 1919–1999* (Washington, DC: Brookings Institution, 1999).

13 James Gibson, *Jacko, Where Are You Now? A Life of Robert Jackson* (Melbourne: Parsons, 2006), 15, 17.
14 Gibson, *Jacko*, 37.
15 Woodbridge, *UNRRA*, vol. 3, 428.
16 UNRRA Needs—Memo, 29 May 1945, in Robert G.A. Jackson Papers, box 1, folder 9, 10–11, Rare Book and Manuscript Library, Columbia University Library (hereafter "RBMLCU").
17 UNRRA Needs—Memo, 11.
18 Chancellor of the Exchequer's Meeting—Memo for British Secretary of State, 30 May 1945, in Robert G.A. Jackson Papers, box 1, folder 9, 11, RBMLCU.
19 Jackson to Herbert H. Lehman—Present State of European Regional Office, in Robert G.A. Jackson Papers, 15 May 1945, box 1, folder 5, 4, RBMLCU.
20 Jackson to Herbert H. Lehman, 5–6.
21 Jackson to Herbert H. Lehman, 6.
22 ERO, "International Mutual Aid: The Task of UNRRA," *The World Today* 2, no. 1 (1946): 35–44, at 37.
23 Weiss and Karetny, "UNRRA."
24 ERO, "International Mutual Aid," 37.
25 ERO, "International Mutual Aid," 42.
26 ERO, "International Mutual Aid," 42–43.
27 Robert G.A. Jackson, "UNRRA: Pattern for World Peace," *The Australian Quarterly* 18, no. 3 (1946): 39.
28 Jackson, "UNRRA."
29 Jackson to Minister of State—Final Report of "Life and Death of the UNRRA," 25 August 1945, in Jackson Papers, box 1, folder 50, 5–7, RBMLCU.
30 Gibson, *Jacko*, 70–71.
31 Quotes in this paragraph from Robert G.A. Jackson Interview conducted by William B. Liebmann, March/April 1978, in Jackson Papers, box 2, folder 4, 166–68, RBMLCU.
32 Craig N. Murphy, "Evolution of the UN Development System," in *Post-2015 UN Development: Making Change Happen?* ed. Stephen Browne and Thomas G. Weiss (London: Routledge, 2014), 35–54; and *The UN Development Programme: A Better Way?* (Cambridge: Cambridge University Press, 2006), 37 and xvi–xvii.
33 Richard Symonds, "Bliss Was it in that Dawn: Memoirs of an Early United Nations Career, 1946–79," Bodleian Library, Oxford University, c.4703, 26. Margaret Joan Anstee (interview 16 May 2014) indicated that Jackson applied his UNRRA experience to subsequent assignments ranging from operations in Bangladesh and Cambodia to the 1969 *Capacity Study.*
34 Eric Helleiner, "Global Governance Meets Development: A Brief History of an Innovation in World Politics," in *Global Governance, Poverty, and Inequality*, ed. Rorden Wilkinson and Jennifer Clapp (London: Routledge, 2010), 42.
35 Andrew Johnston, "Isolationism and Internationalism in American Foreign Relations," *Journal of Transatlantic Studies* 9, no. 1 (2011): 7–20; and Cornelis A. van Minnen, ed., "The Roosevelts: Nationalism, Democracy and Internationalism," Lectures by David K. Adams, Carl-Ludwig

Holtfrerich, Edmund Morris, and Arthur M. Schlesinger at the Roosevelt Study Center, 19 September 1986.

36 Ben Shephard, "'Becoming Planning Minded': The Theory and Practice of Relief 1940–45," *Journal of Contemporary History* 43, no. 3 (2008): 405–19, at 410.

37 Richard Jolly, Louis Emmerij, and Thomas G. Weiss, *UN Ideas That Changed the World* (Bloomington: Indiana University Press, 2009).

38 Weiss and Karetny, "UNRRA."

39 Quoted by William I. Hitchcock, *The Bitter Road to Freedom, A New History of the Liberation of Europe* (New York: Free Press 2008), 247.

40 Reinisch, "'Auntie UNRRA' at the Crossroads," 71.

41 Akira Iriye, "The Making of a Transnational World," in *Global Interdependence: The World after 1985*, ed. Akira Iriye (Cambridge, Mass.: Harvard University Press, 2014), 705.

42 Thomas G. Weiss, *Global Governance: Why? What? Whither?* (Cambridge: Polity Press, 2013).

43 Marvin Klemme, *The Inside Story of UNRRA* (New York: Lifeline, 1949), 12.

44 Rebecca M. Kysar, "The Sun Also Rises: The Political Economy of Sunset Provisions in the Tax Code," *Georgia Law Review* 40, no. 2 (2006): 335–57.

45 Theodore J. Lowi, *The End of Liberalism: Ideology, Policy, and the Crisis of Public Authority* (New York: Norton, 1969).

46 Chris Mooney, "A Short History of Sunsets," *Legal Affairs*, January/February 2004, available at: legalaffairs.org/issues/January-February-2004/story_mooney_janfeb04.msp.

47 Quoted by Gibson, *Jacko*, 75.

48 Gibson, *Jacko*, 71.

49 Jonathan W. Kuyper, "Designing Institutions for Global Democracy: Flexibility Through Escape Clauses and Sunset Provisions," *Ethics & Global Politics* 6, no. 4 (2013): 195–215, quotes in this and the following paragraphs are found on 198, 199, and 200.

50 Jackson to Richard K. Law, Foreign Office—Present State of UNRRA, 15 May 1945, in Robert G.A. Jackson Papers, box 1, folder 3, 8, RBMLCU.

51 This and the following two quotes are from Jackson to Sir Edward Jackson—State of UNRRA, 13 July 1945, in Jackson Papers, Folder 15, 5, RBMLCU.

52 Jackson to Sir Edward Jackson—State of UNRRA, 6.

53 Richard Cupitt, Rodney Whitlock, and Lynn Williams Whitlock, "The (Im)mortality of International Governmental Organizations," in *The Politics of Global Governance*, 2nd edn, ed. Paul Diehl (Boulder, Colo.: Lynne Rienner, 2001), 58.

54 This and the following two quotes are from Robert G.A. Jackson Interview with Jonathan Power, 1983, in Jackson Papers, 25, RBMLCU.

55 This and the next quote are from Memorandum from Grace R. Fox to Jackson—Including Draft of "UNRRA and the Struggle for the Continuation of International Relief," by Thomas J. Maycock, 26 June 1947, box 1, folder 45, 80, RBMLCU.

56 Fiorello H. LaGuardia, "Proposal for a United Nations Emergency Food Fund," 11 November 1946, in Fiorello H. LaGuardia Documents Collection—UNRRA Series, box 26B1, folder 6.

57 Messages Received by the Director-General on the Closing of UNRRA Missions in Europe, 15 July 1947, in Sir Robert G.A. Jackson Papers, box 1, folder 48, 8, RBMLCU.
58 Reinisch, "'Auntie UNRRA' at the Crossroads," 71.
59 Kofi A. Annan, "What is the International Community? Problems without Passports," *Foreign Policy*, no. 132 (Sept.–Oct. 2002): 30–31. See also, Thomas G. Weiss, *Governing the World? Addressing "Problems without Passports"* (Boulder, Colo.: Paradigm Publishers, 2014).

6 Toward universal relief and rehabilitation

India, UNRRA, and the new internationalism

Manu Bhagavan[1]

- **Indian internationalism and the idea of One World**
- **Relief and rehabilitation during World War II**
- **The end of UNRRA and the birth of a new internationalism**
- **Conclusion**

"India" had been involved in the United Nations even in its wartime
incarnation, inasmuch as the British Crown brought the colonized territory into World War II and, in turn, voted to support various institutions created to deal with the challenges wrought by the conflict.
Among the most prominent of these was the United Nations Relief
and Rehabilitation Administration (UNRRA), the mission of which
was to aid countries suffering from the military campaigns. The British
government of India strongly signaled its support even as the subcontinent weathered the effects of one of the worst famines ever
encountered in the region.

UNRRA was based in the United States and led by several men who
considered themselves friends of India, most notably famed New Yor-
kers Herbert Lehman and Fiorello LaGuardia. Over several years, the
UN Relief and Rehabilitation Administration pushed to create an
Indian office and to incorporate Indians into its administration based
in the United States, in a good faith effort to circumvent charges of
imperial complicity. So the agency's leadership was especially surprised
when they ran into resistance from India's anticolonial icons. UNRRA
was too blind to the pernicious stranglehold of imperialism. The
encounter thus exemplifies colonial India's efforts to challenge and
undo great power or global North or Western control of UN bureaucracies from the outset, and to reset both the tone and the substance of
international relations by insisting on shared responsibilities and
mutual respect.

Indian internationalism and the idea of One World

As World War I drew to a close, US president Woodrow Wilson released his blueprint for renewing the world and ensuring a lasting peace. His Fourteen Points argued for a League of Nations, a global forum for debate, decision making, and the resolution of conflicts. Wilson was never able to sell his plan to his own people, and the United States rejected participation in the nascent international union. Without full great power support, the League withered on the vine, its roots of support too shallow to give the structure meaningful strength, and too tangled in competing interests to provide clarity of direction for growth. Yet the League ultimately did bear fruit, for Wilson's proposals found fertile reception in many parts of the non-Western world, which saw in it the seed of a postcolonial future.

Among those most enthused by Wilson's initial grand scheme was Jawaharlal Nehru, scion of an illustrious Indian political family, educated at England's Harrow School and Trinity College, Cambridge, and ally to Mohandas Gandhi, who had made a name for himself challenging the British in South Africa on matters of race and in India on matters like indigo. Wilson seemed to speak to these very issues, and quickly came to be associated with egalitarian ideals. His failure to make the dream a reality was disappointing, and the ineffectual League was found wanting. However, Nehru saw the potential. Over the coming years, he and Gandhi would agree that the idea of the international was key to fundamentally changing the existing colonial order.[2]

In the immediate moment at the end of World War I, Gandhi channeled his energies into the Non-Cooperation Movement, which also gained propulsion from several other outcomes of that war: the dismembering of the Ottoman Empire into mandates that led to the Khilafat Movement; bitterly received Janus-faced (and -bodied) reforms delivered by secretary of state for India Edwin Montagu and Viceroy Lord Chelmsford; wartime powers of sedition that continued to restrict people's freedoms; and the infamous Amritsar massacre. When the killing of police in the town of Chauri Chaura led Gandhi to call off the campaign, Nehru realized that they needed to play a long game. He brooded over the twin failures of the Wilsonian vision, or what was understood to be his vision, and Gandhi's activism, and pondered on the best way forward.

By the 1930s, Gandhi and Nehru were in agreement that India's nationalism had to conform to what they called "progressive internationalism." Their ideas were hazy yet, but were rooted in a firm belief that all of humankind was connected, as were structures of power. Disassembling those structures required humans working together across what they perceived to be artificial boundaries.

While Nehru wished to be clear about the internationalist aims of the Indian National Congress, Gandhi counseled restraint. He suggested that such an idea had to grow organically, respecting input and difference of opinion from all quarters. Leadership, Gandhi argued, meant the stating of the goal followed by rightful inward conduct, and an acceptance that only the nature of a journey could be controlled, not the precise path that needed to be traveled. Nehru took these words to heart and mulled on strategy. As the decade progressed, these ruminations took on new urgency, as Adolf Hitler began menacing Europe even as a global economic depression was taking its toll.

The lightning takeover by Axis forces of many parts of Europe and the subsequent German assault on the Soviet Union in 1941 had the Western Allies on the back foot. British and American planners were centrally concerned with the fate of India, which served as a strategic bulwark against Japanese forces, an oasis for displaced European refugees, and a source of men and resources to aid the military effort. Planners also feared that another Indian anticolonial campaign might distract from the war.

So in early 1942 a group of American leaders came up with an innovative, even daring plan. With the blessing of Britain's US ambassador, Lord Halifax, the secretary of the National Association for the Advancement of Colored People (NAACP), Walter White, proposed that the United States send a delegation to India to assure Gandhi and others of American transparency and good intentions. Wendell Willkie, the 1940 Republican presidential challenger to Democrat Franklin Roosevelt, would lead a team that would talk openly of American racial problems, and declare support for an end to imperialism of all kinds. The idea had support from many writers, intellectuals, and politicians, including the Roosevelts themselves. British prime minister Winston Churchill eventually vetoed Willkie's trip to India, on the grounds that it might legitimize Gandhi and Nehru and their cause.

Instead, Willkie boarded a plane called *The Gulliver* and traveled around the world. When he returned to the United States in August 1942, he made a radio address indicating that India had been on everyone's mind, and that the world had to find a way to come together, end racism and imperialism, and create a system free of political despotism and economic exploitation. His remarks became a sensation, sent Churchill into an apoplectic rage, and were turned into a bestselling book called *One World*.

While Willkie never made it to India, Roosevelt reached out through other ambassadors, most notably the Chinese Kuomintang's Chiang Kai-shek and his wife, who established warm relations and good rapport with the anticolonial leadership. Nonetheless, the Chiangs were rebuffed in their attempt to keep the Indians from launching another anticolonial campaign. Gandhi and Nehru both agreed that the British needed to quit India, but the famous August 1942 declaration was the latter's, adopted in favor of a version put forth by the former.

Nehru's Quit India Declaration was one that broadly laid out his internationalist vision. Arguing that the Axis had to be defeated at all costs, Nehru urged that India be made free, for a free India, he pledged, would stand with the Allies in their fight, and would invest real meaning and power into their rhetoric of liberty and justice for all. He called for a world federation, pooled resources for the common good, and a new global defense force meant to keep the peace.

Gandhi, Nehru, and most anticolonial leaders were immediately imprisoned for challenging British authority in a time of war. It was in his cell in 1943 that Nehru first read Willkie's book and saw in it tremendous symbolic power. *One World* encapsulated many of Nehru's own hopes, and Nehru embraced the concept.

Over 1944 and 1945, Nehru's sister, Vijaya Lakshmi Pandit, went on a lecture tour of the United States, arguing forcefully for India's independence and challenging imperialism in all its forms. She made many friends and allies during this time, especially in New York City, where everyone from Roger Baldwin (first executive director of the American Civil Liberties Union) and Pearl Buck (Pulitzer and Nobel Prize-winning author), to power couple Henry and Clare Booth Luce (he the publisher of *Time* and *Life* magazines and she one of the first women in the US Congress and a Republican star) and Fiorello LaGuardia (the city's larger-than-life mayor) was won over by her charm, beauty, and intellect. As part of her efforts, she debated with Churchill's former parliamentary secretary Robert Boothby on the radio, emerging the clear victor and a national celebrity. Shortly thereafter, with all the clout she had accumulated thanks to her impressive performances, she led a counter-delegation of race-conscious internationalists to San Francisco where the new United Nations Organization was being born. There she charged that there was a wide gap between the idealistic and inclusive rhetoric used for public consumption and the more shadowy shenanigans taking place in backroom deal making. Specifically, moves were afoot to use language like "trusteeship" to allow the new institution to perpetuate the old imperial order while making it sound as if it were not.

While she attracted much attention, Pandit ultimately failed to alter the text of the new United Nations Charter. The British government saw the UN as a body that would allow colonialism to continue. By 1946, however, Pandit, Nehru, and Gandhi decided that the United Nations was too important to dismiss, and indeed they saw it as the first step to One World, still a broad euphemism for an internationalist order that went beyond the old Westphalian system. Pandit returned to New York where, in one of the UN's first orders of business, she led the General Assembly by a two-thirds majority to condemn the state of South Africa for its racist discriminatory policies. This victory established that Article 2(7) of the Charter, the domestic jurisdiction clause, did not prevent the UN from affecting internal matters of member states if universal questions of justice were involved.

This set the stage then for the development of the international human rights instruments, conversations for which began mere weeks after Pandit's victory. For Nehru, and for India, it meant two things. First and foremost, it meant that the UN could be made to serve larger ideals. The Indians decided to take the Charter at face value, using the very rosy language that the imperialists had successfully inserted into it against them. Second, the UN was a good that had to be defended even as it had to be de-imperialized. Such a UN would then serve as a stepping stone to the now clarified ultimate objective of One World: federal, democratic world government.[3]

Relief and rehabilitation during World War II

Just as Nehru was reading Willkie's book, considering its significance, half a world away the US president, Franklin D. Roosevelt, was shepherding through an agreement between 44 nations to provide relief and rehabilitation to those impacted by the ongoing war. Roosevelt's actions were part of a larger strategy to secure a lasting world peace, a strategy that he had begun to lay out in January 1941 when, in his State of the Union speech, he argued that all people everywhere were entitled to four basic freedoms: freedom of speech and worship, and freedom from fear and want.[4] This was further developed in August of that same year when the president and Britain's prime minister, Winston Churchill, agreed to an Atlantic Charter that promoted cooperation and equality and served as a broad statement of principles for what purpose the war was being waged.[5]

The Atlantic Charter was received rapturously by many in the colonized world, who saw in its calls to "respect the right of all peoples to choose the form of government under which they will live" a dramatic challenge to authoritarianism in all its forms, including its imperial incarnation.[6] Churchill blanched at the very idea that the Atlantic Charter would have any negative impact on the idea of empire, and hastened to clarify that its application was limited by context.

Roosevelt did not agree with his companion from across the pond, and he continued to chide Churchill for his stale views. Indeed, it was American insistence on the universal applicability of the Atlantic Charter that informed Willkie's worldview and served as a foundation for his antiracist and anti-imperialist conception of *One World*.

Several months before Willkie found himself in conversation with the NAACP and others on a world tour, on 7 December 1941 the Japanese attacked the United States at Pearl Harbor, and the Americans officially entered the war. On New Year's Day in 1942, those who stood against the Axis regimes signed the Declaration by United Nations, entering into a new, global alliance.[7]

Soon after the United States was fully and openly engaged with winning the war, concrete planning got underway on ways to build cooperation and further the goals laid out in the Four Freedoms and Atlantic Charter, and Willkie's tour was very much part of that overall agenda. It was just over a year after Willkie's return to the United States that, under the direction of Roosevelt, the United States rallied the Allies and their affiliates to establish UNRRA, the formal signing taking place on 9 November 1943. The primary objective of this new body was to "plan, coordinate, administer or arrange for the administration of measures for the relief of victims of war in any area under the control of any of the United Nations."[8] Each member state would be represented by a delegate who would sit on the central council, which was to be executively led by a director-general.

India was a signatory in Washington, but as it was still under Crown rule, its participation was not one of democratic consent. The Americans recognized this problem—there was a vocal lobby in the country advocating for India's independence, and their ranks included the Roosevelts themselves. So India's signature was accepted with a "reservation or statement to the effect" that it was subject to "ratification or legislative approval."[9]

The Montagu-Chelmsford reforms of 1919 that many South Asians found distasteful (because the principle of dyarchy only devolved less-important powers to the local population) nonetheless established the Central Legislative Assembly whose members had some authority over certain matters. The 1935 Government of India Act served as a proto-constitution and allowed for national elections to the Assembly. The body in the early 1940s therefore had some legitimacy, though it remained tainted in the eyes of many simply because it was part of the colonial system of administration.

Despite the complex political environment, the Central Legislative Assembly considered the UNRRA agreement in September 1944 and opted to uphold it. Several months later, in early 1945, the legislature voted unanimously to make a contribution to UNRRA of 8 crores (80 million) of rupees (approximately equivalent to $24 million at the time, or $257 million in 2014).[10]

At the same moment as UNRRA was created, one of the worst famines of the twentieth century was occurring in Bengal. This famine was not a "natural disaster" but was the result of bad policy decisions and perhaps even willful disregard by Churchill, who wanted to preserve reserves at his disposal for postwar needs closer to home.[11] Millions died, either directly from starvation or from disease. Access to food resources began to improve at the end of 1943, but the famine's effects continued to be felt throughout 1944.

Although the famine and support for UNRRA were not directly linked, their temporal proximity conjoined them, along with long-standing grievances of colonial exploitation of native resources. Even so, there was widespread support for the contribution to UNRRA, even as there was recognition that 80 million rupees was a heavy burden to bear.

At the UNRRA Council's first meeting, delegates agreed that each member state should make a contribution "approximately equivalent to one percent of the actual income of the country." Exceptions were made for countries hurting from the war (for which relief was due) and for those "suffering from peculiar situations." The Crown government of India reviewed the situation and concluded that they fit this latter category for three reasons: first, there was no reliable information on national income; second, there was in fact a very low per capita income; and third, India was itself impacted by the war, including by famine and other shortages. As a result, the government concluded that they could not figure or pay the proposed 1 percent and instead came up with what was regardless a quite sizeable figure.[12] UNRRA administrators were broadly cognizant of just how big a sum this was for India although it only made up 1.27 percent of the international agency's nearly $1.9 billion budget, funded by 31 "non-invaded countries."[13] However, they assuaged themselves and, they thought, the Indians as well, by highlighting the fact that 90 percent of each country's contribution was to be used for procurement of surplus goods at cost from the same country.[14] As it was initially worked out, India specifically would provide pepper, tea, raw cotton, cotton waste, raw jute, linseed, peanuts, coir yarn, and jute manufactures.[15]

For the American leadership of UNRRA, Indian participation was of tremendous importance because it helped to truly internationalize the organization, and the Asian imprimatur extended its legitimacy.

The Indians, for their part, were by now guided by the 1942 Quit India Declaration, which committed India in terms of its sense of mission to defeating the Axis and to building up the edifice of a world federation. However, they regardless remained committed to overturning Western imperialism and white supremacy. So, right from the outset of their first formal meetings in July 1945, the Indians, who interfaced with UNRRA through their Commerce Department—led by Jawaharlal Nehru's cousin R.K. Nehru—gently chided UNRRA for being somewhat undemocratic, and they demanded more inclusion of Indian voices. Among India's first suggestions to the UNRRA delegation was that the agency in India should be represented by an Indian, that it should open a permanent office in India, and that more Indians should be added to the UNRRA staff. The agency, attentive to local perceptions and with an eye to receiving a second contribution, was receptive to these requests.[16]

So when Henry Atkinson was dispatched to India in November of that year, he was told to establish an India office, to seek out an Indian to head it, and above all to be tactful toward Indian sensitivities. He was to do nothing to "offend" his hosts while at the same time to seek out procurement of goods from what was now thought of as the first contribution, in the hopes of securing a second.[17]

He set out with due diligence to accomplish these tasks, adopting official policies to advance his agenda. Within a few weeks, Atkinson had determined that there was a "highly unbalanced scarcity of Indians in UNRRA service," for there was "not a single Indian national among the thousands of Class I UNRRA employees."[18] A few weeks later, in January 1946, UNRRA officially created an India office. However, the environment for action had already become more hazardous, as by then government officials concluded that India was going to face food shortages on a national scale that year, brought on by colonial policies, drought, and wartime restrictions on the transfer of goods.[19] Indian officials in the Commerce Department cautioned against announcing the new local office "because of the misunderstanding that would probably be created in the public mind by the natural supposition that UNRRA was coming into India to bring in food."[20] For the same reason, Indian officials counseled changing the name of the new office, discarding "UNRRA Liaison Office," even though signs bearing this title had already been printed. Atkinson obliged, and the agency ultimately settled on calling their new bureau the Procurement and Recruitment Liaison Office. Atkinson also held a number of meetings with Indian officials regarding the food situation and tried privately to work with Washington to secure additional non-UNRRA resources, winning approval to release "surprop" canned milk, only to find that the hoped-for resources had already been shipped elsewhere. These efforts were kept secret since they did not bear fruit and Atkinson was worried that UNRRA would face "adverse reaction" as a result.[21]

Simultaneously, Atkinson began diplomatic efforts to secure a second contribution from the Indians amounting to an additional 4 crores of rupees, or half the original amount received. Some groups in India opposed it altogether while others favored compromising.[22] Eventually, the Central Legislative Assembly decided on 18 April 1946 to support a second contribution in the amount of 2 crores of rupees, "subject to the condition that the situation be reviewed by the Government at the end of September, and that no commitment of funds be made before then."[23]

The end of UNRRA and the birth of a new internationalism

Just prior to the Indian vote in favor of a second contribution, New York's favored son, Fiorello LaGuardia, stepped into the role of director-general and immediately into controversy as well. Longtime president of the US-based India League J.J. Singh, who had worked closely with Pandit on her US tour, called his former ally "inhuman" and charged that the former mayor had requested the Combined Food Board (the US and UK joint wartime agency) to divert wheat shipments meant for India to UNRRA destination countries instead.[24] LaGuardia felt the charge grossly unfair, but the issue hinted at underlying resentment of UNRRA's work.

The main concern had to do with why India was not itself a recipient nation of UNRRA aid. The agreement establishing the agency had indicated that any country victimized by the war could be helped if there was need, and India felt that it met that bar, since it was home to many refugees, had sent contingents of soldiers, was serving to assist the war in various other ways, and was suffering numerous shortages, incurring further misery for its people. UNRRA's position by decision of its council was that aid was only to be given to countries directly invaded by the Axis powers. India, though, had in fact been invaded, with Japanese incursions on the Andaman and Nicobar Islands and parts of Nagaland and Manipur, a point UNRRA eventually conceded. However, the agency felt that India was so vast, with incursions only on its periphery, that it could financially manage with its own resources.[25] This, of course, further upset the Indians, who felt the agency simply did not grasp the nature of colonial exploitation and the brutal conditions under which they had been forced to live and work. As recently as February of that year, Jawaharlal Nehru denounced grain rationing mandated by the Crown, thundering at a mass meeting that if "there is a famine in India, I call on the people to revolt against the government and I warn the government to be prepared to face it."[26]

Just weeks after the legislative vote supporting a second contribution, an Indian official told the agency that India believed that UNRRA should wind up its operations quickly and that its mandate should be taken over by the new United Nations Organization.[27] There were two meanings to read into this claim. One, straightforward, was that relief operations were continuing and that the new world body had a responsibility to ensure proper completion of relief and rehabilitation. However, a second reading was that the Indians also felt that American control of the agency, however well intentioned, was ultimately neither democratic nor truly international. Only a takeover by the UN Organization, and the creation of a forum wherein imperialism in its overt and covert forms could be challenged, would address this issue.

In September 1946, a new interim government took power in India, with Jawaharlal Nehru at its head. This new structure, while not without some controversies of its own, was much more legitimate than its predecessors, and most saw it as a precursor to independent, postcolonial rule.[28]

UNRRA was not caught unawares. It had courted the anticolonial leadership over the course of the year, and agency officials met personally with Nehru and Gandhi, and the Mahatma in particular praised their work.[29] LaGuardia, who saw Gandhi as a saint and had personally supported the cause of Indian independence, crafted a carefully worded letter of congratulations, which he had hand-delivered to Nehru shortly after the interim government assumed power in September. In it, the UNRRA director-general parried lingering doubts about his views stemming from J.J. Singh's charges, and insisted that he was a strong advocate for India in all appropriate forums, including the "food allocating authorities in Washington."[30] Significantly, at that same moment, ships carrying nearly 25,000 tons of wheat were diverted to India from UNRRA stocks (which totaled 100,000 tons) provided by the United States to assist with the food shortage, even though in the end those resources could not be used because of a seamen's strike.[31]

Meanwhile, UNRRA had made progress in incorporating Indians into its staff, going from zero as of 31 December 1945 to 25 Class I employees scattered over Washington, China, London, and New Delhi, and 12 Class II employees hired for local service in New Delhi, all by 31 October 1946.[32] The acting American head of the Indian office,

Henry Atkinson, took great pride in announcing his replacement in Amarjit Singh on 27 October 1946.[33]

For all this, the Indian public and press remained skeptical, and indeed through September 1946 were "very critical of the Central Government and sensitive to the export of any commodities by the Central Government which might seem of use to India."[34] The mood changed when Nehru's government accepted interim authority, but the sentiment was still the same, and the new assembly promised and proved to be more responsive. Within the next two months, they revisited the decision of their predecessors and decided that a second contribution could not be made, however much they supported the idea of international relief in principle. During the legislative debate, the most serious charges leveled against UNRRA all involved its general obliviousness to structural imperialism. Legislators claimed that there were no actual surpluses to provide, and took as particular examples jute, which had otherwise been successfully bartered with Argentina for food, and cotton, which was desperately needed by many people in India.[35]

LaGuardia and his associates all lobbied hard, but to no avail. Without the second contribution, UNRRA's India-based activities had to be wound down over 1947, and its offices eventually shut in 1948.

UNRRA was dissolved but its responsibilities were incorporated into various new, international organizations tied to the UN. Displaced persons came under the jurisdiction of the International Refugee Organization (IRO), health services would be made part of the World Health Organization, food problems would be addressed by the General Assembly and the Food and Agriculture Organization, and a new fund for children would be created to look after the needs of this special segment of the population.[36] In short, authority over so many matters of relief and rehabilitation were disaggregated and democratized, brought under the international jurisdiction of the United Nations Organization. Underscoring that this meant that the colonized world would now have greater control over their resources, not for the purposes of selfishness but with the aim of ending historic exploitation, Nehru told the IRO at the very outset that he wholly supported its mission and purpose, but that countries would have to be free to support it within their means.[37]

Conclusion

India's relationship with UNRRA in the mid-1940s reveals the complex nature of internationalist ideals in the mid-twentieth century, and the varying, often competing visions that were vying for supremacy at the time. UNRRA as it was conceived by Roosevelt and operated by the United States was beneficent and international in scope and function. It sought to create offices all over the world and to incorporate nationals from its various member states into its staff. It directed the resources it collected to the needs of allies regardless of their political systems and brought significant relief to millions not only in Europe, but China as well. This relief was not just in immediate emergency supplies, but in tools and resources needed for reconstruction, to allow devastated communities to stand back up on their own. It was an agency of meritorious mission and actual achievement.

Nevertheless, UNRRA was conceptualized as a coalition of states under Washington's clear and express leadership. Although they wished to help, and both openly and privately sought to do just that, they ultimately displayed a tin ear to the many anguished cries about the layered and deadly nature of the colonial system and its absolute control over all aspects of economies under its thumb. To those who wished to upend imperialism, simply having the government change hands was insufficient. The entire edifice, and indeed the architecture of global relations, had to be torn down and built anew. The Nehru–Gandhi grand strategic objective of One World aimed to do just that, and they needed a strong and successful United Nations Organization in order to actualize their dream. By challenging UNRRA, despite admiring it, they hoped to send a clear signal that nice words and good intentions were no longer sufficient.

In the immediate aftermath, the Indians were quite successful. The United Nations was a highly respected and important organization throughout the 1950s and early 1960s, even as the Cold War cast a chill over all international relations. For domestic reasons, though, the Indians began to turn away from multilateral diplomacy linked to international organization thereafter.[38] By the 1970s, American political impulse led to a weakening of the General Assembly and a strengthening of the Security Council, along with a corresponding rise in US influence and control—so much so that today the UN is primarily criticized as an undemocratic body wholly subservient to US interests.[39]

In this sense, the story of India's relationship with UNRRA in the 1940s remains incomplete. For the health of the international organization, the world's people, and each member state, the UN continues to need to be made more democratic and less imperialistic. For this to happen, the United States needs to relinquish some power and control to allow the United Nations more equally and justly to incorporate the voices of the global South, even as much of the world's impoverished peoples rely on the UN for critical services. Only such an institution will be able to provide vibrant global governance, legitimate enough truly to uplift all of the world's peoples, and to address the border-crossing transcendent crises of our times: state and non-state terrorism, financial and health pandemics, and climate change.

Notes

1 I would like to thank my research assistant Sarah Alshawish, the volume editors Thomas G. Weiss and Dan Plesch, as well as Pallavi Roy, Rahul Rao, and other contributors for their valuable help and feedback.
2 This is not to suggest that Wilson was the source of all forms of internationalist thought. Indeed, empire itself was in one sense an international formation. The Russo–Japanese War had helped spur "non-Western" internationalist thinking, and Lenin popularized another alternative. However, Wilson's ideas really caught fire and helped lead all of this earlier thinking in new directions, and they were particularly relevant to anticolonial movements. See Cemil Aydin, *The Politics of Anti-Westernism in Asia* (New York: Columbia University Press, 2007); Erez Manela, *The Wilsonian Moment* (New York: Oxford University Press, 2007); Mark Mazower, *Governing the World* (New York: The Penguin Press, 2012); Mithi Mukherjee, "'A World of Illusion': The Legacy of Empire in India's Foreign Relations, 1947–62," *The International History Review* 32, no. 2 (2010): 253–71.
3 This section is a summary of Manu Bhagavan, *India and the Quest for One World: The Peacemakers* (New York: Palgrave Macmillan, 2013).
4 See www.fdrlibrary.marist.edu/fourfreedoms.
5 avalon.law.yale.edu/wwii/atlantic.asp.
6 avalon.law.yale.edu/wwii/atlantic.asp.
7 avalon.law.yale.edu/20th_century/decade03.asp. While the "United Nations" has since been understood as a euphemism for the Allies, distinct from the international organization of the same name created several years later, Dan Plesch has recently shown that in fact many arms of the sprawling bureaucracies that would comprise the UNO after its inception in 1945 actually emerged while the war was still raging and made up what he terms the "wartime United Nations." Dan Plesch, *America, Hitler and the UN: How the Allies Won World War II and Forged the Peace* (London: I.B. Tauris, 2011).
8 www.ibiblio.org/pha/policy/1943/431109a.html.
9 www.ibiblio.org/pha/policy/1943/431109a.html.
10 Further Grant Proposed for UNRRA, 18 April 1946, document no. F.7/1/46-DPS, in file 298; Second Indian Contribution (self ref doc 106). Memorandum Covering Replies to Queries Raised by the Honourable Member for Commerce, Question 3, file no. 298; Second Indian Contribution, box S-0528-0563, file S-1416-0000-0016. This and all UNRRA-related documents cited in this chapter come from the United Nations Archives, UNRRA files, AG-018-033, India Mission-Procurement and Recruiting Office, 1945–48. Each file is from a specific box and folder; box and folder numbers are provided the first time a particular folder is cited only. Modern dollar equivalents were calculated using: stats.areppim.com/calc/calc_usdlrxdeflator.php.

11 See Amartya Sen, *Poverty and Famines: An Essay on Entitlement and Deprivation* (New Delhi: Oxford University Press, 1999 [1981]); and Madhusree Mukherjee, *Churchill's Secret War: The British Empire and the Ravaging of India During World War II* (New York: Basic Books, 2010).
12 Annex No. 2, Letter from R.K. Nehru to Mason, 28 July 1945, in file no. 282, "Report of Mr. Sayre & Indian Procedure," box S-0528-0562, file S-1416-0000-0004.
13 Memorandum to I.I. Chandrigar, 12 November 1946, 2, file no. 298, Second Indian Contribution.
14 Interview with Pandit Nehru by Henry Atkinson, 1946, Henry Atkinson's Report, attachment 24, box S-0528-0562, file S-1416-0000-0006.
15 R.K. Nehru to Mason, 28 July 1945.
16 Letter from Francis Sayre to Governor Herbert Lehman, Director-General, 30 July 1945, file no. 282, Report of Mr. Sayre & Indian Procedure.
17 File no. 285, Henry Atkinson's Report, 48.
18 File no. 285, Henry Atkinson's Report, 33.
19 Memo of an Interview with Dr. V.K.R.V. Rao, 11 February 1946, Henry Atkinson's Report, attachment 37.
20 Assessment of Commerce official Pillai as recorded by Atkinson, Henry Atkinson's Report, 32.
21 Henry Atkinson's Report, 54.
22 Interview with Pandit Nehru by Henry Atkinson, 1946, Henry Atkinson's Report, attachment 24.
23 Henry Atkinson's Report, 5.
24 Cable, 13 April 1946, file no. 298, Second Indian Contribution.
25 Message to Viceroy, file no. 299, Administrative-General, Letter from LaGuardia to Nehru, 9 September 1946, file no. 234, "LaGuardia," box S-0528-0565, file S-1416-0000-0037. The former mayor clarified that "UNRRA is prevented by the rules of our international charter from sending food to India, which is in a position to pay for relief supplies."
26 Nehru, quoted in a story titled "Darker Races Not Helped Despite Gifts to UNRRA," *The Afro-American*, 16 February 1946, 8.
27 Interview with Ramaswami Mudaliar, 2 May 1946, Henry Atkinson's Report, attachment 30.
28 Henry Atkinson's Report, 38.
29 Henry Atkinson's Report, 39. Interview with Pandit Nehru by Henry Atkinson, 1946, Henry Atkinson's Report, attachment 24.
30 Letter from LaGuardia to Nehru, 9 September 1946, file no. 234, "LaGuardia."
31 Copy of a report from *The Hindustan Times*, 5 September 1946; and Extract from Dr. Rajendra Prasad's Broadcast on 23 September 1946, also *The Hindustan Times*, 24 September 1946, 2, of Letter from Henry Atkinson, Acting Chief of the UNRRA Office, India, to Joseph Lilly, Director of Public Information, UNRRA Headquarters, Washington, DC, 17 September 1946, file no. 288, Public Information, Box S-0528-0562, file S-1416-0000-0009. Also, Memorandum to I.I. Chandrigar, 12 November 1946, 2, file no. 298, Second Indian Contribution.
32 Memorandum to I.I. Chandrigar, 12 November 1946, 2, file no. 298, Second Indian Contribution.

33 UNRRA India Press Release, 27 October 1946, file no. 305, Public Relations Press, box S-0528-0563, file S-1416-0000-0022.
34 Letter from Henry Atkinson, Acting Chief of the UNRRA Office, India, to Joseph Lilly, Director of Public Information, UNRRA Headquarters, Washington, DC, 17 September 1946, file no. 288, Public Information.
35 "A Note on Proceedings of the Indian Legislative Assembly on November 18, 1946, When the Question of India's Second Contribution was Debated," file no. 298, Second Indian Contribution.
36 Interview with Pandit Nehru by Henry Atkinson, 1946, Henry Atkinson's Report, attachment 24.
37 RAG-2/73-1/02B, United Nations archives, New York. Telegram from the Secretary of External Affairs to the Secretary-General of the United Nations regarding the International Refugee Organization, September 1946; and also Letter from the Member for External Affairs (of the Interim Government of India) to the UN Secretary-General, 30 July 1947. India would not join the IRO immediately because of the financial commitment, but eventually did join. The IRO operated from 1947 to 1952 and then was succeeded by the Office of the UN High Commissioner for Refugees. See www.answers.com/topic/international-refugee-organization.
38 For further details, see Manu Bhagavan, "India and the United Nations, or Things Fall Apart," in *The OUP Handbook of Indian Foreign Policy*, ed. C. Raja Mohan, Srinath Raghavan, and David Malone (Oxford: Oxford University Press, forthcoming 2015).
39 See, for instance, Vijay Prashad, *The Poorer Nations* (New York: Verso, 2012), 6, 114; and Mazower, *Governing the World*, 330–432.

III
Economic development

7 The United Nations and development

From the origins to current challenges

John Burley and Stephen Browne

- **Wartime planning for postwar economic and social cooperation**
- **The road to San Francisco**
- **Lessons for the evolution of the UN development "system"**
- **Conclusion**

The United States dominated wartime planning for the new world organization. It sought international economic and financial cooperation as the means to maintain and expand the capitalist postwar liberal order of open markets and free trade. This ambitious agenda was very largely focused on the center of the world economy in North America and Europe: issues of particular concern to the periphery in Africa, Asia, and Latin America were essentially ignored.

Yet development is now one of the principal purposes of the United Nations, taking well over half of the resources available to the UN system as a whole. The planners of the new "general international organization" brought into being at San Francisco had in no way envisaged such a possibility. Moreover, development requires a coherent approach, but the UN Charter provisions for such concerted international action have proved inadequate to the task.

This chapter explores how development became part of the pursuit of international cooperation, as an "add-on" to the institutional machinery established in 1945.[1] It looks first at the wartime planning for postwar economic and social cooperation. It then reviews the evolution of the UN's programs for development before drawing some general conclusions.

The United Nations has contributed to the evolution of the theory and practice of development, through the analysis of trends and problems and through direct support for national development. This chapter covers both such contributions, with a focus in particular on the latter. Also running through the chapter is the theme that the post-1945 emergence of development as a principal purpose of the United Nations and the decentralized nature of the UN system have together created an unprecedented challenge: is the system today in its present form capable of successfully confronting the myriad interrelated economic, environmental, financial, and social problems?

Wartime planning for postwar economic and social cooperation

From the early days of World War II, and in light of the perceived failure of the League of Nations to prevent aggression, it was self-evident that a new international organization would be required at its end with capacity both to preserve peace and security and to promote economic stability and prosperity. That objective—enshrined in president Franklin Roosevelt's Four Freedoms speech in January 1941 and the objectives set out in the Atlantic Charter in August 1941 and then developed as a multilateral legal instrument in the 26-nation Declaration by United Nations of 1 January 1942—guided the intense preparatory work for the new organization.

The organizational scheme for the UN system was the product in the main of several years of work by a group of dedicated officials in the US State Department. Broadly speaking, there were in the US administration two groups of planners: the realists and the free traders, on the one hand, who argued in favor of a postwar liberal order that the United States by virtue of its economic size and entrepreneurial spirit would naturally dominate; and the idealists, on the other hand, who sought to internationalize the New Deal as a way of organizing and regulating the postwar order.

Diplomats, economists, international lawyers, and technical experts were involved in the series of wide-ranging debates in the State Department, the Treasury, and other US government departments. Research groups and various individuals also contributed to the process. At the nucleus of this work was Leo Pasvolsky, special assistant to Secretary of State Cordell Hull, who through "indefatigable hard work, knowledge and discretion, [was] the indispensable proponent of the Charter."[2] From 1942 onward, they reached out to the other United Nations governments in a multitude of consultations.

The road to San Francisco

Work on what became the Charter provisions on international economic cooperation began in earnest in 1942. The starting point was the Anglo-American discussion on the implementation of Article VII of the Lend-Lease Agreement, which entitled the United States to request British "consideration" of the elimination of imperial trade preferences in return for American wartime economic and financial support. In response, the UK Treasury offered John Maynard Keynes's plan for an international clearing union. Washington's counteroffer was in the form of Harry Dexter White's stabilization fund and of an International Bank for Reconstruction and Development that would be specifically linked, unlike Keynes's proposal, to the United Nations. These proposals and the ensuing discussions eventually led to the UN Monetary and Financial Conference at Bretton Woods and the establishment of the International Monetary Fund (IMF) and the World Bank. They also ushered in a series of consultations on other technical subjects such as agriculture, labor, education, health, civil aviation, and telecommunications, which in turn led to the establishment of other international agencies preceding and accompanying the UN Organization. Naturally, also, the question arose of how all these agencies would work together.

The State Department planners were fully aware of the need to include in the overall structure—"a large tent" as Cordell Hull put it—arrangements for both peace and security, and economic and social cooperation. The 1930s were a constant reminder of how terrible economic conditions of that time had contributed to nationalistic and war-like behavior. In addition, the planners were guided by several key considerations specifically related to economic and social issues, including lessons learned from the League of Nations. Also relevant to the story are functionalism and the events at Dumbarton Oaks and the UN Conference on International Organization that created the Charter at San Francisco.

The legacy of the League of Nations

Most observers regard the League of Nations as an unmitigated failure. This is only partly true. Recently published research has resurrected the League's economic, financial, and social work in the latter 1930s and its influence on the establishment of the United Nations.[3] Alexander Loveday, a Scottish statistician educated at Cambridge and de facto head of the Economic and Financial Organization (EFO) of the League, is the key player here. Pasvolsky used to represent the United States in meetings of the League on economic issues in the mid- to late 1930s, at which Loveday was active, and the two remained thereafter in close touch, especially after the EFO migrated from Geneva in 1941 to resume its activities in the United States at the invitation of the Institute for Advanced Study at Princeton.

In the late 1930s, Washington became genuinely interested in, and highly complimentary of, the League's work on economic and financial issues. The United States had remained an active member of the International Labour Organization (ILO) and sought ways to make its collaboration more effective.[4] Simultaneously, Loveday, with the belated support of the League's secretary-general, Joseph Avenol, used the crisis surrounding the League of Nations to advance reform of its institutional machinery. Inherent in this effort were two objectives: the clearer separation of the League's work on economic, financial, and social cooperation from the political arena; and the consequential attempt to allow non-members (i.e., mainly the United States) greater participation in that work.

Thus was born the Bruce report, or more formally: *The Development of International Cooperation in Economic and Social Affairs.*[5] An independent committee of experts with proven experience of League affairs, which was chaired by the former Australian prime minister Stanley Bruce, recommended in August 1939 a new structure for the League's economic and social affairs. The report's presentation of the need for international economic and social cooperation reads unerringly like a similar report would today. It was still-born, given the outbreak of war a few days following its publication, but the Bruce recommendations for a Central Committee for Economic and Social Questions provided a template for discussions on what would eventually become the UN's Economic and Social Council (ECOSOC).

Once installed in Princeton, Loveday oversaw the preparation of a much-appreciated overview, *The Transition from War to Peace Economy* (1942–43).[6] It "shaped the architecture of economic and financial policy through its globalised interpretation of the crisis ... international cooperation was the key," Patricia Clavin wrote. "The commitment to full employment remained a desired goal, [subject to] ... the liberation of international capitalism ... [it was] a powerful case for institutionalised cooperation."[7]

Loveday also continued his extensive networking. He was close to Frank McDougall, another Australian who had worked with the League on agriculture and nutrition and who plotted with Eleanor Roosevelt to encourage her husband to convene the first of the series of conferences on international organizations, on agriculture. He regularly helped Pasvolsky and others in the State Department, the Treasury, and other US agencies. He advised on the establishment of the UN Relief and Rehabilitation Administration (UNRRA) and the Food and Agriculture Organization (FAO). Moreover, he expressed his concern about how the functions of the new institutions would relate to one another: "he was

anxious there should be one 'overall political and/or economic world organisation of which these various functional bodies should be a part'."[8]

Loveday and others were prescient in their comments about the
evolving international architecture. So why has almost all of the literature about the establishment of the United Nations ignored their
contributions? In fact, Loveday was instrumental in downplaying the
League's experience. He insisted that "reference to the League's pioneering contribution to institutionalised cooperation [be] knowingly
cast aside ... He wanted the successor organisations of the League to
be new and distinct ... and for the new UN organisations, through
comparison with the failed League, to be branded a success."[9]

Functionalism

Another influential thinker was David Mitrany, a Romanian-born
British historian and political theorist associated with the "functionalist"
approach to international relations. He had also worked for the League
and knew Loveday and Pasvolsky. In his 1934 *Progress of International
Governance* and numerous other publications, Mitrany argued that
international cooperation should be based on those issues that unite—
rather than divide—people; that technical issues should be separate
from political ones; that each technical issue should be handled on an
autonomous basis; and that solutions to problems should be sought by
function, not form.

It is evident that the proposals for international organizations were
strongly influenced by the successful experience of the US administration in the 1930s in putting in place the structures for the New Deal to
combat economic depression and high unemployment. Indeed, Mitrany
claimed to take his main model for functional international cooperation from the New Deal, especially the Tennessee Valley Authority.
Some argue, in fact, that the postwar international architecture was
modeled on an internationalization of the New Deal,[10] on the basis of
the "regulatory state" introduced in the United States in the 1930s that,
in the American view, could be generalized worldwide. What is clear is
that the policy of holding separate international conferences on each of
the functional areas in effect confirmed the "functionalist" approach to the
organization of a new postwar order.

In mid-1943 Roosevelt initially preferred a decentralized system without
any coordinating central mechanism. Subsequently, State Department planners asked themselves whether there should be one organization with semiautonomous branches, similar to what Bruce had
suggested for the League, or a coordinating structure with a more

powerful capacity for direction. These debates reveal the relevance of postwar planning to present-day considerations regarding reform of the United Nations to which we return. The basic architecture of the embryonic UN system was determined several months before Dumbarton Oaks. In December 1943, Cordell Hull spoke of "agencies for cooperation in economic and social activities brought within the framework of the international organisation."[11] By July 1944, this became "each specialised economic or social organisation or agency should be brought into relationship with the general international organisation,"[12] the phrase that found its way into the Charter.

In a sense, the choice between alternative structures was determined even before the Dumbarton Oaks consultations of August–September 1944. Roosevelt began the series of conferences establishing the UN and the functional bodies with the subject of food and nutrition, in Hot Springs, Virginia, in May 1943, because he felt it would be easier to explain to domestic opinion the need for such international action. UNRRA was established in November 1943. The ILO gathered in Philadelphia in May 1944. The UN Monetary and Financial Conference took place in July 1944.

The timing and the outcome of the various conferences clearly suggest there was no master plan for the creation of what became the UN system. The ILO case is especially instructive as it was established in 1919 under a separate agreement as part of the League but largely autonomous. The United States was an active member of the ILO, and in the 1930s the New Dealers much appreciated the ILO's approach to labor problems. Its unique tripartite structure (employers, workers, and governments) created almost 100 years ago in a fit of imaginative foresight has stood the test of time. Earlier, the State Department had considered the relationship of the ILO to the general international organization if the latter were to have an overall economic agency, but the Philadelphia gathering paved the way for the ILO to become the first UN specialized agency. It also foreshadowed some of the problems that were to emerge: "if the Philadelphia Declaration had been taken literally by those who voted for it, the ILO would have developed into the master agency among the emerging family of functional international bodies."[13]

Dumbarton Oaks and San Francisco

Before and at Dumbarton Oaks, the Union of Soviet Socialist Republics (USSR) initially wanted the central organization to deal solely with political and security questions. Ambassador Gromyko demonstrated that 70 percent of the League's work in the 1930s had focused on economic and social issues: if this were repeated in the new organization, attention would be diverted from what Moscow considered to be the more important responsibility of securing peace and security. For Washington and London, a satisfactory resolution of the differences with the USSR regarding the use of the veto in the Security Council and membership of the new organization were more important than economic issues, especially after the successful conclusion of Bretton Woods a few weeks earlier. A limited compromise between the USSR and the UK–US delegations at the end of Dumbarton Oaks on the veto issue enabled the Soviets to remove their opposition to including economic and social issues within the framework of the new organization.

Loveday and others were greatly disappointed with the outcome of Dumbarton Oaks, which significantly reduced the intended authority of ECOSOC compared to the original US tentative proposals. Although "history had taught the League that economic, financial, social and security concerns had to be woven together as much as possible,"[14] the necessary institutional linkages were being lost. Bretton Woods had established the framework for postwar economic and financial relations, the UN would handle security, and the ILO was being re-launched. To counteract the emerging consensus on the postwar architecture, Loveday redoubled his efforts: the preparation of the second part of the report on *Transition from War to Peace* was speeded up for publication in early 1945, and he resumed lobbying his contacts in Washington and elsewhere.

There were some gains at San Francisco, but the essential architecture remained as agreed at Dumbarton Oaks. Three points are relevant. First, as a result of pressure from the smaller powers,[15] ECOSOC's status was elevated to that of a principal organ, the same as the Security Council and General Assembly, a clear indication of the importance that they would attach to the UN's responsibilities for promoting economic and social progress. Second, San Francisco went a little beyond Dumbarton Oaks in expanding the powers of the General Assembly and of ECOSOC regarding economic and social issues. However, the conference did not, for reasons explained below, clarify or explain what those powers and functions really meant. Third, on the basis of the outcome of Dumbarton Oaks, San Francisco agreed, in Charter Article 57 (1) to arrangements whereby specialized agencies, established by "inter-governmental agreement" and with "wide international responsibilities ... in economic, social, cultural, educational health and related fields" would be "brought into relationship" with the United Nations organization through agreements that would define the areas for mutual cooperation.

The implications of San Francisco

The creation of the United Nations in 1945 was an act of high statesman-ship. However, in terms of development, it designed an institutional struc-ture that failed to anticipate the needs of millions of people around the world, and which is now clearly failing to meet contemporary challenges.

The State Department and Treasury planners were preoccupied not with development but with preserving the liberal capitalist postwar order. As one prominent American political scientist observed early on, "the ground rules for international economic cooperation that were drawn up in the 1940's under the leadership of the United States were aimed primarily at preventing actions found harmful by the major powers during the 1930's, not at promoting practices helpful to the emerging nations."[16] A multilaterally agreed regime providing special treatment for poor countries was unheard of in those days.

The other main critique concerns the decentralized nature of the international system agreed in San Francisco, with the weak requirements for concerted international action. The foremost historian of the Charter, Ruth Russell, who worked closely with Pasvolsky at the State Depart-ment, commented in their history of the UN Charter: "The basic deci-sion made at Dumbarton Oaks, and confirmed at San Francisco, was that the relationship to be established between the specialised agencies and the world Organisation would be one of co-ordination and co-operation, rather than one of centralisation and direction."[17]

Although San Francisco did add the responsibility that the "Organisation shall make recommendations for the coordination of the policies ... of the Specialised Agencies," it is striking that the debates were almost silent on such issues as the objectives of coordination, on what should be coordinated, and how. Loveday and others were clear in pointing out the consequences: the coordination of economic and financial policy on an intergovernmental level would become far more difficult as a result of the abandonment of the "integrated architecture of the League for the specialist structure of the UN organisations."[18]

After Bretton Woods and before San Francisco, Henry Morgenthau and Dexter White were adamant that the United Nations "was never going to tell the World Bank or the IMF what to do," even though both would become specialized agencies of the UN. As John and Richard Toye comment: "this tension between the formal UN status and the de facto operational independence of the IMF and the World Bank has been a constant feature of the international scene ever since."[19]

Clavin is right in stating that the Bruce report provided a template for the future ECOSOC but wrong in claiming that ECOSOC is a "carbon copy"[20] of the Central Committee proposed by Bruce. Bruce would have had the new League Committee "direct and supervise"[21] the work of the specialist League groups. In contrast, Charter Article 67 (1) states that ECOSOC "may coordinate the activities of the specialised agencies through consultation and recommendations," which is a totally different concept. Another important difference is that Bruce, following League practice, would have enabled the new committee to co-opt experts in their personal capacity whereas ECOSOC is exclusively inter-governmental although occasional receiving expert advice. The alleged similarity between the new postwar order and the US regulatory state also breaks down. Part of the New Deal reforms involved the estab-lishment of a strong central body, namely the Executive Office of the President, following the 1937 report of the Brownlow Commission; nothing similar was proposed for the United Nations.

In fact, neither Dumbarton Oaks nor San Francisco addressed issues of coordination and coherence, nor for that matter did the theories of func-tionalism. The functionalists proposed that organizations should be created to fulfill a need, but once satisfied, the organizations should be closed. Such an approach has proved irrelevant at the international level. There is also nothing in functionalism that suggests how to eliminate overlapping responsibilities between different technical organizations working in related fields—for instance, where does a crosscutting issue like water belong?

The structure was in fact complex and burdensome. It would involve not only significant cooperation among intergovernmental organizations but also efficient coordination at the national level among all the national ministries to be engaged in UN affairs. Member states were aware of the problem in 1945. The Preparatory Commission to the United Nations contains the following paragraph under the heading "Responsibility of Individual Members for Co-ordination":

> While the United Nations, and particularly its Economic and Social Council, has the task of coordinating the policies and activities of spe-cialized agencies, this task can be performed only if Members indivi-dually will assist in making co-ordination possible. The acceptance by each Member of this responsibility for harmonizing its policies and activities in the different fields covered by the specialized agencies and the United Nations will prevent confusion and conflict and enable the United Nations to achieve the purposes ... of the Charter.[22]

This was remarkably prescient. Member states still do not adequately coordinate their national positions, and the UN has been unable to fulfill its coordinating role.

Since the system was to be decentralized, there was no way member states would agree on the need for a "central brain," whether at the intergovernmental or secretariat level. In 1945, most governments conceived of the secretary-general's role in a manner similar to that of the functions of the League's secretary-general, namely as the chief administrative officer at the service of member states. The major powers certainly did not envisage an activist secretary-general, and they subsequently sought to elect malleable secretaries-general, but there have been at least a few surprises.

In summary, the Charter provisions to ensure coherence or action on a system-wide basis were extremely limited. There was no definition of the purposes of coordination, and there was a major lacuna in the architecture, namely ways and means to ensure consistent actions by member states in the UN system's governing bodies.

Lessons for the evolution of the UN development "system"

This section reviews how the United Nations initially assumed the mantle of development thinking, by calling upon some of the same economic pioneers who had been attracted to the League of Nations. Inevitably, compared with the heady optimism that accompanied the UN's birth, its subsequent evolution was bound to fall short of the aspirations of its founders. Nowhere would this be truer than in the complex and variegated sphere of development, of which the evolution was unforeseen, and for which the UN was unprepared.

By the late 1950s, although the UN could no longer claim an exclusive leadership role, its development organizations continued to be a source of original ideas. In the meantime, the UN's operational role grew up around its technical assistance programs, which first the United States and then other donors were prepared to finance.

Ideas and operations never meshed well in the UN, however. Although such problems were recognized early, all subsequent attempts at reform have failed to make a genuine "system" out of a set of separately governed organizations. While some UN planners had advocated a strong center for the UN, ECOSOC was not designed to be an authoritative overseer.

Early development ideas

There was no consensus on what development really entailed. Or more precisely, there was a steady evolution of thinking about how its synonym, economic progress, could be achieved. Prewar economic theory had long been preoccupied with business cycles, and the League's economists, under Loveday, studied the international transmission of depressions. Between the economic stimulus of World War II and the Korean War, the focus was on full employment, which has its place in the Charter. Nicholas Kaldor, future Nobel laureate W. Arthur Lewis, and others contributed to the debate. Reflecting the economic orthodoxy of the day, development thinking was shaped around factors of production and the supremacy of capital. It was the World Bank, rather than the UN, that led in making these arguments, applying neoclassical paradigms, backed by substantial concessional loans: there was never a more distinctive and persistent example of "money talking." Nevertheless, the purpose of the IMF still includes ensuring high levels of employment, and that of the World Bank improving labor standards.

A further concern of fundamental importance to developing countries, and a long-term preoccupation of the UN, was their declining terms of trade. Hans Singer in the UN's Department of Economic Affairs and Raúl Prebisch in the Economic Commission for Latin America (ECLA) advanced arguments that were more fully elaborated in a 1949 paper from the UN Secretariat called *Relative Prices of Exports and Imports of Under-developed Countries.*[23] However, the Prebisch-Singer thesis was not without controversy, being construed as an attack on neoclassicism and the capacity of markets to self-correct.

There is no doubt, though, about the longer-term impact that theories of unequal exchange in trade were to have. From 1946, the UN began drafting the charter for the International Trade Organization (ITO), which included provisions for "underdeveloped" countries to protect their fledgling industries in the interests of development. The charter was agreed at a conference in Havana concluded in 1948, but US president Harry Truman withdrew it from consideration by the Senate, and the ITO never came into being. However, concerns over declining terms of trade led to the creation in Geneva in 1964 of the UN Conference on Trade and Development (UNCTAD) as a forum for the negotiation of more preferential conditions and of a fairer global economic balance in general, and later to the establishment of the International Trade Centre (ITC) for the provision of trade information.[24]

In the 1940s and early 1950s, the UN was the center of creative thinking about development. Just as the League had done, the world organization attracted some of the most original economic minds during its early years.[25] The UN had at least three principal centers of research excellence: in New York at the Department of Economic Affairs (with Singer, Ragnar Nurkse, and Theodore Schultz); in Geneva at the Economic Commission for Europe (ECE) (Gunnar Myrdal and Nicolas

Kaldor); and in Santiago at ECLA (Prebisch). Over time, with the expansion in development research in academia and within development institutions, the UN's primacy was inevitably lost, but it still retained the capacity for original analysis. In the 1970s, the ILO developed the influential "basic needs" approach to development. In the 1980s came UNICEF's work on *Adjustment with a Human Face*,[26] followed since 1990 by the annual *Human Development Report*. UNCTAD's annual *Trade and Development Report* has challenged the prevailing orthodoxy. These examples of original research undertaken by renowned UN experts, however, lacked sustainability. Research became proprietary to each host organization and was barely acknowledged—let alone shared—by the rest of the system. The UN has also failed to translate its own ideas into practice through its operations, which followed a separate course of technical skills development.

If financial capital and trade were the headline items in the development debate to which the UN was initially an active contributor, there was another crucial strand in the argument championed by the UN: human capital and institution building. This third "gap" was not ignored by development theorists. However, the UN was the real incubator of skills development from a very early stage, and technical assistance became the basis of the UN's development operations.

Development operations

Technical assistance was to be the UN's vehicle to build human capital by enhancing skills in developing countries, impelled by the rapid pace of decolonization. It was championed by David Owen, head of the UN's economic department, and became the basis for the UN's other principal role in development: operations. In the first meetings of ECOSOC and the General Assembly, the Chinese delegation proposed a technical assistance program for the UN, recalling that China had benefited from the League's largest such program, in health, during the 1930s and 1940s.[27]

The UN needed organizational capacity and funding, which from the outset were closely linked. The specialized agencies were the core of an inchoate UN development system. However, following Mitrany's functionalism, they were conceived as essentially cooperative ventures, forming epistemic communities of consultation and helping to develop technical norms and standards. To become purveyors of advice, organizations were required to sign up and field technical advisers.

When UNRRA terminated activities in 1947, its remaining funds were distributed among three specialized agencies—the World Health Organization, the Food and Agriculture Organization, and the UN

Educational, Scientific and Cultural Organization—as well as two UN organizations—UNICEF and the International Refugee Organization (which became the Office of the UN High Commissioner for Refugees)—making it easier for them to offer assistance to developing countries. Member states also agreed to include in the UN budget a small fund for "advisory social welfare services," an area not covered by the specialized agencies. In 1948, the General Assembly approved a Technical Assistance Administration (TAA) program in the UN Secretariat. The timing was fortuitous because a month later, in early 1949, US president Truman called for a "bold new program" through the UN "for making the benefits of our scientific advances and industrial progress available for the improvement and growth of under-developed areas."[28]

This "point four" speech opened the door the same year to the Expanded Programme of Technical Assistance (EPTA) as a fund for all technical assistance by the UN system. ECOSOC established a Technical Assistance Committee (TAC) to oversee a Technical Assistance Board (TAB), chaired by the secretary-general and comprising the heads of the specialized agencies. The TAB would be responsible for receiving requests for assistance and passing these on for approval by the TAC. In the first pledging conference in June 1950, donors provided $20 million to the EPTA (over $200 million in equivalent present value).

Owen was the main architect of the EPTA, and became the executive chairman of the TAB, but the TAA, the world's first multilateral aid agency, needed a competent head and Owen sought the services of Prebisch. Secretary-General Trygve Lie did not appoint him, instead opting for Hugh Keenleyside, a Canadian diplomat. This unfortunate precedent has been described as "one of the most unfortunate decisions in the history of the UN's development network," because it meant "rejecting the principle that the UN's development chief should be one of the most respected economists from the developing world."[29]

The EPTA did, however, facilitate UN coordination, mainly because it was a single source of funding for almost all the technical activities of the emerging development system. However, lacking a technical assistance head with the knowledge and stature to exercise strategic oversight and adjudicate how best the funding should be apportioned, the UN reverted to a typical bureaucratic solution, known as "agency shares," awarding each organization a fixed percentage of available funds. Owen himself was not happy with this supply-side arrangement. He wanted developing country views to be instrumental in determining allocations, and he appointed "resident representatives" in the field to act as facilitators.[30] From three at the start of the EPTA in 1950, the number grew steadily and was over 70 when the United Nations Development

Programme (UNDP) was created in the mid-1960s. The obvious tensions in trying to reconcile country needs with agency-apportioned funding have never since been fully resolved. From the mid-1950s, ECOSOC called for a loosening of agency shares (finally abolished in 1961) in favor of more deliberate "country programming." However, the agencies were determined to ensure that they were present in every country allocation and resident representatives became targets for agency advocacy.

The absence of genuine country ownership was not only a UN problem because it has always applied to aid in general. From the outset, however, Owen had been determined to establish principles of partnership in UN programs. He and others reasoned that a requesting country was more likely to receive pertinent advice and support if it involved some financial obligation. Various cost-sharing schemes were devised including "standard basic assistance agreements" (SBAAs), which Owen asked countries to sign with the TAB. Governments requesting assistance were expected to assume responsibility for a substantial part of the costs of technical services. Over the period 1950–64, during which donor countries pledged $400 million for the EPTA, hard currency contributions from developing countries amounted to $45 million. Much more significant, however, was an estimated $900 million in equivalent local costs borne by the beneficiaries.[31]

However, the SBAA and other partnership agreements—which were modeled on the cost-recovery conditions determined by the League of Nations for its technical assistance—began to unravel from the early stages. Many developing countries were willing to share costs in principle, but they perceived the incongruity between UN agency entitlement and recipient obligations. Resident representatives came under pressure from both governments and agencies to soften or waive the conditions of the SBAAs.

Partnership principles would in any case have been difficult for the UN to sustain. Aid, including technical assistance, has never been development "cooperation" in the true sense of that word; led by the bilateral agencies, it became a form of free patronage.[32] During the 1960s its rapid growth was bound to undermine the UN's cost-sharing efforts. Moreover, UN operations across the system have steadily lost their multilateral flavor. Being predominantly supported by earmarked funding from the major donors, UN technical assistance has come to resemble bilateral assistance.

Another funding source came into being in 1958. The UN had earlier proposed the establishment of a Special UN Fund for Economic Development (SUNFED) to support large capital investment projects through grants and soft loans. It was debated for almost a decade because of US and UK opposition to a funding facility governed by the General Assembly. In October 1958, a modest special fund was eventually agreed in resolution 1240 (XIII), but it "would be directed towards enlarging the scope of the UN programmes of TA [technical assistance] so as to include special projects in certain basic fields." The real prize went to the World Bank, which in 1959 established the International Development Association (IDA) specifically for the purpose of extending concessional loans to developing countries. The IDA had many of the same objectives as SUNFED and was to be funded from donor replenishments on a triennial basis, augmented by profits from the Bank's other operations.

The IDA confirmed the readiness of donors to set up a major new funding facility within the multilateral system, but in the World Bank over which they could exert control. It helped to establish the World Bank—although formally a UN specialized agency—as a major operational rival of the UN development system, attracting generous donor support that might otherwise have been directed to the United Nations. Tensions grew between New York and Washington: the neoclassical models of the latter trumped the human development priorities of the former, and the World Bank did not manifest the same concerns for disadvantaged countries (such as the least developed). If the results of World Bank dominance had been better in terms of development results, then the UN would have found it less able to be so righteously critical. As it is, developing countries lost out on both grounds—an indication, perhaps, of the failings of the postwar institutional architecture.

The Special Fund brought another giant of postwar development into the UN arena. Paul Hoffman, who had successfully managed the Marshall Plan, became its head and by 1966, thanks to his fundraising efforts, the resources of the Special Fund had grown to $100 million, larger than the EPTA. In that year, in a rare example of UN rationalization, the Special Fund and EPTA were merged, creating the UNDP. Hoffman became its first administrator and established a pattern that would not be broken for over 30 years: the UN's largest donor would provide the administrator, since the UNDP was intended to be the central funding mechanism of the UN system.

Bifurcation of ideas and operations

The United Nations could no longer claim to be the principal fount of development thinking after the 1950s. It nevertheless remained a source of world-changing ideas, and many Nobel laureates have been associated with the world organization, in contrast to the World Bank.[33] Different parts of the UN, drawing on principles of universality and humanitarianism, have pioneered thinking on human rights, gender equality, fairer economic relations, social development, environmental sustainability, human security, and human development. The UN has always recognized the importance of institutional and capacity development. Many of these ideas and concepts have led to the establishment of key norms and standards that provide benchmarks for development progress. Long before the Millennium Development Goals (MDGs), the UN was setting development goals. In statistical standards and population data, the UN remains the point of reference.

The UN has been less successful in pooling its best ideas and in using them as a basis for its technical assistance activities. The bifurcation of ideas and operations is due in part to organizational factors. ECOSOC never had the authority or power to "govern" the nine specialized agencies, which have their own independent intergovernmental structures, three of which (International Telecommunication Union, Universal Postal Union, and ILO) long predate the UN.

The UN's so-called development system was never established as a coherent "system" but instead comprised specialized agencies that were newly and separately created, together with pre-existing organizations that were, as we saw above, "brought into relationship" with the UN. Lacking a cohesive design, the new system would have needed a smart center within the UN to guide it, but there was no such thing and thus no strategic oversight. When the UNDP was established in 1966, it had dual functions of funding and coordination, but it has not actually taken the latter function seriously, substituting it for "allocation."

In fact, the problems of non-coordination have become worse over time. Even as the EPTA was being created with the support of Western donors, the specialized agencies were tapping into their own sources of funding from the same countries. By the time that the UNDP came into existence as the system's central funding mechanism, the dispersion of sources had widened considerably.

To make matters more complex, the UNDP decided in the 1980s to play down its role as chief sponsor, reduce funding to other UN bodies, and go after the same donors to fund its own programs. It became, in effect, not a UN coordinator but competitor. As a consequence, the technical assistance programs of many of the smaller UN organizations—designated as "implementing agencies" of the UNDP, and to that point still dependent on UNDP funding—almost collapsed.

Coordination has also been made more complex by the addition of new organizations, created in response to emerging concerns: in the 1960s, UNCTAD, the ITC, and the UN Fund for Population Activities (UNFPA, later the UN Population Fund); in the 1970s, the UN Environment

Programme (UNEP), UN Habitat, the International Fund for Agricultural Development (IFAD); in the 1980s, the UN Industrial Development Organization (UNIDO, previously an entity of the UN Secretariat); and in the last decade UN Women as an amalgam of four pre-existing entities, and the World Tourism Organization, previously outside the UN system. In parallel, more and more individual organizations set up their own country representative offices, so that today there are over 1,000, each with their own staff and administration. Such resource duplication could only prevail in the absence of a unified perception of the system.

Attempts at reform

The United Nations has been cognizant of this untrammeled dispersion of efforts, but because of the origins of the system described earlier, the UN has been unable to prevent it. After the UNDP was set up, Robert Jackson was asked by the UNDP Governing Council to produce a comprehensive blueprint for reform. He saw the need not just for a center, but for a smart one, with an "organized brain to guide it."[34]

The *Capacity Study* was pragmatic as well as radical, but its recommendations were watered down after intergovernmental scrutiny. The "consensus" that emerged called for stronger country programming based on specific allocations of funding by country (indicative planning figures). More authority was to be given to resident representatives over the UN funds and programs, but not over the specialized agencies in the same country, as the *Capacity Study* had proposed. New UNDP regional bureaux were supposed to align with the UN's regional commissions but instead became independent and powerful. The outcome thus fell far short of what would have been needed to give the UN greater coherence in its development activities. For example, its longest chapter was devoted to a single UN-wide information system that would have greatly facilitated cohesion; such a system is as far away in today's electronic era as it was then.

In 1975 a group of 25 experts was convened to study the workings of the UN system, this time at the behest of the developing countries. Its report,[35] however, was received with virtual indifference by the UN's most senior officials. Notwithstanding the reluctance of the Secretariat, discussions led to resolution 32/197 in 1977, which endorsed a good part of the report's recommendations, including the appointment of the director-general for development and international economic cooperation and the designation of resident coordinators of UN operations in each country. The director-general (also a recommendation of the *Capacity Study*) was appointed, but the incumbents of the position, limited resources, and weak commitment on the part of the Secretariat meant that the UN development system never found the brain to guide it. At the country level, the designation of resident coordinators was a welcome step, but then—as now—the posts (mostly filled by the UNDP) had little effective influence while field representatives of all other UN organizations continued to answer to their respective headquarters.

The most recent system-wide reform proposals came from a high-level panel on system-wide coherence in 2006. One of its proposals was the consolidation of four existing entities into a single new organization, UN Women. It was a small but significant step toward rationalization. Another recommendation was for the UN to "Deliver as One" at the country level—that is, with one leader, one program, one budget and, where appropriate, one office. This recommendation has been partially implemented in some countries, but a recent evaluation determined that the one-UN approach had significantly raised transaction costs, suggesting that full integration was a better solution than convergence. The report also recommended the establishment of a UN sustainable development board "to drive coordination and joint planning between all funds, programs and agencies to monitor overlaps and gaps," and a high-level "political forum" for sustainable development has now been set up under ECOSOC auspices.[36]

High-level conferences to discuss specific development concerns have long been a tradition at the UN. Following several such meetings in the 1960s and 1970s, the practice of holding summits of heads of state and government began in the 1990s, culminating in the largest ever (to that time) development summit in September 2000. The outcome of this summit, the *Millennium Declaration*, was a remarkable document that set out the principles for a peaceful, well-governed, and progressive world in General Assembly resolution 55/2. Five years later, in October 2005, an even more comprehensive development blueprint was agreed by an even larger summit in General Assembly resolution 60/1. These were products that could only have come from the UN.

Converting these ideas into practice remains the challenge. Eight MDGs were extracted from the 2000 declaration. They constituted an agenda of sorts for the UN development system although it took several years for all organizations to acknowledge their importance. However, the less politically palatable but nevertheless more important agenda represented by the totality of these declarations provides the way forward for the United Nations. Development is not viable without human security, sound governance, and the guarantee of individual rights and freedoms—all mentioned in the declaration but not in the actual MDGs.

Deliberations on the post-2015 agenda suggest how the United Nations could best tackle the weaknesses inherent in its past: the bifurcation of ideas and operations, and the challenge of coherence. First, aligning the UN's ideas and operations will require much greater attention to assisting countries to meet the global norms and standards that they have agreed rather than pursuing numerous sector-based skills projects that non-UN sources can provide better. Second, the unique value of the UN is in its range of roles across peacekeeping, humanitarian relief, promotion of human rights, and development. The UN is most urgently needed in situations of insecurity, fragility, and peace building, and the challenge of coordination is now greatest across the entire system, and not merely among the development organizations.

Conclusion

There is much to learn from the history of how the UN's development operations have been an add-on to the Charter provisions for international economic and social cooperation. The world organization carried over from the League an important role of development think tank. Initially with a virtual monopoly on original development thinking, it has continued to incubate ideas that have influenced the global development agenda. However, there has always been an institutional bifurcation between ideas and practice. For this and for other reasons associated both with the structure of the UN system and with donor financing, most of the best ideas have remained just that.

Paradoxically, operations have also suffered because of the nature of their origins. While many of the system's organizations would not have come into being without the enthusiasm for the UN to tackle key issues of development, these separately constituted bodies became impossible to meld into a genuine system. Their increasingly dispersed funding sources and the support that each receives from different functional ministries have always been the main obstacles to the creation of a more unified system. While the UN subscribes to closer collaboration, its cumbersome coordination mechanisms have slowed its ability to respond to contemporary development challenges, which often demand interdisciplinary approaches. Whether it is in confronting the spread of poverty, the consequences of climate change, the instability of financial systems, the possibility of conflict stemming from competition for resources, the rapid transmission of disease, or cyber security, UN development organizations should adopt more integrated and coherent responses.

UN development operations are beholden to the ultimate authority of member states, but while intergovernmental bodies are the only legitimate basis for drawing up universal conventions and norms for subsequent national ratification and implementation, the requirements for consensus hinders operational innovation. Not surprisingly, therefore, new non-UN funds and mechanisms have sprung up, for example in the health and environment fields, which have mixed governance structures, and which have been more nimble in their development operations.

History teaches us that the concerted international action that the world needs will not be achieved on the basis of the UN Charter. While genuine reform of UN development operations is essential for whatever post-2015 agenda is agreed, the lack of committed multilateralism renders such reform more unlikely. Must we wait for another San Francisco moment?

Notes

1 The authors are grateful to the participants at the London writers' workshop in May 2014, especially Margaret Joan Anstee and Richard Jolly, for their useful comments on an earlier draft, as well as Patrizio Civili, Ian Kinniburgh, Khalil Hamdani, and Craig Murray for their helpful suggestions.
2 Stephen C. Schlesinger, *CNN's Diplomatic License*, 24 December 2004.
3 Patricia Clavin, *Securing the World Economy: The Reinvention of the League of Nations* (Oxford: Oxford University Press, 2013).
4 "Letter of 2 February 1939 from Cordell Hull to the League," quoted by Victor-Yves Ghébali, *La Société des Nations et la Réforme Bruce, 1939–40* (Geneva: Centre européen de la Dotation Carnegie pour la paix international, 1970), 16–17.
5 League of Nations, *The Development of International Cooperation in Economic and Social Affairs*, Report of the Special Committee, document no. A.23.1939, 1939.
6 League of Nations, *The Transition from War to Peace Economy*, Report of the Delegation of Economic Depressions, Part I, Geneva, Series of Publications, Economic and Financial, II, A.
7 Clavin, *Securing the World Economy*, 290–93.
8 Clavin, *Securing the World Economy*, 296.
9 Clavin, *Securing the World Economy*, 283, 304.
10 Anne-Marie Slaughter, "International Law and the Protection of the New Deal Regulatory State," in *Multilateralism Matters: The Theory and Praxis of an Institutional Form*, ed. John Gerard Ruggie (New York: Colombia University Press, 1993), 125–56.
11 "Memorandum from Secretary of State to the President, 29 December 1943," in US Department of State, *Postwar Foreign Policy Preparation, 1939–45*, 576–81.
12 *United States Tentative Proposals for a General International Organization* (Washington, DC: USDA, 1944).

13 Ernst Haas, *Beyond the Nation-State* (Stanford, Calif.: Stanford University Press, 1964), 156.

14 Clavin, *Securing the World Economy*, 326.

15 Australia, Egypt, Ecuador, Honduras, Mexico, New Zealand, and Venezuela all spoke in favor. Vol. 10, records of Committee II/3, United Nations Conference on International Organization, 1945.

16 Robert E. Asher, "International Agencies and Economic Development," *International Organization* 22, no. 4 (1968): 433.

17 Ruth B. Russell and Jeanette E. Muther, *A History of the United Nations Charter* (Washington, DC: Brookings Institute, 1958), 797.

18 Clavin, *Securing the World Economy*, 356.

19 John Toye and Richard Toye, *The UN and Global Political Economy* (Bloomington: Indiana University Press, 2004), 23.

20 Clavin, *Securing the World Economy*, 337–38.

21 League of Nations, *Report of the Special Committee* (Geneva: League of Nations, 1939), Official No. A.23.1939, 19–21.

22 Report of the Preparatory Commission of the United Nations, document PC/20, 23 December 1945, chapter 3, section V, paragraph 43.

23 United Nations, *Relative Prices of Exports and Imports of Under-developed Countries* (New York: UN, 1949).

24 Stephen Browne, *The International Trade Centre* (London: Routledge, 2011).

25 Janez Stanovnik, an early Yugoslav delegate to the UN (and later the executive secretary of the ECE), was scarcely exaggerating when he said: "There was no one single great name in economic writings in the period of 1945 to 1955 who was not in one way or the other associated with the United Nations." Oral History transcript from the United Nations Intellectual History Project, CD-ROM (New York: Ralph Bunche Institute for International Studies, 2007).

26 Giovanni Andrea Cornia, Richard Jolly, and Frances Stewart, *Adjustment with a Human Face* (London: Clarendon Press, 1987).

27 Gilbert Rist, *The History of Development* (London: Zed Books, 1997); and Craig Murphy, *The United Nations Development Programme: A Better Way?* (Cambridge: Cambridge University Press, 2006).

28 *US Department of State Bulletin*, Washington, DC, 30 January 1949, 123.

29 Murphy, *The United Nations Development Programme*, 56–7.

30 They were initially recruited by the UN's Technical Assistance Administration and in 1952 came under the authority of David Owen and the TAB.

31 Mahyar Nashat, *National Interests and Bureaucracy versus Foreign Aid Programmes, 1949–75* (Stockholm: Ministry of Foreign Affairs, 1995), 138–39.

32 Stephen Browne, *Aid and Influence* (London: Earthscan, 2006).

33 Richard Jolly, Louis Emmerij, and Thomas G. Weiss, *UN Ideas That Changed the World* (Bloomington: Indiana University Press, 2009).

34 United Nations, *A Capacity Study of the United Nations Development System*, vol. I (Geneva: UN, 1969), para. 31.

35 Report of the Group of Experts on the Restructuring of the Economic and Social Sectors of the UN System, *A New United Nations Structure for Global Economic Cooperation* (New York: UN, 1975).

36 Report of the Secretary-General's High-level Panel on UN System-wide Coherence, *Delivering as One* (New York: UN, 2007), 44.

8 Financing gaps, competitiveness, and capabilities

Why Bretton Woods needs a radical rethink

Pallavi Roy

- **An unsustainable system?**
- **The beginnings of the IMS**
- **Main debates at war's end**
- **The agency of developing countries**
- **The need for a Bretton Woods 3?**
- **Conclusion**

The international financial institutions (IFIs) of the Bretton Woods System (BWS), namely the International Monetary Fund (IMF) and the World Bank (the Bank henceforth), were meant to overcome collective action problems among countries and help solve market failures in financing on a global scale (at least outside the "Iron Curtain"). The system worked for a while and contributed to the rapid global growth in the post-World War II period. However, it then unwound spectacularly in 1971 when US President Richard Nixon ended the pegging of the US dollar to gold, spurred on by West German, Swiss, and French redemptions of dollars for gold.

Partly as a consequence, the 1970s and 1980s were decades of global stagnation, high inflation, and high unemployment in the developed economies while many developing economies languished even more. The world economy started looking rosier from the 1990s as capital started flowing to developing economies, and trade expanded under the aegis of the World Trade Organization (WTO). Earlier in the 1980s a few economies like South Korea, Taiwan, Malaysia, and Thailand had "emerged," and by the end of the 1990s China was emerging as the world's economic powerhouse and the Indian subcontinent was also displaying steady growth rates of gross domestic product (GDP). China's manufacturing growth helped boost demand for African and Latin American commodities and its purchases of US Treasury bills financed the growing budget deficits of the United States and helped keep the Yuan low against the dollar. This new system of global payments began to be described by analysts as Bretton Woods 2 (BW2), in which exchange rates were managed by some emerging economies to uphold their export-oriented economies and the dollar was once again the reserve currency of choice, this time informally as opposed to the formal mechanism of the BWS, allowing the United States easily to finance its current account deficit. This system is not without its critics who feel that the US deficit position is unsustainable.[1]

However, the current international monetary system (IMS) is unsustainable for other reasons, explored in the first section below. The central and most critical issue of international political economy that grows from history, beginning at Bretton Woods in 1944, and explored in this chapter is how the current world economic order can resolve the gap in financing for capability development. The chapter discusses the need to implement new institutions that can design and implement financial instruments that suit the needs of developing economies. It begins by examining why the current system is unsustainable—ironically having failed to address the problem that had led to the collapse of the original BWS. The chapter then explores the origins of the Bretton Woods global payments system, the immediate imperatives behind it, and how far it was able to solve the problem of capability building.

An unsustainable system?

This chapter posits that the real reason for this unsustainability is the failure of BW2 to address the critical problem that also led to the failure of the original BWS—the permanence of payment surpluses and deficits in many countries. The new BW2 system might reflect the continuing dominance of the United States as the global superpower, in military and economic power, but there has been a significant change in power structure with China's emergence as an economic powerhouse with substantial and persistent dollar surpluses. The financing situation, however, remains unchanged with the United States running a permanent deficit balanced largely by China's payments surplus. In the case of the original BWS, surpluses and deficits were not meant to be permanent. The IMS was supposed to provide solutions so that deficit countries could move back into surplus, and surplus countries using their reserves were to help countries in deficit. By the late 1960s, however, the United States was in permanent deficit and other countries had to maintain surpluses to balance the world economy, and the unraveling of the original BWS was in part linked to this problem.

As indicated earlier, according to much current discourse the real problem is how to reduce US deficits and how to get China to reduce its surplus. While this adjustment is necessary according to a large body of literature,[2] the necessity is not an immediate one given that the United States is not about to lose its reserve currency status very soon. The critical issue is that the global payments system, whether the initial Bretton Woods system or the so-called Bretton Woods 2, has not addressed the most important problem underpinning the payments deficits of developing countries. This problem of financing the development of organizational and technical capabilities in emerging enterprises and sectors is crucial, so that the competitiveness required for addressing trade imbalances can be acquired. This specific problem should not be confused with the broader issue of "capacity development" that can encompass investments in institutions, human capabilities, and so on. While these latter aspects of development are also important, we are concerned with a more specific capability because without its development, developing countries in particular are unable to engage in the global trading system in a sustainable way.

"Capability development" refers to the processes through which firms learn to organize modern production methods in order to achieve international competitiveness. This capability, in turn, requires financing the process of learning. Learning is only successful if the financing comes with credible conditions, and the disciplining mechanisms and the governance agencies that oversee the financing cannot be significantly distorted by rent-seeking interests.[3] The development of globally competitive sectors and in particular the development of a broad-based employment-generating manufacturing sector is essential for sustaining development in labor-surplus developing economies. The absence of a global financial architecture that can provide the financing for developing these capabilities has contributed to the instability of the global payments system. A later section outlines the framework of capability development in greater detail.

Persistent deficits constrain the financing abilities of developing countries, and that financing capability is the basis for achieving capital accumulation. Industrial development and, in particular, the development of a broad-based employment-generating manufacturing sector is essential for sustaining development in labor-surplus developing economies that least have access to financing. Hence, any new global system should address this gap in financing, and despite the huge amounts disbursed by both Bretton Woods institutions, the financing provided by the IMF and the Bank has yet to cater to capability development or broad-based manufacturing in developing countries.

For too long the Bank moved away from project financing to lending for governance or bureaucratic reform, and the IMF focused on conditional lending that only took into account "macroeconomic stability" (or the balance between inflation and employment and size of the budget deficit). Even though both the Bank and the IMF have recently made changes to their lending policies, they are still far from addressing the pertinent financing needs identified above. The problem is compounded by the fact that the global power balances that led to the creation of the BWS have changed substantially, thereby making it even more difficult for a new financing paradigm to be created. Hence, a radical shift is required in the task of creating a new global financing system that will adequately address the needs of the global South.

Members of the Organisation for Economic Co-operation and Development (OECD) countries, on the one hand, are credible states with large productive tax bases and do not face much difficulty in persuading surplus emerging powers like China to finance their debt. Thus, the United States finds such favor among lenders, helped in no small amount by the fact that it is also the world's leading economic and military power. Developing countries, on the other hand, have weaker state capacity as they are still negotiating the fraught process of transitioning from pre-capitalist to capitalist economies, and they also often lack credibility as debtors given the vulnerable state of their economies. Their tax base is smaller, and they have lower credibility in attracting the long-term lending that is so necessary for development financing. What is today readily available for OECD countries needs to find its way to Bangladesh or Chad, and BW2 has no tools to achieve these investments on a significant scale. Yet global stability in the longer term is dependent on the sustainable growth of developing economies. If there is a global crisis looming, it is the crisis of underdevelopment brought on by a dearth of financing opportunities in the very countries where potential growth is very high. Instead, the capital that does find its way to developing countries is "hot money" or short-term capital flows that are volatile and dependent on capricious sentiments and the availability of liquid financial instruments.

The critical issue of international political economy that is explored in this chapter is how the current world economic order can solve this gap in financing for capability development. It discusses the need to implement new institutions that can design and implement financial instruments that suit the needs of developing economies. The next section explores the origins of the Bretton Woods global payments system, the immediate imperatives behind it, and how far it was able to solve the problem of capability building.

The beginnings of the IMS

The United Nations Monetary and Finance Conference, held at Bretton Woods in 1944 and more popularly known as the Bretton Woods conference, brought together 730 delegates from 44 governments. They were as disparate as the United States, Liberia, Bolivia, British India, Mexico, the Soviet Union, Iceland, Poland, the United Kingdom, and China among many others. Some were imperial powers, some colonies or in varying degrees co-opted by larger countries, and a few were countries trying to build their polities and economies independent from larger powers. The conference was also convened during World War II and therefore under circumstances that were far from ideal. It became a stage for the changing dynamics of the international political economy, with British imperial power on the wane, American power on the ascendance, and colonies, especially Asian ones, getting restive about their dependent status.

Despite this, what the Bretton Woods conference achieved was a relative harmonization of interests among disparate countries in terms of setting up two seminal institutions that were to help finance and, where necessary, refinance development over both the short term and the long term. The IMF was set up to provide short-term financial assistance for countries that were facing balance-of-payments (BoP) crises. The World Bank, initially called the International Bank for Reconstruction and Development (IBRD), would provide long-term financing. The IMF was the cornerstone of the negotiations, and its chief responsibility was to provide liquidity to countries that needed it.[4] This provision was predicated on the understanding that the economic crisis of the inter-war years was a result of freely floating exchange rates that held countries hostage to external pressures and limited their role in currency management, much to their detriment. A fixed exchange rate that would still allow countries enough room to intervene in currency markets was therefore necessary, but maintaining or "defending" a fixed rate regime also required adequate liquidity in the form of foreign exchange to deal with short-term imbalances and flexibility within countries to adjust their prices and productivities so that deficits, in particular, were not permanent.

The IMF was envisioned as the institutional answer to help countries gain access to this liquidity. In the case of a large payments deficit, a country could experience a sudden shock to its economy if it has to adjust rapidly. This disequilibrium made access to liquidity important, and this was the role of the IMF. It would be useful to parse the main debates at Bretton Woods and also to explore the oft-ignored agency of developing countries at the conference.

Main debates at war's end

Not surprisingly, recently discovered transcripts found by an economist in the uncatalogued section of the library at the United States Treasury reveal that the most contentious debates at the conference took place around the IMF and its role.[5] Interestingly, not all of the important debates were on the "dollar-sterling" issue that many historians have identified as the overriding concern at the conference.[6] While the conflicting British and American positions about the reserve currency and adjustment mechanisms (discussed below) in the world economy certainly took center stage, the transcripts throw light on some other important debates that saw developing countries take on the developed ones and at least in some cases achieve important concessions. Recent work by Eric Heilleiner has also provided robust evidence of the involvement of developing countries in the conference, not just as spectators.[7]

One of the most critical debates concerned the nature of the IMF's functions. Was it going to concentrate on economic development of both developed and developing countries—in the sense of focusing on full employment for the former and aiding in the development process for the latter—or would its mandate be the narrower one of smoothing over temporary BoP crises? The debate summed up the widely diverging policy imperatives for developing and developed countries. For the former, economic development and strategies for industrialization and "catching up" were far more important than developed-country imperatives of full employment and social welfare; however, in the end, it was the latter's interests that dominated, given the balance of power in the world. Hence, at this stage financing for capability development was not even part of the conversation, which in the large part remained restricted to addressing BoP crises. Given the economic context of the interwar period, even this was a significant achievement, but the system still did not go as far as it should and could have gone, because had the United States wished, the developing countries' agenda could also have emerged as a priority.

The other keenly discussed issue was how the IMF would deal with the "debt legacy."[8] Colonies like Egypt and India were demanding that they be allowed to use the sterling credits that the British had provided in return for goods exported to them by their colonies during World War II; at that point, they were unable to use them because of exchange controls imposed on them by the UK government. This measure would have made the IMF responsible for a direct legacy of the war, a role that the United States, United Kingdom, and France opposed. Among other issues, and one that seems anodyne now—the composition of the current account—also saw divisions drawn between developed and developing countries. The question of quotas and how they were to be paid for was hotly contested and divided the delegates. The reason to highlight these seemingly small victories is that they were conceded at a time when the world was deeply divided but developing countries had little agency. There are lessons for what can be achieved today in light of the changed power structures: the developing world can negotiate harder to design a global financial architecture that is more inclusive and equitable.

At the time, the BWS was defined by the competing recommendations of the British and American delegations about what the international monetary architecture would resemble. This chapter does not examine the intricacies of the differences as there is more than ample literature on the subject.[9] The British delegation led by John Maynard Keynes mooted the idea of an International Clearing Union (ICU), which would have the authority to create a new currency (bancor) that would act as a reserve currency. Overdraft facilities to the tune of $26 billion would also be provided to countries with a BoP deficit so that they could borrow without fulfilling strict conditionalities. The system would have worked like a conventional banking system in which surpluses would be lent out to countries with a deficit just like deposits in a bank are lent as loans. His proposal also put forward corrective measures that were to be taken both by creditor and debtor countries when conventionally the burden of adjustment fell on the debtor.

Counterfactuals have little place in historical analysis, and there is no telling what might have happened if Keynes's plan had been implemented. Nonetheless, there is little doubt that Keynes's plan was sounder than the American one presented by Harry Dexter White, a technocrat at the US Treasury, and not a very senior one at that. However, White became the prime mover at Bretton Woods because he was negotiating from a position of strength as the chief US representative. The plan by White did not include the ICU, and the overdraft facility was finally whittled down to $8.8 billion. The proposal of the creditor's taking on liabilities was also struck down because the United States was clearly the largest creditor at the time, and was replaced by a watered down "scarce currency clause" as a compromise with the British.[10] Most significantly, the bancor was one of the first proposals to be dismissed during negotiations prior to the conference, and the US dollar was to emerge as the reserve currency. This was later to become the BWS's undoing, as presciently highlighted by Robert Triffin.[11] It was the White plan, though it remained broadly Keynesian, which came to be adopted at Bretton Woods. However, some of the issues highlighted earlier in the section were keenly debated between developing and developed countries.

The agency of developing countries

The stage seemed to have been shared the most by White and Keynes; their interactions, not always cordial, have been well documented.[12] However, a fresh look at the composition of the conference is instructive in order to shed light on how developing countries played a role. The conference was organized into three commissions, and each had a number of committees. For instance Commission One, which was dealing with the IMF and was chaired by White, had four main committees, eight ad hoc committees, and a Special Committee on Unsettled Problems, among others. Commission Two was headed by Keynes and responsible for charting the course of the IBRD. However, it is clear from the transcripts that Commission One was the heart of the conference, and Keynes attended many meetings of that commission too. Commission Three dealt with "other means of financial cooperation" and was headed by Eduardo Suarez of Mexico. It was largely a forum to make recommendations on topics that could not be made a part of the two main commissions. Its most significant recommendation was the dissolution of the International Bank of Settlements, which nonetheless survives to this day.[13]

In each of these commissions and committees, voices from the delegates of developing countries reverberated loudly, including from then colonized countries like Egypt and India. It would appear from the transcripts that China and India were among the harder negotiators. The IMF's role in economic development was keenly debated, and India and Australia wanted the IMF's remit to be broader. While this view was not approved, concessions were nonetheless made and changes were made to the draft of the Bank agreement to lay greater emphasis on concerns of late development—although the term "late developers" was not widely used then. Latin American countries were the key players in the negotiations that led to a greater emphasis on economic development, given that they shared a long history of engagement with the United States through the latter's "Good Neighbor" policy that Franklin Roosevelt had initiated in the 1930s. This had established financial relationships with the United States upon which Latin American countries drew at Bretton Woods.[14]

The other issues debated for developing countries were voting rights, quotas, and the components of the current account. Little success was achieved in the former case but a more significant success was achieved by countries like China, Greece, and India—all of which received a significant share of income from remittances—to include them in the current account. Given that the BWS did not allow convertibility on the capital account, placing remittances in that account would have made such a crucial source of income off-limits for the current account of these countries.[15]

On the issue of the management of postwar debt, countries like India and Egypt bargained hard, with the threat of India leaving the sterling area looming large if British debts to India were written off.[16] However, in this instance the two countries were not able to reach a satisfactory conclusion due to opposition from the United Kingdom and France with its French franc zone similar to the sterling area; the United States did not want to antagonize two key allies.[17] While the United Kingdom made some pronouncements to placate Egypt and India, it was well after Bretton Woods, in the 1950s, that London reached some sort of settlement on the sterling balances with Delhi.[18]

A quick look at the composition of committees also reinforces the analysis and the argument that developing countries were not completely devoid of agency at the conference. Three out of the four main committees of Commission One were headed by delegates from developing countries (Committee Two was headed by Pavel Maletin, the deputy finance minister of the Soviet Union). Committee One discussed the "Purposes, Policies, and Quotas of the Fund" and was chaired by a member of the Chinese National People's Party, or the Kuomintang—the diplomat and historian Tingfu Tsiang, who later served as Taiwan's permanent representative at the UN. This committee decided among other things that quotas would be reevaluated after five years. Committee Three, on "Organization and Management of the Fund," was headed by Artur de Souza Costa, Brazil's finance minister, and was responsible for the provisions on super-majorities and calls to the IMF board of governors mentioned above. Committee Four concerned "Form and Status of the Fund" and was chaired by Manuel Llosa, a Peruvian legislator, and deliberated on aspects of the IMF "on paper."[19]

The autobiography of Chintamani Deshmukh, a key member of the Indian delegation who later became the governor of India's Central Bank, reveals an interesting sideshow at which the Indian delegation threatened to leave the conference because it was being provided with too small a quota. The threat worked, and in the end India was provided a quota that ensured it remained a permanent member of the IMF's executive board for 25 years.[20] It also reveals that Keynes's ideas were not popular among many British colonies largely because of his insistence on the United Kingdom's debt being forgiven, which would have meant a loss for countries holding sterling balances. Unfortunately, Deshmukh does not provide sufficient details of the negotiations to determine what led to this success, but one can only imagine that neither Washington nor London wanted a participant with as large a territory and population as India's to leave the conference at a time when they needed to build a consensus around their ideas of the international financial system. However, developing countries were not able to wrest any concessions in terms of industrial development even though the Bank was created to help countries like India and Egypt. In its first couple of decades of operation, the Bank undertook extensive project lending, which did not come with any institutional mechanisms that would involve disciplining to prevent rent seeking and ensure successful implementation. Such a mechanism should be an important part of any new financing system.

Even this limited success on the part of developing countries at the Bretton Woods conference was, of course, a marked departure from the manner in which the League of Nations operated. If anything the League, an attempt by European powers after World War I to regulate international economic affairs, is used as an example of how *not* to construct international consensus. As Eichengreen writes, the construction of an international monetary order is an historical process, and the older order does find itself reflected in the new in some way.[21] The League's biggest achievement came in 1927 with the International Economic Conference in Geneva. Participation was of 194 delegates and 157 experts from member states, along with observers from the United States and the Soviet Union. Key issues were trade and granting "most favored nation" status, a matter of WTO deliberations even today, and the cartelization of large industries. As Louis Pauly writes, the real success of the League is the legacy of "multilateral economic surveillance" that the IMF and the Bank also carried forward.[22] There were senior members of the League's Economic and Financial Organization and the Economic Intelligence Service (EIS), like Per Jacobsson of Sweden, J.M. Fleming and Louis Rasminsky, both British and from the EIS, and Jacque Polak from the Netherlands, also of the EIS, who served in the IMF in its initial years. Hence, there was a modicum of continuation in both policies and personalities in the early IMF. The BWS architects also learned from the cardinal mistake of the League: the automaticity principle in the international economic order did not hold—that is, the belief that markets would create order on their own without monitoring while the League would act as a "temporary buffer" between markets and its members.

This principle was set aside during the Bretton Woods negotiations by consensus, but in many instances the United States used the conference to put forward its agenda and succeeded. In that sense, the trade-offs that Washington was willing to make were the least costly ones. John Ikenberry highlights that the US use of its hegemonic power also reflected its wish not to be seen as coercive, especially with its European allies, and this desire limited its postwar agenda.[23] The normative aspect of the US agenda is girded by the fact that coercion would be unproductive. The United States also saw the IMF and the Bank as factors in preventing developing countries from becoming part of the communist bloc. Hence, the financial order that emerged after the Bretton Woods conference was a result of both liberal and realist calculations. While US hegemony carried the negotiations forward, they were made possible through the "breakpoint" that had been reached during the war. It was imperative to find a solution to the problems facing the world order in the years around 1945, and this motivation provided the opportunity to fuse world interests, in whatever limited but as yet unprecedented manner, at Bretton Woods.

In terms of institutional economic analysis, World War II proved to be an exogenous shock for the international order that provided the incentives to overcome collective action problems of coordinating the interests of the various representatives. The realization was that everyone should follow similar rules in their own self-interest rather than engage in the type of free-riding and ultimately self-defeating behavior that results in each country trying to devalue currencies to gain an advantage. Without this shock, coordination problems and free-riding incentives would have led to similar problems to those that the League faced and ultimately led to its demise. In the mid-1940s the global distribution of power was also such that it allowed the United States to define the distribution of benefits (as a result of the creation of the IMF and the Bank) in its favor almost unchallenged. This global "political settlement" made the distribution of global power compatible with the definition of institutional rules with a specific distribution of global benefits.[24]

As a result, the BWS was relatively quickly and successfully implemented by the 1950s. Countries adhered to the formal rules of the newly created system for a while because they saw the benefits compared to the previous system and did not perceive the bargaining power to achieve anything better, which made for a strong and sustainable institutional order as long as the underlying distribution of power across countries was stable. The "rules of the game"[25] were compatible with the global distribution of power in the new financial order. The postwar power structure or political settlement was thus an important independent variable that influenced the creation of the new system.

However, as US deficits grew from the late 1950s, they also grew larger than its gold stock and confidence in the dollar was gradually undermined as Triffin had argued.[26] The needs of European countries were no longer being fulfilled by the system. US deficits were growing due to increased social welfare spending but mainly due to the war in Vietnam. The Europeans and Japanese were concerned about this seemingly excessive ability of the United States to finance its liabilities and began questioning the credibility of the dollar by making far too frequent demands on the gold holdings of the United States than the system formally demanded, given that the system had invested the responsibility of economic stability to the United States. As a result, the equilibrium in the "political settlement" between the distribution of power and distribution of benefits was slowly coming undone, leading to its dissolution in 1971.

A recent history of the Bretton Woods conference pins its US-centric outcome, which came at the expense of the United Kingdom, on White's Soviet sympathies. Of course, his pro-Soviet views and interactions with Moscow are no secret for historians of Bretton Woods. However, a new book observes that White's secret association with the Soviet Union and his admiration of its economic program were responsible for the loss of British positions in Bretton Woods. As Benn Steil writes, "What even his closest colleagues were generally unaware of, however, was that White's vision involved a much closer American relationship with a new, rising European power [meaning the Soviet Union], and that he was willing to use extraordinary means to promote it."[27] White died in 1948 soon after testifying that he was not a communist but after having resigned his position as US representative to the IMF in 1947.

Despite the "fatal flaws" inherent in the system, there can be little doubt that the results of the Bretton Woods conference led to unprecedented positive results for the world economy. World output grew at an annual rate of just below 5 percent, and world industrial production at 5.6 percent every year at least until the mid-1960s. Due to the provision of a closed capital account, short-term, or "hot money," flows were absent and capital flows were largely long term in the form of foreign direct investment (FDI). The combination of capital account controls and space for domestic policymaking worked to redress some of the contradictions of external and internal balances. Inflation was low and per capita income reached its highest since 1879.[28] The Bank was actively involved in financing projects linked to economic development like power projects or transportation. The Marshall Plan played a complementary role. However, the policy architecture that it used was still under the BWS framework, which had a positive effect on at least some developing economies, especially in Latin America and East Asia. Nonetheless, such growth was inadequate because of the crucial financing gap of building credibility. Yet the concessions wrested by developing countries surely foreshadowed what might be possible if a similar negotiating table is set with a menu to redraw the contemporary global financial architecture.

The need for a Bretton Woods 3?

Both the original BWS and the current BW2 have failed to address the problem of financing economic development in developing countries. After the collapse of the BWS in 1971, the IMF still maintained its role as a provider of liquidity and even started getting more involved in the economies of developing countries through programs like structural adjustment policies and Poverty Reduction Strategy Papers. Enough criticism has been leveled against both,[29] but it is worth repeating that in the IFIs' efforts to provide macroeconomic stability, the key principle of capability development was never addressed. Capability development remains the heart of the problem of development and is a supply-side issue that needs to be urgently addressed.

Capability development has two challenges: developing know-how in organizational capabilities, literally how to organize modern production at all levels but particularly within firms; and financing the period of low returns or even loss-making when an organization is going through this learning process.[30] It is widely known that developing countries fail to achieve competitiveness even when they import the appropriate machinery and have the appropriate skills because their firms and other organizations lack the organizational capability to produce efficiently. Capability development is an extension of Kenneth Arrow's "learning-by-doing" analysis, but when financing is available for economies and firms to improve their organizational capabilities, they also have to put in a high level of effort that needs to be monitored in order for them to develop the relevant organizational capabilities.[31] Otherwise, the financing fails, the firms become bankrupt, and the country has to be bailed out. The global failure to develop institutional mechanisms for financing capability development is one of the central constraints to the development of global financing arrangements that could drive enhanced development.

While technology for mature industries is relatively freely available for developing countries, they are usually unable to develop the requisite organizational capabilities to achieve competitiveness even with their comparative advantage of low wages. This situation results because their organizations and firms do not yet have the internal routines and processes to organize production well enough to achieve competitiveness.[32] Of course, this would not be true of all developing countries. Their institutional and political success in developing organizational capabilities varies widely as this broad group includes relatively successful countries like China (the outlier in this group); intermediate countries like Malaysia, Indonesia, South Africa, and India; as well as many poor countries in sub-Saharan Africa and elsewhere in which organizational capabilities are less developed.

Learning-by-doing is most fundamental in poor countries but is also necessary in many sectors, even in more advanced economies of the global South. India, for instance, has a sophisticated auto and auto-components industry but lacks a semi-conductor sector despite having a skilled pool of engineers and having attempted to develop these capabilities for many years. Learning-by-doing necessarily requires a sustained but short period of "loss financing" as organizations build up their capabilities. As with all financing arrangements, it also necessitates that investments in the learning process be monitored because monitoring goes hand-in-hand so that such financing is used effectively and not captured for alternative purposes.[33]

The current world economic order, however, possesses neither the financial instruments for financing firms in developing countries nor an institutional framework for monitoring efforts in learning appropriately even if financing were available. At a more fundamental level, policy priorities are not even directed at helping governments develop such instruments. While capital flows, especially short-term ones, are highly mobile, technological capabilities are not,[34] which is precisely the reason why economies require financing to acquire technological capabilities. This type of radical developmental thinking should be the framework for Bretton Woods 3.

Conclusion

What would a desirable global payments system look like for developing countries, and is such a system politically feasible given the power and interests of the dominant players in the world system? Available financing is either short term, through the capital market often with high rates of interest, or comes from the IMF and the Bank, which do not lend with capability development in mind. The global imbalances in payments indicate massive surpluses at the global level that do not find productive avenues of investment precisely because many of the countries with the largest surpluses lack the capabilities to use them productively. These surpluses are directed into US Treasury bonds that are destabilizing and cause asset imbalances because advanced countries cannot generate high rates of real growth given their already high levels of per capita income.

Hence, what is required is an international bank so that surplus countries can buy bonds issued by a global institution like a revamped IFI, and that institution can direct funds for capability development to poor countries where growth prospects are by definition high. Investors could potentially derive good returns, and developing countries could grow. Critically, such a change requires new thinking about the criteria for managing global financing flows and the institutional mechanisms for monitoring effort and performance in investments for capability development.

The change in voting rules in 2009 at the IMF did little to alter the rules of the game effectively. In fact, Jan Kregel[35] builds on Hyman Minsky's theory of financial fragility and describes a large part of the lending by international agencies as a "Ponzi scheme" in which over-indebted countries borrow to pay-off debts.[36] There is an obvious and critical need for strong global institutions that can penetrate developing-country economies and provide credible lending with institutional developments that can sustain effective investments in capability development. The Group of 20 (G20) has not provided the leadership required, and the Group of 77 has a nominal presence and lacks a strong consensus on the way forward. The IMF and the Bank in their current form cannot perform this function.

The discourse of "foreign expertise and local futility" against which one of the Bank's foremost economists, Albert Hirschman, railed during his stint in Colombia in the 1950s (as detailed by his biographer) still exists in a compounded manner within the IMF and the Bank.[37] Perversely, ruling coalitions in developing countries often use this aberration to their benefit to capture some of the rents from policy lending by the IFIs by following their policies on paper when they know these are unlikely to deliver any developmental benefits. The cynicism on all sides in the global aid and policy business can unleash a vicious cycle of adverse growth outcomes, growing debt burdens, and periodic write-offs. Of course, Hirschman-style experiments are too uncertain in the current context as developing countries need faster results. Hirschman argued that countries learn how to solve problems by experimenting and learning from mistakes. However, experimenting along lines that are unlikely to be enforceable in particular political settlements is liable to be wasteful and unacceptable for the IFIs providing the resources.

The political context of experimentation was not part of Hirschman's framework. Experiments have to be based on credible institutions in a country that can limit the waste from failed experiments by not attempting types of financing that cannot be policed in that political context, and by ensuring that institutions exist that can credibly impose conditions for particular types of financing that ensure high levels of effort in learning. On the one hand, this issue will be hugely contentious even before the various sides arrive at the negotiating table. Least developed countries want concessions that other developing countries will oppose, and developing countries have different sectoral and technological interests that may be conflicting. Developed economies, on the other hand, will need an assurance of returns to their investments in developing countries and the assurance that institutions exist to ensure losses are detected early and thereby limited, and that gains are declared and shared.

The challenge is to identify and agree the governance structures that could make such a global financial structure work. Solving this problem might appear implausible in light of the current global political power structure, but the creation of the Bank and the IMF undoubtedly would have been deemed impossible in the interwar years. A radical shift is the only way forward.

It is an irony of the current IMS that countries that have solved the problem of financing capability development have done so largely by using protective and interventionist mechanisms that operated outside the global financial system. These instruments have become progressively more difficult to imitate because of changes in the global trade architecture, especially through the WTO, and because most countries do not have the internal political structures that allowed a few countries to operate these financing systems. South Korea in the 1960s and 1970s and China since Deng Xiaoping, for instance, used subsidies and import protection, along with currency intervention in the case of China, to develop capabilities. Most developing countries do not have the internal political structures that would allow them to replicate such strategies.

In an increasingly open trading framework, and given the inability of most developing countries to provide indirect financing to their emerging sectors to develop competitiveness, the world requires global financial institutions that are radically different in design. A sustainable world financial system needs multilateral institutions with the appropriate institutional capabilities effectively to provide the requisite financial flows that could fill this glaring gap. History shows that the earlier attempt, the BWS, was not the best that could have been achieved. It did, however, lay the foundations for world economic growth, and there are crucial lessons that emerge from the experience. The Bretton Woods conference represented an attempt at multilateral institution building that was radical for its time. If we are to achieve a more sustainable global order for ours, it should be built on a global financial system that allows the rapid development of new productive capabilities across countries, communities, and regions that would indeed represent a dramatic break with the past.

Notes

1 See Barry Eichengreen, *Global Imbalances and the Lessons of Bretton Woods* (Cambridge National Bureau of Economic Research, 2004); Morris Goldstein and Nicholas R. Lardy, *China's Role in the Revived BWS: A Case of Mistaken Identity* (Washington, DC: Institute for International Economics, 2005); and Nouriel Roubini and Brad Sester, "Will the Bretton Woods 2 Regime Unravel Soon? The Risk of a Hard Landing in 2005–6," paper written for the Symposium on the "Revived BWS: A New Paradigm for Asian Development?" Federal Reserve Bank of San Francisco and UC Berkeley, San Francisco, February 2005.
2 Goldstein and Lardy, *China's Role in the Revived BWS*; and Roubini and Sester, "Will the Bretton Woods 2 Regime Unravel Soon?"
3 Mushtaq Husain Khan, "Technology Policies and Learning with Imperfect Governance," in *The Industrial Policy Revolution: The Role of Government Beyond Ideology*, ed. Joseph Stiglitz and Yifu Justin Lin (London: Palgrave Macmillan, 2013).
4 Benjamin J. Cohen, "Balance-of-Payments Financing: Evolution of a Regime," *International Organization* 36, no. 2 (1982): 457–78.
5 Kurt J. Schuler and Andrew Rosenberg, *The Bretton Woods Transcripts (excerpts)* (New York: Center for Financial Stability, 2013).
6 John Gerard Ruggie, "International Regimes, Transactions, and Change: Embedded Liberalism in the Postwar Economic Order," *International Organization* 36, no. 2 (1982): 379–415; and Richard Gardner, "Sterling-Dollar Diplomacy in Current Perspective," *International Affairs* 62, no. 1 (1985): 21–33.
7 Eric Heilleiner, "The International Development of Bretton Woods: North South Dialogue in the Making of Postwar Order," introductory draft chapter, forthcoming 2014.
8 Heilleiner, "The International Development of Bretton Woods."
9 Cohen, "Balance-of-Payments Financing," 457–78; Richard Cooper, *Is There a Need for Reform?* (Boston, Mass.: Federal Reserve Bank of Boston, 1984), Conference Series 28, The International Monetary System: Forty Years after Bretton Woods; Raymond F. Mikesell, *The Bretton Woods*

Debate: A Memoir (Princeton, N.J.: Princeton University Press, 1994); Louis W. Pauly, *The League of Nations and the Foreshadowing of the International Monetary Fund* (Princeton, N.J.: Princeton University Press, 1996); and Robert Skidelsky, "Keynes, Globalisation and the Bretton Woods Institutions in the Light of Changing Ideas about Markets," *World Economics* 6, no. 1 (2005): 15–30.
10 The clause said that if the IMF ran out of stocks of a country's currency, it could be declared a "scarce currency." Members could then discriminate against the country's goods in their trade policies. In 1944 the dollar was expected to become scarce, but scarcity did not happen because of the Marshall Plan.
11 Robert Triffin, *Gold and the Dollar Crisis: The Future of Convertibility* (New Haven, Conn.: Yale University Press, 1960).
12 Schuler and Rosenberg, *The Bretton Woods Transcripts (excerpts)*; and Benn Steil, *The Battle of Bretton Woods: John Maynard Keynes, Harry Dexter White, and the Making of a New World Order* (Princeton, N.J.: Princeton University Press, 2013).
13 Schuler and Rosenberg, *The Bretton Woods Transcripts.*
14 Heilleiner, "The International Development of Bretton Woods."
15 Schuler and Rosenberg, *The Bretton Woods Transcripts.*
16 S.R. Tomlinson, "Indo-British Relations in the Post-Colonial Era: The Sterling Balance Negotiations," *The Journal of Imperial and Commonwealth History* 13, no. 3 (1985): 147; Reserve Bank of India, *RBI History: Problems of Plenty*, volume II (Mumbai: Reserve Bank of India, 1998), 598.
17 Schuler and Rosenberg, *The Bretton Woods Transcripts.*
18 Reserve Bank of India, *RBI History: Problems of Plenty*, 598.
19 Schuler and Rosenberg, *The Bretton Woods Transcripts.*
20 Chintamani Deshmukh, *Course of My Life, The Centenary Edition* (Hyderabad, India: Orient Blackswan, 1996), 127, 141–45.
21 Barry Eichengreen, *Globalizing Capital: A History of the International Monetary System* (Princeton, N.J.: Princeton University Press, 2005), 5.
22 Pauly, *The League of Nations.*
23 G. John Ikenberry, "A World Economy Restored: Expert Consensus and the Anglo-American Postwar Settlement," *International Organization* 46, no. 1 (1992): 289–321.
24 Mushtaq Husain Khan, *Political Settlements and the Governance of Growth-Enhancing Institutions* (London: SOAS, 2010).
25 Douglass North, *Structure and Change in Economic History* (New York: W.W. Norton, 1981).
26 Triffin, *Gold and the Dollar Crisis.*
27 Ben Steil, *The Battle of Bretton Woods: John Maynard Keynes, Harry Dexter White, and the Making of a New World Order* (Princeton, N.J.: Princeton University Press, 2013), 5.
28 Anna J. Schwartz, "Do We Need a New Bretton Woods?" *Cato Journal* 20, no. 1 (2000): 21–25.
29 Alison Marshall, Jessica Woodroffe, and Petra Kjell, *Policies to Roll-back the State and Privatize? Poverty Reduction Strategy Papers Investigated* (Helsinki: UNU-Wider, 2001), WIDER Discussion Papers World Institute for Development Economics, No. 2001/120. See also Frances Stewart and Michael Wan, *Do PRSPs Empower Poor Countries and Disempower the*

World Bank, or Is it the Other Way Round? (Oxford: University of Oxford, 2003), Queen Elizabeth House Working Paper Series, October 2003; and Joseph Stiglitz, *A Single Economic Model Does Not Suit Whole World* (Geneva: Global Policy Forum: 2004), available at: www.globalpolicy.org/component/content/article/209-bwi-wto/42773.html.

30 Khan, "Technology Policies and Learning with Imperfect Governance."
31 Khan, "Technology Policies and Learning with Imperfect Governance."
32 Khan, "Technology Policies and Learning with Imperfect Governance."
33 Khan, "Technology Policies and Learning with Imperfect Governance."
34 Mario Cimoli, Giovanni Dosi, and Joseph E. Stiglitz, *The Political Economy of Capabilities Accumulation: The Past and Future of Policies for Industrial Development* (Pisa, Italy: Santa Anna School of Advanced Studies, 2008).
35 Jan Kregel, *External Financing for Development and International Financial Instability* (Geneva: UNCTAD, 2004).
36 According to him, there are three kinds of loan financing: hedge, speculative, and ponzi. Hedge financing is when creditors are able to pay back both principle and interest; speculative is when regular interest payments have to be made, but the future is uncertain and there is a risk of default; and ponzi is when creditors have to borrow even to pay back the interest. See Hyman Minsky, *The Financial Instability Hypothesis* (Annandale-on-Hudson, NY: Bard College, 1992).
37 Jeremy Adelman, *Worldly Philosopher: The Odyssey of Albert O. Hirschman* (Princeton, N.J.: Princeton University Press, 2013), 321.

9 Stable agricultural markets and world order

FAO and ITO, 1943–49

Ruth Jachertz

- **The nutrition approach to surplus and shortage**
- **Increased consumption, food production, and market expansion: the Hot Springs conference**
- **Postwar shortages and the FAO's plan for the World Food Board**
- **Commodity policy in the ITO**
- **The FAO's International Commodity Clearing House**
- **The end of the ITO and the future of commodity agreements**
- **Conclusion**

In May 1943, while World War II devastated Europe, a group of scientists met for two weeks in the plush surroundings of a remote Virginian resort hotel.[1] There they attended a technical and expert conference on food and agriculture as official delegations of their 44 respective home countries. For many, the travel had been dangerous, difficult, and long, but the experts were driven by a mission: to ensure lasting peace in the postwar order by increasing food production and restructuring agricultural markets. They were assured by the backing of US president Franklin Delano Roosevelt, who had initiated this gathering. This meeting in Hot Springs, Virginia, was the first in a series of conferences called by the United Nations, the term used for the Allies fighting against the Axis powers.[2] The conference on food and agriculture was followed by several others, most notably the UN Monetary and Financial Conferences in Bretton Woods, which established the International Monetary Fund and the International Bank for Reconstruction and Development, and in Dumbarton Oaks, which laid the foundation for the United Nations Organization at the UN Conference on International Organization in San Francisco.

Access to food was widely regarded as one of the key elements necessary for establishing lasting peace.[3] For the delegates in Hot Springs, it was obvious that agricultural production and agricultural trade had to be seen in conjunction. Only stable international markets provided incentives for producers while providing consumers with a reliable food supply. The Hot Springs conference, therefore, not only led to the creation of the UN Food and Agriculture Organization (FAO), but also influenced the commodity policy envisioned in the charter for the proposed International Trade Organization (ITO).

Although only a small percentage of agricultural products reached world markets, regulation was considered essential because fluctuations could have devastating effects on the overall goal of price stabilization. Foremost in the minds of all postwar planners was a fear of a repetition of the situation after World War I: a breakdown of international agricultural markets, unsellable surpluses after the end of the war-induced artificially high demand, and, after the financial crash of 1929, the ensuing Great Depression, which had hit agriculture especially hard.

Since virtually all governments wanted to maintain their domestic protection of agriculture, trade in agricultural products was never seriously considered as a free market. Instead, international commodity arrangements were supposed to create the stability necessary for an expansion of production and international trade.

This chapter sketches the "worldwide solutions" to commodity trade suggested by the FAO and ITO and outlines the reasons why they were stillborn. As important as describing the ultimate failure of the plans is to uncover the reasons why these plans were drawn up in the first place. In other words, why did smart, ambitious people with sound political instincts believe their equally ambitious plans involving worldwide cooperation stood a chance of being accepted by governments? There was a window of opportunity for this kind of worldwide plan, but it closed quickly. The last part of the chapter briefly outlines further developments in agricultural markets in the absence of an international organization.

The nutrition approach to surplus and shortage

Allied plans for the postwar world began astonishingly early. The planners were guided by their wish to avoid the mistakes after World War I.[4] The main concern for the food sector was the "specter of surplus"—a buildup of unmarketable surpluses, followed by even lower prices, the eventual breakdown of international markets, and another depression, which had affected the agricultural sector especially hard in 1929.

However, there never really had been a surplus problem, argued scientists and political activists concerned with nutrition. Surpluses only meant that commodities could not be sold in regular markets, but the demand for food in the population was apparent. Looking at nutritional needs, therefore, production before the war had been inadequate.[5] The solution was to turn nutritional needs into effective demand. The nutrition approach combined employment, health, and social justice policies; it had been championed by progressive British groups and popularized by the League of Nations, which regarded "under-consumption" as the cause of the Great Depression. To increase consumption and improve their nutritional status, people needed assured income provided by full employment and insurance benefits.

Increased consumption then would stimulate both local production and trade in foodstuffs and lead to economic growth.[6] The two key people to develop this nutrition approach within the League of Nations were former Australian prime minister Stanley Melbourne Bruce and his long-time collaborator Frank L. McDougall.[7] Bruce, then the Australian representative, gave a "rousing speech" to the League's Assembly in September 1935 on the "marriage of health and agriculture," which centered on the revival of trade between the industrialized and the agricultural countries to make it possible for immense numbers of people to get more and better food.[8] The concept was so convincing that the assembly established two bodies, a Technical Commission on Nutrition to consider food requirements, and a Mixed Committee to report on nutrition in relation to health and agriculture and on the economic aspects of the subject.[9] *The Physiological Bases of Nutrition* and *The Relation of Nutrition to Health, Agriculture and Economic Policy*, published in 1936 and 1937, respectively, became the League's most popular publications.[10]

Increased consumption, food production, and market expansion: the Hot Springs conference

According to legend it was McDougall who persuaded Roosevelt to hold an international conference on long-term problems in food and agriculture.[11] While it is doubtful that the conference rested on McDougall's initiative only, it is quite possible that he was influential in making food the topic for a first wartime international conference.[12] Roosevelt's keen political instincts led him to embrace this positive topic, which resonated well with his own slogan "freedom from want."[13] The United States invited all United Nations and those Latin American republics that had broken off diplomatic relations with the Axis powers to a technical and expert conference on food and agriculture.[14] The conference took place from 18 May to 3 June 1943 at the Homestead Resort.

Most debates in Hot Springs were informed by the League's work on the role of nutrition, but while there was widespread agreement on the tenets of the nutrition approach—"that food production must be greatly expanded, but that to produce more food is useless unless markets are created to absorb it by a widespread increase in consumer purchasing power"[15]—the sections debating the role of nutrition and those pondering appropriate trade arrangements produced quite different ideas about the meaning. The nutrition section gathered the more enthusiastic and idealistic nutrition experts, who felt that the time had come to apply their research and finally feed humanity on a nutritional standard. Section III contained views from more hardnosed economists about how best to avoid surpluses, and whether an expansion of output was really feasible. Most agreed on the usefulness of commodity agreements for market stabilization but those had to be studied further.[16] Furthermore, there was no agreement on where best to coordinate these agreements—in the proposed new international organization for food and agriculture or in a separate trade organization.

The Hot Springs conference created the UN Interim Commission on Food and Agriculture—to advise on the structure the UN Food and Agriculture Organization, which was formally inaugurated with the signing of its constitution at the Chateau Frontenac in Québec on 16 October 1945. As the first specialized agency, the FAO predated the actual United Nations Organization by eight days, since the UN Charter entered into force on 24 October 1945. In the United States, the deliberations over the FAO's establishment were anxiously watched to gauge the extent of support for the new multilateral project. Thus, the US Senate's ratification of the UN Food and Agriculture Organization's constitution on 21 July 1945 was seen as an important indicator of strong support for the United Nations system as a whole when the Charter was still under negotiation.[17]

In the preceding two years, the Interim Commission on Food and Agriculture was under the leadership of Canada's ambassador to the United States, Lester B. Pearson, who had worked on the institutional set-up and the goals of the envisioned food organization. For him, this appointment marked the beginning of his long involvement with the United Nations—later in his roles as foreign minister and prime minister. In a section written by McDougall, who was chairman of the review panel, the interim commission report stressed the familiar topic in the League of Nations that enlarging effective demand by providing employment and income would increase production while preventing the creation of surpluses. McDougall even claimed that the FAO would show that the "welfare of producers and welfare of consumers are in the final analysis identical"—the conflict between producers interested in high return and consumers interested in low prices would dissolve when seen in the "larger framework" of unfulfilled demand on the side of the consumers and the untapped production potential of farmers.[18] the FAO's first director-general, the esteemed nutritionist and fiery fighter for social policies John Boyd Orr, gathered a small staff in the temporary the FAO headquarters in Washington, DC. Their first task was to gather data on the dramatic world food situation.

Postwar shortages and the FAO's plan for the World Food Board

During the war, there had been many conflicting forecasts on food needs in the postwar period. Generally speaking, the British started to worry earlier about impeding shortages; until the latter half of 1944, the US War Food Administration was preoccupied with the danger of domestic surpluses rather than with possible food shortages in liberated areas.[19] Perception in the United States changed slowly, and only started to change substantially in the spring of 1945.[20] Secretary of Agriculture Clinton P. Anderson did not believe the more negative reports produced within his own department and failed to grasp the extent of the damage inflicted on world agricultural production. Only in early 1946 did he realize that there was no world surplus, but a massive food crisis with threats of starvation in Europe and Asia.[21]

FAO's *1946 World Food Survey*, based on data "covering 90 percent" of the world population, warned of a shortage of staple grains of grand proportion.[22] It calculated a lack of 10 million tons in wheat equivalent for cereals, which spelled hunger for large parts of the world. An alarmed Boyd Orr called for an emergency meeting on the world food situation in May 1946 in Washington, DC. In order better to allocate food supplies on a worldwide basis, the delegations formed an International Emergency Food Council (IEFC).[23] This step was almost revolutionary because earlier the United States and the United Kingdom had resisted giving Canada (a food-surplus country) a seat on the wartime Combined Food Board. That board was now dissolved into the new body with a much larger membership. The IEFC's membership was open to any country represented on one of its 16 commodity committees and was served by the FAO secretariat. Most staff were seconded from the Foreign Agriculture Service of the US Department of Agriculture. The IEFC relied on voluntary donations by member countries and then allocated these foodstuffs to the UN Relief and Rehabilitation Administration, other relief agencies, and individual countries.[24] In hindsight, this innocuous technical body marked the high point of international collaboration, because even the United States as the largest producer followed the IEFC's recommendations for its export policy.[25]

At the same conference in May 1946, delegations requested that the FAO director-general develop proposals dealing with the long-term agricultural situation. How could production, distribution, and consumption be organized to prevent both shortages and surpluses? Orr and his staff developed a plan for the World Food Board (WFB) to be operated by the FAO. A massive increase in production was technically feasible, the report argued, but this increase would only materialize if world market prices were reliable and farmers could plan and plant accordingly.[26] Stable prices would result in more trade, which in turn would provide better nutrition for consumers and more income for producers. To this end, the WFB relied on operating buffer stocks.[27] To operate the stocks, it would fix a price for each commodity and then array minimum and maximum prices within 10 to 15 percent of this initial price. When the world price rose to the high, the WFB would release its stocks onto the global market; when prices reached the minimum, it would purchase and store the surpluses. Recognizing that "underdeveloped" countries lacked capital to buy much-needed fertilizer, machinery, pesticides, and seeds, the WFB also envisaged a credit facility to provide long-term credits. In addition, it would use some of its reserves for famine relief and for concessionary sales to poor countries that could not otherwise meet their food needs.[28]

At the core of the World Food Board lay the notion that increased trade with all its attendant benefits would only materialize in regulated markets, not in a resort to a free market.

The World Food Board versus commodity policy in the ITO

The delegates at FAO's second conference in September 1946 in Copenhagen were aware that US support was crucial for the WFB. When US under secretary of agriculture Norris E. Dodd expressed his government's support for the plan, there was thus "a sigh of relief."[29] The conference agreed that "international machinery" was necessary and asked a preparatory commission to discuss Orr's proposals and other recommendations. The 18-member Preparatory Commission under the leadership of Bruce met for three months of intensive work.[30] At the first meeting, Dodd informed the delegates that Washington was reversing its position. The State Department had convinced President Harry Truman that agricultural trade should fall within the responsibility of the proposed trade organization.[31] The discussions on the ITO's charter, which contained a chapter on international commodity agreements, were in full swing. Most delegates to the FAO were members of the departments of agriculture and assumed that the FAO should receive oversight over agricultural trade. However, the delegates to the ITO preparatory committee unanimously agreed that since the ITO had the overall mandate over trade, there should be no separate responsibility over agricultural trade.[32] In the end, FAO's governing bodies had to agree, and Bruce, the head of the FAO committee discussing the world food proposals, asked the members of the ITO delegations to attend his group's meetings and to advise on the proper course.[33] In deference to the ITO's mandate, the Preparatory Committee's report did not embrace the World Food Board.[34]

The Preparatory Committee supported many of the WFB's ideas—which is not surprising considering that it had been written by Bruce with the help of McDougall. It retained the concept that an increase in consumption held the key to functioning markets. While it embraced the commodity proposals in the ITO's proposed charter in principle, it stressed that these agreements should contribute to fair prices for consumers and producers alike; avoid restrictions on production and stimulate expansion of consumption and improvement of nutrition; and encourage shifts in production to areas in which the commodities in question could be most economically produced. Furthermore, it envisaged that these agreements would include provision for famine reserves, price stabilization reserves, and sales at concessionary prices to "needy" countries.[35] In order to keep commodity trade and the general food situation under review at the highest political level, it advised the FAO to set up a council composed of political representatives, which was immediately established. Crucially, though, the report did not insist on the FAO's oversight over trade in agricultural products, and thus responsibility fell to the ITO.

Commodity policy in the ITO

Official negotiations on the proposed International Trade Organization had been initiated by the United States. At its first meeting in February 1946, the UN Economic and Social Council (ECOSOC) passed a resolution calling for a conference on trade and employment. During 1945, a multiagency staff committee in the US administration developed *Proposals for Expansion of World Trade and Employment*, which it published for "consideration by the peoples of the world."[36] After the team under assistant secretary of state William L. Clayton received feedback—not from the world, but rather from the United

Kingdom—they elaborated the draft into the *Suggested Charter for an International Trade Organization.*[37] This document became the basis for the discussions at the Preparatory Committees in London from 15 October to 26 November 1946; the drafting session at Lake Placid, New York, from 20 January to 25 February 1947; and the Preparatory Commission in Geneva from 10 April to 21 August 1947.

Much of the debate on the ITO's charter can be interpreted as an underlying conflict between proponents of free trade and those advocating for regulations adapted to individual countries' needs—such as provisions for the continuance of special trade relationships and trading blocs, the protection of infant industries, and the primacy of national employment guarantees over trade obligations. The United States was the most forceful proponent of free trade at least as perceived by other negotiators.[38] In Washington, however, this position was far from uncontested. Large parts of the US population distrusted free trade, and within both parties the issues were hotly debated; even within the administration itself, there was no consensus.

Crucially, even the US proposals for free trade did not extend to so-called primary products. The fundamentally different treatment of trade in primary products as opposed to trade in industrial goods was based on the special role accorded to agriculture everywhere. All countries had agricultural price- and income-support policies that predated the war. These measurements were further extended during the war, through price controls, rationing, production control, subsidies, and control over trade. Free trade might better be viewed as an ideology than an overall policy for the agricultural sector. The appeal of free trade only extended to those areas where it would not hurt US commercial interest. Highly industrialized countries, including most importantly the United States, could export industrial products at competitive prices and were wealthy enough to subsidize their agricultural sector at prices above the world market. Australia, as a newly industrializing country, therefore was the most vocal opponent to the US proposal.[39] For them, as for other developing countries, the protection of their infant industries was as important as gaining markets for their export commodities.

Despite these diametrically opposed positions, the 18 countries present in London and Geneva managed to arrive at a set of compromises and come up with a joint proposed charter.[40] There were no apparent fundamental conflicts on commodity policy. The delegates were united in their wish to avoid a return to the depressed years of the 1920s and 1930s and shared the feeling that they were trying to break new ground in creating "deliberate multilateral action" in a field that had seen individual agreements, but never before an integrated approach.[41] A hint at possible disagreements in the future was the question of "fair" prices for products. Newly independent India raised the question that commodity agreements should not only deal with disequilibria, but with maintaining stable prices over a longer time. The FAO observer supported this notion and reminded all discussants that 70 percent of the world's population were farmers and that thus low prices could not be the solution. In the end, the commodity chapter avoided the question about how to determine a fair price for individual products.

The comparably harmonious atmosphere of the small preparatory groups quickly evaporated when 65 countries met at the UN Trade and Employment Conference in Havana beginning on 21 November 1947. An exasperated US delegation found the Latin American countries a "most consistent and difficult source of opposition."[42] The Latin Americans had come to Havana disappointed by the results of the Chapultepec conference in spring 1945, at which Washington had proposed an Economic Charter of the Americas that did not share their positions on industrialization, income redistribution, and increased standards of living.[43] At Havana, they consistently tried to find ways to insert these positions into the draft charter.

The commodity chapter was left mainly intact, but the seemingly minor change of the phrase "prices fair to consumers and remunerative to efficient producers" into "such prices as are fair to consumers and provide a reasonable return to producers" came about after heated debates on proposals by the delegations of Ceylon, Cuba, El Salvador, Mexico, the Philippines, Uruguay, and Venezuela on prices accorded to producers.[44] At stake was the already familiar question of how a "fair" price could be determined, and the claim that not only the most efficient producers should be taken into account. During the war, the United States and Canada had become the most efficient large-scale producers, and other producers feared for their market share if only efficient if counted.

On 24 March 1948, participating states finally signed the Final Act of the Havana Conference. Chapter VI described the circumstances under which the need for commodity agreements might arise and prescribed general guidelines for their operations. Although such agreements were in principle contrary to the expansion of free and unhampered trade, primary commodities were different from other traded goods and as such could still be included in the ITO charter. Demand for agricultural products was highly inelastic and price fluctuations due to harvest failures and speculation had been violent, thus necessitating agreements to stabilize markets.[45] Intergovernmental commodity agreements might afford a breathing space when production and consumption could not be adjusted as rapidly as necessary or when a country aimed to develop secondary industries based upon domestic production of primary commodities. Furthermore, the protection of natural resources might form another reason for an agreement. Reflecting on the wartime management of scarce resources, Chapter VI also endorsed the equitable distribution of a primary commodity in short supply as sufficient reason for an agreement. In contrast to earlier agreements on single products, the ITO guidelines stipulated the inclusion of importing countries.[46]

The charter distinguished between control agreements, which would regulate and curb production or set prices, and "all other agreements." The only acceptable reasons for control agreements were unsellable surpluses and widespread unemployment related to that specific commodity. All experience with international commodity agreements (ICAs) had so far been based on controlling production and prices. For the future, though, the chapter foresaw agreements with the express purpose of increasing production and consumption. This novel feature had been mainly promoted by the United Kingdom, Australia, and India, and it became part of the charter in the Geneva meetings.[47]

The charter foresaw the ITO's main task as convening conferences at which ICAs would be negotiated. In preparation, the ITO could install study groups and it would review the ICA's operations. In the case of disputes, the ITO would act as the arbitrator.

The commodity chapter enshrined an exception to free trade—the regulation of agricultural products with potentially significant market shares—as a part of the proposed the ITO. The agreed goal was to avoid wild price fluctuations, but the question of how high prices should be was contested. Many developing countries depended on the income generated by export of their primary products. They were therefore especially interested in ICAs that achieved higher revenue and would have preferred agreements among producers only.[48] At the same time, the ITO's commodity chapter specifically included consumers. This equal focus on consumers was shared by the FAO staff, who, although supportive of developing country producers, argued for making consumers' needs the basis for increasing trade.

The FAO's International Commodity Clearing House

The Havana Charter stipulated that it would come into force if a majority of the governments that had signed the Final Act ratified it within one year. Because of the prominent role of the United States in drafting the ITO Charter, the majority of countries waited for ratification by the US Congress, where the process dragged.[49] However, in the commodity sector, action was needed. The "spectre of surplus" loomed again. At the heart was the dilemma of the dollar gap. North America was not only the most prolific producer of food, but also of industrial products. The rest of the world relied on its production capacities but did not have the dollars to pay for it. The FAO lamented the United States' growing market share in international farm trade (25 percent in 1947), which left consumers vulnerable to output variations in the United States. The solution lay in greater volume of trade distributed between more market participants and greater stimulation of production in the "underdeveloped areas." However, these were ideas for the future as well. At that moment it was essential that the United States did not curtail its production because its products were sorely needed in a world that was still recovering from war.[50]

Aside from the dollar gap, which threatened surpluses, there were ongoing negotiations on an international wheat agreement, and prewar agreements on sugar, coffee, and tin were up for renewal. Therefore, ECOSOC passed a resolution on April 1947 that "pending the establishment of the ITO," members should adopt as a general guide the commodities chapter of the Geneva draft and the report of the preparatory commission on world food proposals of the FAO. At ECOSOC's request, the UN secretary-general also appointed a small coordinating committee to foster adherence to these principles and to keep developments under review.[51]

Since this committee had no real power and the ITO was still in limbo, the FAO Council in June 1949 asked its new director-general, Norris E. Dodd, to study the problem of accumulation of surpluses in hard currency countries and existence of shortages of these commodities in soft-currency countries. Dodd was trying to salvage at least parts of Orr's plan. He commissioned a small group of experts under the leadership of University of California economist John B. Condliffe, who had been a member of the League of Nations Economics Intelligence Service.[52]

The commission came up with the plan for a redistributive scheme on a global scale. The vehicle would be the International Commodity Clearing House (ICCH). It requested contributions based on member states' gross national product to an overall operating budget of $5 billion, which it would use to purchase food surpluses in the dollar area. It would then sell these for soft currencies. The latter would in the long run be used to finance a system of buffer stocks administered by the ICCH. Furthermore, foodstuffs would be channeled to needy nations at concessionary prices. In introducing the plan, Dodd took great pains to explain that the ICCH would work through regular trading channels. However, the delegates at the FAO conference in December 1949 were so critical of the main features of the plan that all thought of creating it was abandoned. Criticism centered on the financial provisions. The scheme would have delayed the introduction of general convertibility and hindered exporting countries from earning hard currency because they had to sell their products for soft currency to the ICCH. In addition, the ICCH scheme would have distorted normal trade patterns to the detriment of other exporting and importing countries.[53]

The conference report frankly admitted that delegates had been unable to envisage any international mechanism designed to deal with commodity problems that would not be subject to the criticisms leveled at the ICCH. The FAO members noted with regret that the ITO was not yet established. Within the FAO secretariat, a Committee on Commodity Problems was created as an advisory body to study the surplus commodity situation until the ITO was established.

The end of the ITO and the future of commodity agreements

The momentum for multilateral cooperation had definitely slowed. The last of the proposed international financial and trade organizations did not have broad-based public support within the United States, and the Truman administration was afraid of jeopardizing its already difficult relationship with Congress over an organization that it considered of secondary importance. Truman thus waited until April 1949 to present the final charter to Congress. Much of the debate about the ITO centered on Articles 3(1) and 21(4b), which linked full employment and trade, an assumption that already in the early Cold War sounded socialist.[54] On 6 December Truman announced that he would no longer seek Congressional approval of the ITO Charter. By that time, major actors no longer felt a pressing need for the organization. Some of the issues that the ITO was meant to address on a multilateral basis were solved for Western Europe through the Organisation for European Economic Co-operation (OEEC) via quota restrictions on intra-European trade and the successful operation as a soft-currency bloc.[55]

There remained an unfulfilled need for a commodity organization, but the FAO secretariat was thoroughly chastened by its experiences with the WFB and the ICCH. The General Agreement on Tariffs and Trade (GATT), which had been adopted in 1947 as part of the Geneva discussions on ITO, accepted commodity agreements as general exceptions to the code of conduct. However, developing countries were left in the unsatisfactory position of not being able to use GATT as a vehicle for promoting commodity agreements.[56]

Conclusion

Many delegates gathered at Hot Springs in 1943 hoped that postwar food policy would be guided by the nutrition approach of the League of Nations. Guaranteed employment, insurance, and decent wages would lead to more income and enable an increased consumption of food and greater variety in diets. Higher demand for food would cause an expansion of production, increased trade and interdependence, and ultimately peace. It thus linked social and agricultural policies at home with international cooperation in trade. Despite or because of the ambitious scope of the project, it generated considerable support in progressive political circles who believed in scientific solutions to social problems. Progressive groups were not alone in demanding cooperation in the food sector because they were joined by producer and consumer organizations that feared another Great Depression. Moreover, there was the very real destruction of agricultural infrastructure and arable land that necessitated new thinking about how to rebuild quickly and efficiently and how to restore trade.

FAO director-General Orr's plan for a World Food Board, based directly on the nutrition approach, had a genuine chance of being accepted by governments. The massive destruction of world agriculture and the specter of worldwide hunger; a sincere belief in the possibility of keeping some of the wartime cooperation in food administration; and the fear that without a stabilization of world market prices the depression in agriculture would return combined to make it an auspicious time for an encompassing plan. However, the FAO's member states in the end did not embrace the plan, mainly because of parallel discussions on the ITO's commodity policy. The open question of whether the US Congress would ratify the ITO Charter hampered discussion of the FAO's International Commodity Clearing House and the interim commission set up by ECOSOC. The Truman administration chose not to fight the battle over the ITO with a Congress that was preoccupied with security issues and the Cold War. In addition, the impetus for cooperation decreased once the specter of starvation in Europe had been avoided and Western European economies were recovering under the Marshall Plan. The United States had been willing to forgo economic gain in order to stabilize Europe via the OEEC, but its generosity did not extend to "the rest of the world," especially those countries under Moscow's influence.

There are two main features of the plans for postwar agriculture that are as valid and elusive today as when they were drawn up. First, the focus on nutrition looked at individual nutritional status rather than effective demand to calculate the "real need" for food. Second, it focused attention on the role of international agricultural markets. Granted, neither the ITO commodity chapter nor the FAO plans were "perfect," because there could be no policy that simultaneously reconciles producers' drive for higher incomes with the consumers' wish for low prices, promotes free trade but safeguards emerging markets, and rewards the efficiency of large-scale farming but keeps small farms alive.

Certainly, an international organization would have made mistakes, but the situation that arose in the absence of such an organization was far worse. It was neither a free market nor regulated cooperation but a chaotic muddling through. There never was agreement on agricultural issues in the GATT until the Uruguay round; instead, the United States was granted a waiver on their agricultural subsidies and the European Union (EU) could install the common agricultural policy without retribution.

There is a large difference between the individual commodity agreements that were negotiated under UN auspices and the more encompassing plans of the FAO and ITO. It is, of course, impossible to tell whether the ITO would have accomplished more than its minimal function of calling study groups and conferences, which is what the UN did with the collaboration of the study groups at the FAO. The novel feature of the ITO's commodity policy—to conclude agreements with the explicit goal of raising nutrition levels—was never formalized.

Comprehensive regulation of trade in agricultural products remained elusive in the coming decades. All attempts in the various GATT rounds to create a more liberal market for agricultural products failed until the Uruguay round. Frustrated by GATT's intransience, developing countries put their hopes in the United Nations Conference on Trade and Development (UNCTAD), but UNCTAD's Integrated Programme for Commodities also was unsuccessful. Exceptions were the heavily traded products of wheat, sugar, and coffee, in which special pacts between producer and consumer countries were ratified and extended on several occasions. They harkened back to prewar agreements. Of the three, the semiprivate International Wheat Agreement, first signed in 1949, was certainly the most important product for food security. However, the 1967 extension failed as a result of separate deals among exporters that aimed to bring the supply situation under control; from that point onward, all economic provisions were suspended, which made all subsequent agreements irrelevant.[57]

The World Food Board was a broad plan, encompassing everything the FAO secretariat deemed necessary for an expansion of production: a credit facility, a food aid arm, a fertilizer bank, buffer stocks, and a board to set minimum and maximum prices. It is a testament to the spirit of cooperation that the WFB was, for a time, even seriously considered as a possibility by many the FAO members. Ironically, the parallel deliberations of the ITO—which displayed the same combination of idealism and necessity—made it plausible to set aside the WFB in favor of the ITO's commodity chapter. However, the switch to the ITO also made it possible to ignore other WFB features, which were taken over only in part by other international organizations. In 1960 member states created the International Development Association as the World Bank's soft-loan facility, and in 1963 the World Food Programme (WFP) became the UN's food aid arm. It took the food crisis of the early 1970s and the drought in the Sahel to establish the International Fund for Agricultural Development in 1976 along with a special fertilizer fund within the FAO. Despite several attempts, the FAO was unable to establish stockpiles or buffer stocks under international guidelines. In the absence of an international organization with jurisdiction over international buffer stocks, it fell to the United States, which since the early 1950s had been building up huge surpluses, to keep the world's food reserves. By the 1960s this function as the unofficial residual supplier was widely accepted and expected. In the early 1970s the US Department of Agriculture finally reached its goal of keeping supply and demand in equilibrium, which in fact upset a highly volatile international market. Quite unexpectedly, the reserve of last resort was depleted precisely when a series of crop failures between 1972 and 1974 threatened many parts of the globe with famine. The situation was aggravated by the absence of a worldwide system of food reserves and a food aid regime dependent on donors' supply situation.

The long-term problems of food and agriculture that were thoroughly discussed in the 1940s would return with regularity over many subsequent decades, with the solutions suggested during the food crises of the early 1970s and again in 2007–08 strikingly similar to those suggested to resolve the postwar food crisis: buffer stocks, distribution of scarce supplies and reliable food aid as short-term measures, an increase in agricultural production in the developing world, and a more just trading system as long-term measures.[58]

Significantly, these crises all had repercussions in rich countries—the 1970s and 2007–08 did not reach crisis proportions in the industrialized countries, but they were addressed as such precisely because the price hikes were felt there. For a short time, food policy was in the limelight because of the specter of widespread starvation, especially in Europe. The more serious problem of under-nutrition and malnutrition, which had so vexed the delegations at Hot Springs, remained a

concern mainly for experts. Thus there is a third lesson from food
policy since World War II: the many forums for discussion and consultation might mitigate some problems—such as avoiding a trade war
between the EU and the United States, or making food aid more
effective, or discussing stakeholder involvement—but they would not
succeed in designing a food distribution system that benefits those who
suffer from malnutrition and hunger.

Notes

1 Research for this chapter was supported by the Volkswagen Foundation,
and logistically and emotionally by my husband and my children. The
writing has benefited from the insightful suggestions of the collaborators
and commentators on this project, especially Katharina Rietzler, Laura
Hammond, Angus Lockyer, Leon Gordenker, John Burley, Thomas G.
Weiss, and Dan Plesch.
2 Dan Plesch, *America, Hitler and the UN* (London: Tauris, 2011).
3 Lizzie Collinghurst, *The Taste of War: World War Two and the Battle for Food* (London: Penguin Books, 2012), Chapter 19.
4 Jessica Reinisch, "Introduction: Relief in the Aftermath of War," *Journal of Contemporary History* 43, no. 3 (2008): 371–404.
5 James Vernon, *Hunger: A Modern History* (Cambridge, Mass.: Harvard University Press, 2007), 125; John Boyd Orr, *Food, Health and Income* (London: Macmillan, 1936); Martin David Dubin, "The League of Nations Health Organization," in *International Health Organizations and Movements, 1918–1939*, ed. Paul Weindling (Cambridge: Cambridge University Press, 1995), 56–80.
6 Sean Turnell, *Monetary Reformers, Amateur Idealists and Keynesian Crusaders: Australian Economists' International Advocacy 1925–1950* (unpublished PhD thesis, Macquarie University Australia, 1999), Chapter 4; Sunil Amrith and Patricia Clavin, "Feeding the World: Connecting Europe and Asia, 1930–1945," *Past and Present*, no. 8 (2013): 29–50.
7 See John B. O'Brien, "F.L. McDougall and the Origins of the FAO," *The Australian Journal of Politics and History* 46, no. 2 (2000): 164–74; Wendy Way, *A New Idea Each Morning: How Food and Agriculture Came Together in One International Organization* (Canberra: Australian National University E-Press, 2013); Patricia Clavin, *Securing the World Economy: The Reinvention of the League of Nations, 1920–1946* (Oxford: Oxford University Press, 2013), 166, sees McDougall's "importance to the development of a League agenda on positive security shine through the archival records." On Bruce, see Ina Mary Cumpston, *Lord Bruce of Melbourne* (Melbourne: Longman Cheshire, 1989); and Alfred Stirling, *Lord Bruce: The London Years* (Melbourne: Hawthorn Press, 1974).
8 Gove Hambidge, *The Story of FAO* (New York: D. Van Nostrand, 1955), citation 46; on McDougall's influence on the nutrition approach, see Way, *A New Idea*, Chapter 6.
9 F.P. Walters, *A History of the League of Nations*, vol. II (London: Oxford University Press, 1952), 749–61, citation 754.

10 *The Problem of Nutrition: Report on the Physiological Bases of Nutrition* (Geneva: League of Nations Publications, 1936); *Final Report of the Mixed Committee on Nutrition: The Relation of Nutrition to Health, Agriculture and Economic Policy* (Geneva: League of Nations Publications, 1937).

11 O'Brien, "F.L. McDougall"; Ralph W. Phillips, *FAO: Its Origins, Formation and Evolution 1945–1981* (Rome: FAO Press, 1981), chapter 2.

12 The executive secretary of the US delegation at Hot Springs recalled that everyone in the State Department was taken aback that the first international conference was to be on food rather than money or trade and placed the responsibility for the theme to Australian influence. Interview with Leroy Stinebower, 9 June 1974, available at: www.trumanlibrary.org/oralhist/stine bow.htm.

13 Clavin, *Securing the World Economy*, 295.

14 Craig Alan Wilson, "Rehearsal for a United Nations: The Hot Springs Conference," *Diplomatic History* 4, no. 3 (1980): 263–82. For a colorful report, see Lionel Charles Robbins's *Hot Springs Diary*. Robbins was a member of the British delegation and negotiated the commodities sections. The diary was sent as an official report to the War Cabinet, digital.library. lse.ac.uk/objects/lse:yak575lex.

15 Hambidge, *The Story of FAO*, 51.

16 *United Nations Conference on Food and Agriculture, Hot Springs, Virginia, May 18–June 3, 1943, Final Act and Section Reports* (Washington, DC: Government Printing Office, 1943).

17 League of Nations Chronology, 1945, available at www.indiana.edu/ ~league/1945.htm.

18 United Nations Interim Commission on Food and Agriculture, *The Work of FAO* (Washington, DC: US Government Printing Office, 1945), 3 and passim.

19 Eric Roll, *The Combined Food Board* (Palo Alto, Calif.: Stanford University Press, 1957), 180–84. Roll was the UK official on the board. Dennis A. Fitzgerald remembers that there were different scenarios in US planning, but that most assumed an early return to surpluses. Interview with Dennis A. Fitzgerald, Washington, DC, 21 June 1971, available at www.trumanlib rary.org/oralhist/fitz.htm. Fitzgerald was concerned with allocation and distribution of foodstuffs during his whole professional career, in the Combined Food Board, the International Emergency Food Council (IEFC), the Marshall Plan, and the Department of Agriculture.

20 Bela Gold, *Wartime Economic Planning in Agriculture* (Oxford: Oxford University Press, 1949), 430–45.

21 Virgil W. Dean, *An Opportunity Lost: The Truman Administration and the Farm Policy Debate* (Columbia: University of Missouri Press, 2006), 28.

22 *World Food Survey* (Washington, DC: FAO Press, 1946), 5.

23 "The Food and Agriculture Organization of the United Nations," *International Organization* 1, no. 2 (1947): 121–23. On the extent of hunger, see Tony Judt, *Postwar: A History of Europe since 1945* (New York: Penguin Books, 2005), 37–39; and Collinghurst, *Taste of War*, 467–81.

24 FAO, *Report of the Special Meeting on Urgent Food Problems, May 20–27, 1946*, (Washington, DC: FAO Press, 1946).

25 "United States policies regarding the problem of critical world shortages in food, fuel and industrial items, editorial note," FRUS 1947, vol. I, 1039–42.

26 FAO, *Proposal for a World Food Board* (Washington, DC: FAO Press, 1946); Amy L.S. Staples, *The Birth of Development: How the World Bank, Food and Agriculture Organization, and World Health Organization Changed the World, 1945–1965* (Kent, OH: Kent State University Press, 2006), 85–94; and D. John Shaw, *World Food Security: A History Since 1945* (Houndsmills, Basingstoke: Palgrave Macmillan, 2007), 15–31.

27 The Delegation on Economic Depression of the League of Nations published the Second Report on Economic Stability in the Post-War World in March 1945; see Clavin, *Securing the World Economy*, 328–40, quote on McDougall, 336. The delegation was informally gathered by Alexander Loveday, the section on buffer stocks developed by Winfield Riefler. Winfield Riefler, "A Proposal for an International Buffer-Stock Agency," *Journal of Political Economy* 54, no. 6 (1946): 538–46.

28 *Report of the FAO Preparatory Commission on World Food Proposals* (Washington, DC: FAO Press, 1947).

29 Russel Smith, "FAO: Copenhagen Story," *The New Republic*, 14 October 1946.

30 *Report of the Conference of FAO, Second Session, Copenhagen, Denmark, 2–13 September 1946*. All reports of FAO Conferences are available at: www.fao.org/unfao/govbodies/gsbhome/conference/conference-reports/en/. There were 16 original members: Australia, Belgium, Brazil, Canada, China, Cuba, Czechoslovakia, Denmark, Egypt, France, India, the Netherlands, the Philippines, Poland, the United Kingdom, and the United States. Argentina participated in all matters concerning wheat, Siam in rice discussions; the Soviet Union was invited but declined.

31 Allen J. Matusow, *Farm Politics and Farm Policy in the Truman Years* (Cambridge, Mass.: Harvard University Press, 1967), 87.

32 London Preparatory Committee to the Conference on Trade and Employment, Verbatim Report of the 7th Meeting of Committee IV, 1 November 1946, E/PC/T/C.IV/PV/7. All reports, minutes and background documentation on ITO deliberations available at www.wto.org/gatt_docs/1946_50.htm (hereafter ITO online).

33 "Message from the Food and Agriculture Organization to the forthcoming United Nations Conference on Trade and Employment," 20 November 1947, E/CONF/2/7; "Telegram S.M. Bruce to Suetens," 14 November 1946, London PrepCom, Meeting of Heads of Delegations, E/PC/T/DEL/9, ITO online.

34 *Report of the FAO Preparatory Commission on World Food Proposals.*

35 *Report of the FAO Preparatory Commission on World Food Proposals*, Chapter V.

36 *Proposals for Expansion of World Trade and Employment*, November 1945 (Washington, DC: Government Printing Office, 1945).

37 *Suggested Charter for an International Trade Organization*, Department of State, September 1946 (Washington, DC: Government Printing Office, 1946).

38 Thomas Zeiler, *Free Trade, Free World: The Advent of GATT* (Chapel Hill: University of North Carolina Press, 1999), Chapters 1–4.

39 Ann Capling, *Australia and the Global Trade System: From Havana to Seattle* (Cambridge: Cambridge University Press, 2001), 26.

40 Member countries were: Australia, Belgium-Luxembourg, Brazil, Canada, Chile, China, Cuba, Czechoslovakia, France, India, Lebanon, the Netherlands, New Zealand, Norway, South Africa, the United Kingdom, and the United States. For a full list of delegations, E/FC/T/INF/2, ITO online.
41 Debates on commodities took place in London in Committee IV, document E/PC/T/C.IV/PV/1 to 9 and in Sub-Committee on II and IV, document E/PC/T/C.II; in Geneva in Commission B, document E/PC/T/B/PV 1 and *Report of Sub-Committee on Chapter VII, 27 June 1947*, document E/PC/T/W/228. Quotation: The Netherlands Delegate at Second Meeting of Committee IV, 19 October 1946, London Prepcom, document E/PC/C.IV/PV/2, all ITO online.
42 "Draft Telegram by the United States Delegation at Habana," Secret, 14 January 1948, FRUS, 1948, I, 830–32.
43 Officially called "Inter-American Conference of War and Peace," 21 February–8 March, 1945. Barry Carr, "Chapultepec Conference," in *Encyclopedia of U.S. Military Interventions in Latin America*, vol. I, ed. Alan McPherson (Santa Barbara, Calif.: ABC-CLIO, 2013), 89–90
44 Interim Commission for the International Trade Organization, *UN Conference on Trade and Employment, Reports of Committees and Principal Sub-Committees*, Geneva, September 1948, 129 and 136.
45 United Nations Conference on Trade and Employment held at Havana, Cuba, 21 November 1947 to 24 March 1948, *Final Act and Related Documents*, see chapter VI for commodity agreements, available at: www.wto.org/english/docs_e/legal_e/havana_e.pdf.
46 US Tariff Commission, *Report on the Havana Charter for an ITO* (Washington, DC: Government Printing Office, 1947), 72.
47 Geneva PrepCom, Report of Sub-Committee on Chapter VII, 27 June 1947, E/PC/T/W/228, ITO online.
48 John Toye and Richard Toye, *The UN and Global Political Economy: Trade, Finance, and Development* (Bloomington: Indiana University Press, 2004), 38–41.
49 H. Milner, *Interests, Institutions and Information: Domestic Politics and International Relations* (Princeton, N.J.: Princeton University Press, 1997), 139–41.
50 Council of FAO, *Report of the 6th Session*, 13–24 June 1949, CL/6, Part II, World Food Situation, FAO Council reports at: www.fao.org/unfao/govbodies/gsbhome/council/council-reports/en/.
51 *Resolution of the Economic and Social Council on Establishing an interim Co-ordinating Committee for International Commodity Arrangements*, 28 March 1947, E/CONF2/C.5/16, ITO online.
52 FAO, *World Commodity Problems* (Washington, DC: FAO, September 1949); Staples, *Birth of Development*, 97–99; Shaw, *World Food Security*, 32–36; John B. Condliffe, "Expert on Monetary Policy, Obituary," *The New York Times*, 26 December 1981.
53 *Report of the Conference of FAO, Third Session*, Geneva, 25 August–11 September 1947.
54 Susan Ariel Aaronsen, *Trade and the American Dream: A Social History of Postwar Trade Policy* (Lexington: University Press of Kentucky, 1996), Chapter 7.
55 "Memorandum by the Secretary of State to the President," Secret, 20 November 1950; "Memorandum by the Secretary of State on Cabinet

Meeting," Secret, 21 November 1950; "Secretary of State to Diplomatic and Consular Posts," Confidential, 4 December 1959; all FRUS, vol. 1 (1950): 782–90.

56 Timothy Josling, Stefan Tangermann, and T.K. Warley, *Agriculture in the GATT* (Houndsmills, Basingstoke: Macmillan, 1996), 18–19.

57 Ronald W. Andersen and Christopher Gilbert, "Commodity Agreements," in *New Palgrave Dictionary of Money and Finance*, vol. 1, ed. Peter Newman *et al.* (London: Macmillan, 1992), 389–92; Christopher Gilbert, "International Commodity Agreements: Design and Performance," *World Development* 15, no. 5 (1987): 591–616; *History of the International Wheat Agreement* (London: International Wheat Council, 1991), unpublished document.

58 Derek Headey and Shenggan Fan, *Reflections on the Global Food Crisis* (Washington, DC: IFPRI, 2010), chapter 4; Christian Gerlach, "Die Welternährungskrise 1972 bis 1975," *Geschichte und Gesellschaft* 31, no. 4 (2005): 456–85.

10 Conclusion

Past as prelude, whither the United Nations?

Dan Plesch and Thomas G. Weiss

- Multilateral cooperation, realism not idealism
- The wide relevance of multilateralism
- Historical grounding for today's global governance
- Adjusting theory
- Future research
- Is good-enough global governance good enough?

The rediscovery of the lost or the suppressed is a recurring theme in literature, mythology, and of course history: the Renaissance itself is a defining example. Much of Western popular fiction since World War II—from *The Lord of the Rings* to *The Chronicles of Narnia* to *Star Wars*—is based on such rediscovery. Our conclusion to this volume is that revisiting the practice of the United Nations at war provides a startling example of the phenomenon of forgotten historical lessons.

In 1945, one London synagogue marked the end of World War II with a service celebrating "The Victory in Arms of the United Nations," and comparable labeling was also used in Christian services. Seven decades later, this packaging seems so odd as to require fact checking.[1] Yet *this* United Nations had not only defeated fascism but had also been building multilateral civilian organizations since 1942. As such, international cooperation for economic and social policies was at the core of Allied national security strategy for the postwar world; the current equivalents of "human security" or "human development" are, in contrast, found on the periphery. The legacy of Allied efforts from 1942 to 1945 merits careful scrutiny as the planet collectively continues to fumble with problem solving in the anarchical world of the twenty-first century.

Rather than try to spell out separate insights from individual chapters, we instead explore the implications arising across the essays about the wartime origins of United Nations and the future of the world organization. Six stand out with implications with a bearing on practice or scholarship: the decision to work multilaterally; the broad substantive and geographic resonance of multilateralism; the relevance of historical inquiry to understanding the contemporary globalizing world; further research for the lines of inquiry sketched here; the implications for theoretical explorations of international affairs; and the underappreciated role of intergovernmental organizations (IGOs) in global governance.

Multilateral cooperation, realism not idealism

The national decisions to work together, and to make the subsequent construction of peace a core part of the original mobilization against fascism, reflect a Realist (or at least realistic) calculation about the merits of multilateral cooperation. To revisit the title of our Introduction, cooperation was a short-term tactic designed to have a synergistic relationship with a more comprehensive, longer-run strategy. The "vision-thing" motivated peoples and kept states allied, and it was made tangible so that the postwar vision was more than propaganda and sought to get as much accomplished as possible before "business-as-usual" returned as the default option for the postwar world order.

Governments pursued traditional vital interests, to be sure, but the wartime United Nations was far more than a temporary and idealistic packaging, a liberal plaything to be tossed aside as soon as the war ended. The Cold War halted this basic multilateral commitment and spawned a far narrower cooperation confined to states within two competing ideological blocs. It is hard not to pose the counterfactual about the shape of contemporary global problem solving had wartime collaboration endured beyond the bloodshed.

None of the chapters here supports the notion that the failed League of Nations made either governments or analysts view as sensible and logical any recommendation for states to rely on might alone after the second war in two decades to end all wars. If that were indeed the case, Allied governments might have insisted on Spartan educational methods to prepare their populations for the next war; reciprocal mass atrocities perpetrated against the Germans; US corporate takeovers of potentially profitable European economies and their empires; and Moscow bombed by a Realist United States as an encore after Nagasaki. While national competition and interest, as always, remained a feature of international politics, something fundamental had changed.

That such traditional solutions and quid-pro-quos did not occur should be puzzling; to win and yet not seek revenge and plant the seeds for the next war was not an approach much in evidence in Western history save in limited form after 1815, but the post-World War II peace was not based on a Metternich-like management of nationalisms but on cooperation among rivals. As the historian Angus Lockyer observed, education in the West, for instance, had been oriented toward training men for war for 500 years.[2] What changed so that the Conference of Allied Ministers of Education during the war sought insights about healing the wounds of war rather than rubbing salt in them?

What changed was the self-destructive mindset of World War I. The 1914–18 bloodletting had such a dreadful impact on so many societies that a widespread revulsion arose against its repetition. That the next war came about driven by even more extreme racist militarism made the attacked governments and peoples more rather than less determined to do better the next time around. In 1948 the commissioners from the UN War Crimes Commission (UNWCC) wrote in their final report:

> One side, that of the Axis, asserted the absolute responsibility of belligerents, who, it was asserted, were under no obligation to respect human rights, but were entitled to trample them underfoot wherever the military forces found them inconvenient for the waging of war. This is the totalitarian war as envisaged by the Axis powers. This doctrine was repudiated as contrary not only to morality but to recognized international law which prescribed metes and bounds for the violation even in war of human rights.[3]

While historians tend to emphasize continuity and political scientists change, these essays contain evidence of both. Each chapter in this volume builds not only on learning from the 1942–45 period but also aims to salvage the viable components from the general wreckage of the League of Nations as part of the foundations for the next generation of international organizations. The efforts to pursue economic and social research, to care for refugees, to pursue human rights, and to charge international secretariats with responsibilities for action were all present in the wartime thinking and practice of the 1940s. To meet these ends, the toxic brand that the League had become was disavowed, but its staff and methods were much in demand as officials sought to avoid an endless repetition of wars of increasing self-destructiveness.

The British and other Europeans were motivated to follow almost any American lead that would—in contrast to the collapsed League of Nations without Washington's participation—involve the United States in the wider world to help in the future control of Germany,

Japan, and, for some, the Soviet Union. However, on war crimes, education, agriculture, and the global economy, European ideas joined those of Australian, Chinese, and Indian officials to shape outcomes.

As at present and for much of the period since its establishment, national policymakers—and certainly those in Washington—have seen little need to invest more political capital in the United Nations although more has been devoted to regional organizations. A fresh look at the effectiveness of and the strong investment in liberal internationalism in order to win World War II could elevate that earlier strategy as a benchmark in comparison with contemporary efforts that deride universal membership organizations.

Since World War II's end, when Franklin D. Roosevelt's multilateral strategy was set aside in favor of Harry S. Truman's visceral anticommunism, the United States has not replicated its success. In sporting terms, the "wins" in the 1991 Gulf War and in the Balkans can be set against the "tie" in Korea, and the major losses in Vietnam, Iraq, and Afghanistan. Who or what led to the collapse of communism and whether the Cold War itself and its duration were necessary is still being discussed by the umpires. The impact of Roosevelt's progressive era strategy, while hotly derided by self-styled Realists, looks remarkable in retrospect.

The wide relevance of multilateralism

Both the substance of wartime efforts and their geographical reach go far beyond the simple morality tale of a military triumph, usually told as an American or Anglo-American story that has arguably become the defining experience of the contemporary world order. Yet the multilateral values of the time as captured in this volume's essays were quickly set aside and, indeed, forgotten in order to emphasize national contributions. As state leaders and publics alike contemplate the problems of the twenty-first century, the striking 1942–45 investments of political, human, and financial capital in projects and programs that recognized the overlap between global and national interests should be revisited. They provide inspiration, if not templates, for contemporary practice.

Moreover, additional lessons arise from the resonance of such an approach worldwide, among states and non-states alike. Contributors to this volume, like a growing number of historians everywhere, share a wider perspective and accompanying conviction: the history of the UN's wartime origins, like the history of any epoch, cannot be understood merely in terms of separate national or even regional histories but should encompass the global context of that moment. As a result, the customary tale of the victory over the Axis powers in World War II being told as an Anglo-American story—with the substantial addition of the Soviet Union's contributions on the Eastern front and an occasional mention of China—should be modified.

As the deliberations took place before the rapid decolonization that followed the war—only 50 states participated in the San Francisco Conference on International Organization whereas today's UN membership numbers 193—it is tempting to simplify the tale. Here, however, the details of Imperial India's and China's contributions to early efforts to pursue war criminals and determine the postwar direction of assistance to forcibly displaced persons and of trade and finance, for instance, are pertinent. Clearly more powerful countries, and especially the United States, had more say during such deliberations, but other voices from countries in what is now called the "global South" were actually present on stage and not merely in the wings, including not only 19 states from Latin America that had long been independent but also others whose independence was more recent: three from Africa (Ethiopia, Liberia, and South Africa); three from Asia (China, the Philippines, and Imperial India); and seven from the Middle East (Egypt, Iran, Iraq, Lebanon, Saudi Arabia, Syria, and Turkey). By the 1970s, of course, decolonization had proceeded apace and two-thirds of UN members would be erstwhile colonies, but the wartime and immediate postwar United Nations was already far more than a Western history even a generation before decolonization was completed. Indeed, rapid decolonization is hard to imagine in the form and with the speed that it took place without these earlier developments.

Twenty-first-century leadership discourse in China and India and elsewhere among emerging powers finds it convenient to accept the Anglo-American mythology—if only as a justification for distancing themselves from the "old order" and the 1945 institutions. A clear appreciation of their own liberation efforts in the context of the wartime deliberations would provide the basis for a new internationalist—dare we say, even a "post-national"—approach to global affairs more suited to contemporary needs and problem solving.

Non-state actors of all stripes sought to shape the postwar institutions—independent commissions studying the lessons of the past for future application, nongovernmental organizations (NGOs) delivering aid or lobbying, and other civil society actors, including the media and business, were involved in the fray. We are hardly the first to remark that the world is more interconnected and interdependent than it used to be. However, the wartime experience already suggested the increased ease of establishing international entities and coalitions of all stripes, and in multiplying their interactions and impact. This reality represented an intensification of the variable geometry of what is now called "transnational relations" or "global governance" before the term was coined in the 1990s, although analysts certainly see evidence earlier.[4] Over the past century, there has been a marked increase in the number and the scope of actors on the world stage, and their burgeoning numbers have been concentrated in non-state actors—specifically in international NGOs and transnational corporations (TNCs).

In doing so, states and non-state actors have cobbled together frameworks for cooperation and actual responses that have produced more order, stability, predictability, and respect for human rights than might have been expected. In short, they have contributed to improving global governance, which goes far beyond a formal system of coordination by state-based entities to embrace an evolving system of multi-sector partnerships. While states are the starting point for analyses of world politics, they are no longer alone in the limelight on the globe's stage, and this situation was already in evidence during and immediately after World War II. The growth of non-state actors has meant more diversity in potential players and partners. The proliferation of actors has continued and is contributing concretely to the shape of contemporary global problem solving.

In short, even in the ultimate world conflagration between states, the state-centric model of traditional international relations failed to capture accurately the international dynamics at play. And more than Western values and notions were on the drawing board and ultimately in the United Nations Charter.

Historical grounding for today's global governance

Going back to the World War II origins of the United Nations is enough to make most social scientists' eyes glaze over—fortunately not those of the contributors to this volume.[5] In addition to the blinkered focus on the present that we lament in the Introduction, another obstacle to better understanding is that mainstream international relations has shifted away from the study of intergovernmental organization and law, toward "global governance."[6] The term itself was born from a marriage between academic theory and practical policy in the 1990s and became entwined with that other meta-phenomenon of the last two decades, globalization. James Rosenau and Ernst Czempiel's theoretical *Governance without Government* was published in 1992,[7] just about the same time that the Swedish government launched the policy-oriented Commission on Global Governance under the chairmanship of Sonny Ramphal and Ingmar Carlsson. Both set in motion interest in global governance. The 1995 publication of the commission's report, *Our Global Neighbourhood*,[8] coincided with the first issue of the Academic Council on the United Nations system's journal *Global Governance*. This quarterly sought to return to the global problem-solving origins of the leading journal in the field, which seemed to have lost its way. "From the late 1960s, the idea of international organization fell into disuse," Timothy Sinclair reminds us. "*International Organization*, the journal which carried this name founded in the 1940s, increasingly drew back from matters of international policy and instead became a vehicle for the development of rigorous academic theorizing."[9]

Employing the term did not, however, eliminate the preoccupations that had motivated previous generations of international relations and international organization scholars because global governance still sought to explore collective efforts to identify, understand, and address worldwide problems and processes that went beyond the capacities of individual states. It reflected a capacity of the international system at any moment in time to provide government-like services in the absence of world government. Global governance encompassed cooperative problem-solving arrangements that were visible but informal (e.g., practices or guidelines) or were temporary formations (e.g., coalitions of the willing). Such arrangements could also be more formal, taking the shape of hard rules (laws and treaties) or else institutions with administrative structures and established practices to manage collective affairs by a variety of actors—including state authorities, intergovernmental organizations, nongovernmental organizations, private sector entities, and other civil society actors.

Perhaps most importantly, the United Nations has been and continues to be an important player in filling some global governance gaps.[10] In fact, the essays in this collection suggest the extent to which the wartime United Nations also played this role *before* the United Nations Organization was born in San Francisco.

It is commonplace to declare borders irrelevant for many of the most intractable contemporary problems, ranging from climate change, migration, and pandemics to terrorism, financial instability, and proliferation of weapons of mass destruction; and that addressing them successfully requires actions that are not unilateral, bilateral, or even multilateral but rather global. Everything is globalized—that is, everything except politics. The policy authority and resources necessary for tackling such problems remain vested in individual states rather than collectively in universal institutions. The classic collective action problem is how to organize common solutions to common problems and spread costs fairly. The fundamental disconnect between the nature of a growing number of worldwide challenges and the current inadequate structures for international problem solving and decision making goes a long way toward explaining the fitful, tactical, and short-term local responses to thorny issues that require sustained, strategic, and longer-run global perspectives and action. Once again, however, a closer scrutiny of 1942–45 demonstrates that more ambitious and cosmopolitan visions can sometimes dominate the more customarily navel-gazing views of governments and their constituents.

Can a more comprehensive framework of global governance help us to attack that basic disjuncture? Contemporary global governance is a halfway house between the international anarchy underlying Realist analysis and a world state. The current generation of IGOs undoubtedly helps lessen some transaction costs and also helps overcome some structural obstacles to cooperation as should be clear to anyone examining international responses to the 2004 tsunami or ongoing humanitarian crises in Libya or the Democratic Republic of the Congo for which we see a constellation of helping hands—soldiers from a variety of countries, UN organizations, large and small NGOs, and even Walmart.

Moreover, while global governance certainly is not the continuation of traditional power politics, it also is not the expression of an evolutionary process necessarily leading to the formation of structures capable of addressing contemporary or future global threats. Nor is it simply bound up with governing the economy over the *longue durée*. Moreover, to speak of "governance" and not "government" is to discuss the product and not the producer. Agency and accountability are absent. In the domestic context governance adds to government, implying shared purpose and goal orientation in addition to formal authority and police or enforcement powers. For the globe, governance is essentially the whole story, what Scott Barrett describes aptly as "organized volunteerism"[11] with the United Nations at its pinnacle.

The plea by many historians to learn lessons from the past to apply to today's and tomorrow's problems resonates loudly, at least for the contributors to this volume and readers who have followed the argument thus far.[12] E.H. Carr commented that history is an "unending dialogue between the past and the present."[13] Yet the ahistorical quality of too much social science and international relations, in particular, is striking. One explanation is the value placed on parsimony, putting a premium on the simplest of theoretical pictures and causal mechanisms. As such, history complicates matters, but it also makes some fundamentals clearer.[14] Self-doubt and reflection flow naturally from historical analysis in a way that they do not from abstract theoretical models.

There is, though, a powerful overriding consideration to which a longer-term perspective leads us. Realists observe that there is no world state—no global Leviathan—and from that conclude smugly that there is only anarchy and self-help, thereby dismissing liberal institutions as a failed dream—and a "pipe dream" at that. The realities of the wartime United Nations and its legacy of institutions lead to a very different conclusion: the fear of conquest and annihilation can drive states into cooperation and institution building. Thus nuclear war and the destructive capacity of industrialized society has created a virtual Leviathan.[15]

Historians may be uncomfortable with the notion of "future-oriented history," but looking back to 1942–45 would have less value-added were it not applied to understanding tomorrow as well. With apologies to card-carrying members of the fan club for history as history, there is a considerable future-oriented value in examining wartime history and in applying lessons to contemporary and future global governance—in asking a set of questions that enable us to work out how the world is, was, and could be governed; in exploring how changes in grand and not-so-grand patterns of governance occurred, are occurring, and *ought* to occur.

We return to the starting point for this volume, namely that the dominance of military and national interest perspectives has meant that the non-military tactics and strategy of 1942–45 are underexplored and underexploited territory. They contain lessons that force a reexamination of familiar ideas and assumptions—and shibboleths—worldwide.

Adjusting theory

We have noted the retreat into abstract theory from the study of international organization by the journal of that name. This development points to wider issues to be considered by theorists—be they Realists, liberal institutionalists, constructivists, or critical in their outlooks.

The liberal idea of building international institutions as a Realist necessity constitutes the main finding from the chapters in this volume. The nuclear age and climate change reinforce the strength of this argument. It is not new to us and is obvious to many people although they do not customarily swim in the mainstream of governmental policy and decision making.

Among the shining intellects of the last century, in parallel with Albert Einstein and Bertrand Russell in their founding statement of the

Pugwash movement, one renowned scholar jumps to mind. "The rational relationship that existed from the beginning of history to 1945 between force as a means and the ends of foreign policy does not apply to nuclear weapons," Hans Morgenthau wrote. "But we continue in large measure to think and act as though 1945 did not mark one of the great watersheds of history where a new age began, as distinct from the age that preceded it as the modern age has been from the Middle Ages or the Middle Ages have been from Antiquity."[16]

"Realists" customarily elevate the early Morgenthau to the Pantheon of founding savants of hard-headed worldviews while ignoring the late Morgenthau.[17] This selective approach makes no more sense than for the clergy of the Catholic Church to use Galileo in defense of the idea that the Sun revolves around the Earth on the basis of what he may have said before he picked up his telescope.

The rediscovery of the wartime United Nations contradicts the conventional wisdom that liberalism was abandoned in the face of the Nazis. Evidence of the wartime United Nations reinforces the policy preferences of liberal institutionalists, albeit under the banner of Thomas Hobbes rather than Immanuel Kant. The historiographical question for theorists is why the wartime UN has not figured centrally, if at all, in their analyses. For those who examine primary sources, it is very much present in the pages of the *Foreign Relations of the United States*, of the mainstream international relations journals of the 1940s, and of newspapers, minutes of town meetings, and university agendas of the day. Indeed, there is something of value in the record of the wartime United Nations for other theoretical orientations as well. For constructivists, for instance, the redefinition of interests in wider multilateral terms was brief but real. For those of a postmodern persuasion, perhaps they should note the need to avoid replicating some of the worst aspects of modernity by being blind to the richness of the past? For those with other critical theoretical perspectives, it may be distasteful to find so much that is positive for working people in the policies of the US government.

Future research

The lack of research into the formative years of today's United Nations—beginning with the signing by 26 governments of the Declaration by United Nations on 1 January 1942 rather than with San Francisco in April 1945—is puzzling indeed. In particular, the archives in the myriad organizations of the UN system and of many governments, with the notable exceptions of those of the United States and the United Kingdom, are often in disarray or even nonexistent. They nonetheless represent treasure troves for serious students of history and politics.

For those card-carrying members of a particular theoretical branch in the field of contemporary international relations, there is much to bring to the fore. The integrated use of different forms of power rather than the sharp dualism of hard versus soft power stands out, as do the examples of twin-track diplomacy and the operation of international coalitions of state and non-state actors. More in-depth digging is required to understand the dynamics not just of such successful contemporary campaigns as those to ban land mines and establish the International Criminal Court but also to those analyzed in this volume that helped create and shape the global institutions of the 1940s.

The role of pre-independence India emerges in several chapters, which reflects the strengths and backgrounds of particular contributors. Clearly, many other developing countries from Latin America as well as a handful of African, Asian, and Middle Eastern ones were active during World War II gatherings, and their precise impact on the shape of postwar intergovernmental organizations merits far greater study than has been the case to date.

The study of the development of the Arab League in Cairo in March 1945 as an initiative to get ahead of any top-down settlement along the lines of Versailles after World War I is a case in point. Revisiting the Arab League as part of the infrastructure resulting from the aftermath of World War II would be inconvenient for scholars of almost all persuasions, who view the world order created in the 1940s as made only in London and Washington.[18]

While the UN system represents what is commonly associated with Western liberal values, the voices of what would eventually be called "underdeveloped" then "developing" then "Third World" and now "global South" countries were registered. They had agency and influenced outcomes. The acceleration of decolonization that Washington and Moscow pushed against the expressed wishes of London and Paris, in particular, was strikingly in evidence and strengthened by the presence of other former colonial possessions. Brian Urquhart—who worked for Gladwyn Jebb in the UK delegation on preparations for San Francisco and was one of the first recruits for the world organization in 1946—recalled that the colonial powers had imagined 50–75 years for the decolonization process with individual colonies being graduated as UN "trustees." However, that timetable changed very quickly indeed: "The avalanche started with the Indian subcontinent in 1947. And once that happened, and with people like Ralph Bunche really pushing, by the mid-1950s it was clear that this was going to be a very rapid process."[19]

Each of the chapters begins to assemble a possible mosaic that requires considerable additional research, both directly into history and then into contemporary policy applications. For example, a study begs to be written comparing the vision of the State Department planners and advisers starting around 1940 with those of recent years—of Sumner Wells and Eleanor Roosevelt, for example, with Samantha Power, Richard N. Haas, Anne-Marie Slaughter, and Ivo H. Daalder or of John Bolton. Or the public archives of the UN Information Organization offer a unique collection of the statements about military and political priorities that the Allies judged essential to publicize in the throes of war—whether a student is interested in what Australia decided to put at the top of its agenda, or to trace the public statements on unconditional surrender.

Our authors have their own research agendas, and we would do them a disservice if we tried to summarize their thoughts about the shape of future research. In our own contributions to the volume, about the UN Relief and Rehabilitation Administration (UNRRA) and the UN War Crimes Commission, we can say that work has barely begun. There is still no in-depth digging underway, for instance, on the realities of democratically run refugee camps and the implications for post-conflict and democracy building today. The 2,000 or more records for the trials conducted under UNWCC auspices in a score of jurisdictions should be assembled in a unified and digitized collection, but the search has barely begun to assemble all those primary documents.

The historiography of international relations—the history of that history—and more particularly of the wartime United Nations as it was set aside by the 1950s is a task that we will not attempt here. However, it is worth puzzling over the following question: why was spending time and resources to think about a better multilateral future not seen as a distraction for governments even at a time when a Nazi and imperial Japanese victory was possible? Such breathtaking confidence and practical vision is obviously in short supply today.

Is good-enough global governance good enough?

All manner of transboundary problems plague a planet composed of sovereign states that recognize no overriding authority save, occasionally, the unity of the Security Council. Three decades ago a celebrated academic title argued for "bringing the state back in."[20] Of course, states had never left, except in a few imaginations. Anne-Marie

Slaughter stimulated an analytical trend with her 2004 book *A New World Order*.[21] It viewed networks of various types—governmental, intergovernmental, and nongovernmental—rather than physical organizations as the key problem-solving formula. More recently, such analysts as Dan Drezner and Stewart Patrick resign themselves to living with the sum of these alternative arrangements and dismiss the universal-membership United Nations as hopeless and hapless. All that we can pursue, apparently, is a multilateral sprawl—in other words, what currently constitutes "good-enough global governance."[22]

Alas, that is not and will not be adequate without a revitalized United Nations as an integral component of a future world order.[23] We are kidding ourselves to be infatuated with various types of mini-lateralisms, or what the *Human Development Report 2013* calls "coherent pluralism."[24]

Those thinking about a future world order in the midst of the last truly global conflagration, beginning with the 1 January 1942 signing of the Declaration by United Nations, were persuaded of the critical importance of multilateral approaches not only to fight fascism *but also* respond to future threats to international peace and security as well as foster postwar economic and social stability. To fast forward, the value of a functioning Security Council was demonstrated in legitimizing and authorizing action to halt Colonel Muammar el-Gaddhafi's murderous designs on Benghazi in March 2011. The reverse could be said about Syria where the costs of finger pointing among the permanent five members were evident. However, even here, when the politics were right and the need arose for a face-saving way to dispose of Bashir al-Assad's chemical weapons, the universal UN was called upon to authorize and work the Organization for the Prohibition of Chemical Weapons. When governments decide to make use of intergovernmental organizations, they work. UNRRA, we should recall, was an important humanitarian *and* strategic weapon until the Cold War made it imperative to pursue narrower channels to assist war victims.

Readers should revisit the wartime convictions of the UN's founding fathers (and a few mothers) in order to keep in mind that contemporary global governance is a second- or third-best surrogate for authority and robust multilateralism. However useful in explaining fledgling international collaboration, it lacks prescriptive power. If global problems require global solutions, we also require strengthened IGOs, especially those of the UN system.

It is worth reflecting upon two puzzling features that distinguish current from earlier thinking, especially the passionate commitment during the 1942–45 period to explore collective responses to collective problems. For both puzzles, the insights from wartime multilateralism as the most realistic approach to a recognized global threat are striking, especially because the numbers of threats to world order—from proliferation and finance, from climate to pandemics—either in isolation or in combination certainly qualify as requiring a wartime-like mobilization.

The first is the dramatically different perspective of today's international relations specialists. Their predecessors interpreted advances in international organization and law not simply as tactical moves that under the circumstances were more effective than unilateral efforts and the law of the jungle; they also observed the march of history and foresaw a growing web of IGOs and public international law as steps in a stumbling yet inexorable (and unfinished) journey toward more authoritative arrangements for the world.

The late Harold Jacobson observed that the march was woven into the very tapestries on the walls of the *Palais des Nations* in Geneva— now the UN's European Office but once the headquarters of the League of Nations. They "picture the process of humanity combining into ever larger and more stable units for the purpose of governance— first the family, then the tribe, then the city-state, and then the nation— a process which presumably would eventually culminate in the entire world being combined in one political unit."[25] The post-Enlightenment period was fruitful in blending science and thinking about how to link individuals in ever-expanding communities. "As man advances in civilization, and small tribes are united into larger communities," was how Charles Darwin put it, "there is only an artificial barrier to prevent his sympathies extending to the men of all nations and races."[26]

Paradoxically then, during much of the twentieth century when states could actually address or attenuate pressing problems, the idea of overarching authority and even world government remained on the fringes of acceptable thinking. In the current century, when states visibly cannot tackle an ever-growing number of life-threatening menaces, such authority is unimaginable, and world government is so beyond the pale that proponents are liable to be placed in the academic equivalent of an asylum. In fact, many observers look askance at and even deride the idea of more muscular intergovernmental organizations of precisely the kind that were on all governmental drawing boards—for education, finance, trade, agriculture, among others—from 1942 to 1945.

The second puzzling feature is that earlier conceptual efforts emphasized the state while grudgingly admitting the capabilities of other actors, in particular IGOs. Now that both civil society and market-oriented groups have become prominent (vis-à-vis states) in international society, the United Nations and other IGOs seemingly are old-fashioned. Although the recognition of the potential and actual contributions by non-state actors is helpful, it should result in something less immodest and unrealistic than a standing ovation. Burgeoning numbers of NGOs and TNCs have resources and energy, to be sure, but why are more robust IGOs an afterthought, if even a thought at all? How can this be the case in a world so obviously lacking institutional machinery to address the inherent problems of globalization, to provide global public goods, and to address serious security challenges? How could such mechanisms have been front-and-center in planning from 1942 to 1945 but unthinkable now?

We should be clear. Local and national jurisdictions remain crucial for local and national problem solving. Subsidiarity dictates using the lowest level of problem solving that works. As Hedley Bull and other students of the English School of international relations have long reminded us,[27] there is more order, stability, and predictability in international politics than the idea of an "anarchical" international system might lead us to believe. Yet self-satisfaction is hardly appropriate given the number and magnitude of global problems requiring global solutions. The current generation of universal-membership IGOs is so anemic and atomized that we need to do more than throw up our collective hands and hope for the best from the hordes of norm entrepreneurs, activists crossing borders, epistemic communities, profit-seeking corporations, and transnational social networks.

Non-state actors can make and have made essential contributions to global problem solving. Not to put too fine a point on it, however, they can do little to manage geopolitical competition safely or control the spread of advanced weapons—let alone eliminate poverty, fix climate change, ensure macroeconomic stability, agree on international standards, or halt mass atrocities. In fact, polycentric approaches can exacerbate fragmentation and distract because decentralized institutional innovations often give the impression of a movement toward a solution when none is at hand.

The downside to date of thinking about good-enough global governance—and again the contrast with the wartime United Nations is instructive—is enthusiasm for what amounts to a "Global Tea Party" while downplaying the actual consequences of ad hoc and inadequate rather than systematic and global multilateral responses. While the private can complement the public sector, it simply cannot do everything better than the public sector, which includes public intergovernmental organizations. Mini-lateralism is helpful in many ways, and there certainly are many potential partners in today's variable architecture of global governance, but their limitations should be obvious as well. Without more robust IGOs, especially universal ones like those launched as a result of World War II, and elements of supranational regulatory power, states and their citizens will not reap the benefits of trade and globalization, discover nonviolent ways to meet security challenges, or address environmental degradation.

No one really knows what the future holds, of course. Without a long-term vision, however, we are obliged to accept the current contours of our unacceptable world order, including the meager organizations that constitute the contemporary UN system. In fact, they are limping along with the same weaknesses that characterized their actual establishment after World War II—although not their possible dimensions considered by planners during the war. Indeed, we require a three-pronged strategy in the decades ahead: the continued evolution and expansion of the formidable amount of practical global governance that already exists; the harnessing of political and economic possibilities opened by the communications revolution that began late in the last century; *and* the recommitment by states to a fundamental revamping and strengthening of the United Nations.

That strategy grows from all the chapters in this volume and flows from the dominant approaches among World War II's Allies. International order has been built and rebuilt on numerous occasions, and yesterday's institutions all too often are ill-equipped to tackle today's problems. We thus return to a question that troubled us, and we hope readers, in the Introduction and one that implicitly underlies this argument: Will the next generation of multilateral organizations arise as a result of unnecessary and unspeakable tragedies—as the United Nations did from fighting fascism and the ruins of World War II? Or could such institutions result from the more deliberate construction of more adequate institutions to address felt needs that clearly do not respect borders?

Contemplating the former option is not soothing even if history informs us that such tragedies are the customary currency for global institutional reforms. Working on such books as this one reflects a guardedly optimistic—although we hope not misplaced utopian—working hypothesis: a human capacity exists for learning and adapting; it is unnecessary to await suffering on a scale that could well dwarf that of World War II.

The need for intergovernmental organizations with teeth is too often short-changed in thinking about global problem solving. Perhaps they have always been too few in number and arrived too late on the scene and with too little state backing. However, in the second decade of the twenty-first century, addressing collective action problems requires, at a minimum, rebuilding or creating more robust IGOs—most clearly in the UN system but at the regional level as well—with wider scope, more resources, and additional democratic authority.[28]

We ignore at our peril a clear message: good-enough global governance is not good enough. Governments still have the prevention of industrialized disaster—whether military or environmental or financial—as their core objective. However, in 1942–45 as now, there were those who did not see the need for urgent action or, worse, sought to preserve their narrow interests at the expense of the nation and the larger international community of states. Then as now, success was hardly guaranteed and victory was a close call. The odds are unknowable, but at least we should reclaim the wartime generation's legacy rather than the militaristic version that predominates foreign policy decision making—across the North and the global South.

The last words belong to Franklin Roosevelt. A few weeks before D-Day with the outcome of the war still in the balance, he sent an address to the delegates gathered in Philadelphia for a session to reaffirm the traditional objectives of the International Labour Organization (ILO) that had been founded in 1919 after World War I:

> I am thinking about Africa. And I am thinking about certain parts of the Near East, the west coast of Africa, the north coast of Africa, and then the eastern end of the Mediterranean. You know where I went. And it is perfectly true that poverty anywhere constitutes a danger to prosperity everywhere.
>
> . . .
>
> I think of a little colony, a little piece of the earth's surface, Gambia, where I happened to have landed from Brazil. Nice, peaceful people, and as the saying goes, poor as church mice. Why mice should be singled out, I don't know. But Gambia is very, very poor.
>
> . . .
>
> Well, when I was there, I wasn't thinking in terms of who should do it, but if they had a little less poverty, that would bring prosperity to a lot more people outside of Gambia. They are kept down because of exploitation. I think that is going to be a new word in the next meeting of the I.L.O., something that I have had in the back of my head a long time, something that says something against exploitation of the poor by the rich—by Governments, as well as individuals.[29]

A month earlier, Roosevelt had sent a message at the conference's opening that retains a haunting contemporary resonance: "We know that the conditions of a lasting peace can be secured only through soundly-organized economic institutions, fortified by humane labor standards, regular employment and adequate income for all the people."[30]

Our theme of past as possible prelude suggests that such insights and visions for the postwar order from 1943 to 1945 remain valid for many twenty-first-century challenges. The question is whether that history can repeat itself.

Notes

1 "Liberal Jewish Synagogue London, Service of Thanksgiving for the Final Victory of the United Nations in the World War of 1939–45 and for the Ensuing Peace, August 19th, 1945," available in the British Library, London.
2 Comments made at the workshop on "Wartime History and the Future United Nations," SOAS, University of London, 16 May 2014.
3 UN War Crimes Commission, *Information Concerning Human Rights Arising from Trials of War Criminals*, document E/CN.4/W/19, 15 May 1948, available at: www.unwcc.org/wp-content/uploads/2013/04/UNWCCUN-HRs-Report.pdf.
4 See, for example, Craig N. Murphy, *International Organization and Industrial Change: Global Governance since 1850* (Cambridge: Polity Press, 1994). For speculation about the pay-offs from using the lenses for other periods, see Thomas G. Weiss and Rorden Wilkinson, "Global Governance to the Rescue: Saving International Relations?" *Global Governance* 20, no. 1 (2014): 19–36.
5 See Akira Iriye, ed., *Global Interdependence: The World after 1945* (Cambridge, Mass.: Harvard University Press, 2014).
6 Thomas G. Weiss, *Global Governance: Why? What? Whither?* (Cambridge: Polity Press, 2013); and Thomas G. Weiss and Rorden Wilkinson, eds., *International Organization and Global Governance* (London: Routledge, 2014).
7 James N. Rosenau and Ernst Czempiel, eds., *Governance without Government: Order and Change in World Politics* (Cambridge: Cambridge University Press, 1992).
8 Commission on Global Governance, *Our Global Neighbourhood* (Oxford: Oxford University Press, 1995).
9 Timothy J. Sinclair, *Global Governance* (Cambridge: Polity Press, 2012), 16.
10 Thomas G. Weiss and Ramesh Thakur, *Global Governance and the UN: An Unfinished Journey* (Bloomington: Indiana University Press, 2010).
11 Scott Barrett, *Why Cooperate? The Incentive to Supply Global Public Goods* (Oxford: Oxford University Press, 2007), 19.
12 Margaret Macmillan, *The Uses and Abuses of History* (New York: Random House, 2009).
13 E.H. Carr, *What is History?* (London: Pelican, 1961), 62.
14 Andrew J. Williams, Amelia Hadfield, and Simon J. Rofe, *International History and International Relations* (London: Routledge, 2012).

15 This argument draws on Dan Plesch, "Introducing the Concept of a Weapons of Mass Destruction Free Zone," *International Relations* 22, no. 3 (2008): 323–29.
16 Hans Morgenthau, *A New Foreign Policy for the United States* (Washington, DC: Council on Foreign Relations, 1969), 208; see Daniel Deudney, "Hegemony, Nuclear Weapons, and Liberal Hegemony," in *Power, Order, and Change in World Politics*, ed. G. John Ikenberry (Cambridge: Cambridge University Press, 2014), 195–232; and Dan Plesch, "Nuclear Disarmament and International Relations: A Failure of a Discipline," Proceedings of the British International Studies Association Nuclear Orders Working Group, Leicester, England, September 2013, available at: bisaglobalnuclearorder.files.wordpress.com/2014/03/leicester-2013-conference-proceedings.pdf.
17 John Mearsheimer, "The False Promise of International Institutions," *International Security* 19, no. 3 (1994/95): 5–49.
18 Stefanie K. Wichhart, "Selling Democracy during the Second British Occupation of Iraq, 1941–45," *Journal of Contemporary History* 48, no. 3 (2013): 509–36.
19 Thomas G. Weiss, Tatiana Carayannis, Louis Emmerij, and Richard Jolly, *UN Voices: The Struggle for Development and Social Justice* (Bloomington: Indiana University Press, 2005), 171.
20 Peter B. Evans, Dietrich Rueschemeyer, and Theda Skocpol, eds., *Bringing the State Back In* (Cambridge, Mass.: Cambridge University Press, 1985).
21 Anne-Marie Slaughter, *A New World Order* (Princeton, N.J.: Princeton University Press, 2004).
22 Daniel W. Drezner, "'Good Enough' Global Governance and International Finance," *Foreign Policy Blogs*, 30 January 2013, available at: drezner.foreignpolicy.com/posts/2013/01/30/good_enough_global_governance_and_international_finance; and Stewart Patrick, "The Unruled World: The Case for Good Enough Global Governance," *Foreign Affairs* (January/February 2014), available at: www.foreignaffairs.com/articles/140343/stewart-patrick/the-unruled-world.
23 This section builds on Thomas G. Weiss, *Governing the World? Addressing "Problems without Passports"* (Boulder, Colo.: Paradigm Publishers, 2014).
24 UNDP, *Human Development Report 2013: The Rise of the South: Human Progress in a Diverse World* (New York: UNDP, 2013), 112.
25 Harold K. Jacobson, *Networks of Interdependence: International Organizations and the Global Political System*, 2nd edn (New York: Knopf, 1984), 84.
26 Charles Darwin, *The Descent of Man and Selection in Relation to Sex* (New York: Appleton and Co., 1897), 122.
27 Hedley Bull, *The Anarchical Society: A Study of Order in World Politics* (New York: Columbia University Press, 1977).
28 For the direct election of national representatives to the UN and other IGOs, see Dan Plesch, *The Beauty Queen's Guide to World Peace* (London: Politicos, 2004).
29 Franklin D. Roosevelt, "Address to an International Labor Conference, 17 May 1944," available at: www.presidency.ucsb.edu/ws/?pid=16509.
30 Franklin D. Roosevelt, "Message to the ILO Conference, 20 April 1944," International Labour Organization, 26th Session, Philadelphia, 1944, Verbatim Record of Proceedings 2, available at: www.ilo.org/public/libdoc/ilo/P/09616/09616(1944–26).pdf.

Index

Routledge Global Institutions Series

Human Development
by Richard Ponzio

The International Monetary Fund (2nd edition)
Politics of conditional lending
by James Raymond Vreeland (Georgetown University)

The UN Global Compact
by Catia Gregoratti (Lund University)

Institutions for Women's Rights
by Charlotte Patton (York College, CUNY) and
Carolyn Stephenson (University of Hawaii)

International Aid
by Paul Mosley (University of Sheffield)

Global Consumer Policy
by Karsten Ronit (University of Copenhagen)

The Changing Political Map of Global Governance
by Anthony Payne (University of Sheffield) and
Stephen Robert Buzdugan (Manchester Metropolitan University)

Coping with Nuclear Weapons
by W. Pal Sidhu

EU Environmental Policy and Climate Change
by Henrik Selin (Boston University) and
Stacy VanDeveer (University of New Hampshire)

Global Governance and China
The dragon's learning curve
edited by Scott Kennedy (Indiana University)

The Politics of Global Economic Surveillance
by Martin S. Edwards (Seton Hall University)

Mercy and Mercenaries
Humanitarian agencies and private security companies
by Peter Hoffman

Contemporary Human Rights Ideas (2nd edition)
Betrand Ramcharan (Geneva Graduate Institute of International and Development Studies)

Protecting the Internally Displaced
Rhetoric and reality
Phil Orchard (University of Queensland)

The Arctic Council
Within the far north
Douglas C. Nord (Umea University)

For further information regarding the series, please contact:
Nicola Parkin, Editor, Politics & International Studies
Taylor & Francis
2 Park Square, Milton Park, Abingdon
Oxford OX14 4RN, UK
Nicola.parkin@tandf.co.uk
www.routledge.com

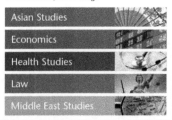